the official *fantasy league*℠ manager's handbook

the official *fantasy league*℠ manager's handbook

by Andrew Wainstein

with illustrations by
Dave Robinson

and contributions
by Fantasy League Managers

CORGI BOOKS

THE OFFICIAL FANTASY LEAGUE MANAGER'S HANDBOOK 1994/95

Andrew Wainstein

A CORGI BOOK 0 552 14287 5

First publication in Great Britain

PRINTING HISTORY
Corgi edition published 1994

Page design, layout and typesetting by Telekinesis.

Corgi Books are published by Transworld Publishers Ltd, 61–63 Uxbridge Road, Ealing, London W5 5SA, in Australia by Transworld Publishers (Australia) Pty Ltd, 15–25 Helles Avenue, Moorebank, NSW 2170, and in New Zealand by Transworld Publishers (NZ) Ltd, 3 William Pickering Drive, Albany, Auckland.

Printed and bound in Great Britain by Cox & Wyman Ltd, Reading, Berkshire

With much love to Sara,
Mom, Dad, Mara Lee, Lannis,
Shaun, Ouma and Oupa.

A big thanks to Chris,
and especially all the team at
Fantasy League.

contents

foreword

nick hancock

Comedian, Radio 5 Fantasy League Champion 1993-94.

The cultural influences of Fantasy Football provide strange phenomena: the impossibility of finding a vacant public telephone at 4:45 on a Friday evening, for instance; or the sight of a frantic man in a pub on a Sunday lunchtime asking complete strangers if they know who takes corners for Ipswich Town. Only the initiated can know what's going on, and if you're a small minded, anally retentitive, statistical pedant like me, then you'll be positively wallowing in the agonies and ecstasies of the game's vagaries. Apparently the game appeals to normal people, too.

I have been appalled at myself for how easily I have been sucked into Fantasy Football's fascination, and took an indecent amount of pleasure in winning my League without being tainted by any Manchester United or Arsenal players. The fact is the game's a blessed release from the serious business of supporting Stoke City: it's a chance to look at the results page without the arteries hardening and even an excuse to look heavenwards at the Premier League.

The only elements of managership that Fantasy Football denies you is the opportunity to make ex-gratia payments to players, or conduct transfers in motorway service stations with huge carrier bags of cash.

With no experience of playing the game at the top level you still get to decide which top players get to play and which ones get to join Paul McGrath in the bar. An opportunity unheard of since, well, since the F.A. appointed Graham Taylor.

Of course, everything has a down side, so beware of the game's dangerous side effect - the possibility of becoming a Fantasy Football bore; because as sure as you are that your side is the conversational equivalent of Carlos Alberto's Brazil, to everyone else they're Tony Adams' Arsenal.

Good Luck.

Nick Hancock S.C.F.C.

introduction

a brief history of Fantasy League

The question "did you have a good weekend?" is usually greeted by "yeah, very relaxing".

An answer of "absolutely awful - just two points" is a dead give-away - they're talking Fantasy League.

Many people reading this book will have been introduced to Fantasy League by listening to it on BBC Radio, watching it on BBC2, or by playing it in the Daily Telegraph or 90 Minutes magazine. You could easily be forgiven for thinking it was a large scale multi-media event launched at the start of 1994. In fact, this could not be further from the truth.

early days

It all started almost four years ago on a computer in a bedroom in North London. I had been vaguely aware of games in the US that allowed baseball and basketball fans to put together teams of real players. The game was a natural success in America because players have always been rated in terms of stats, so compiling teams was a simple case of adding up the stats on each player. But could it work on English football? Surely not. Apart from goals, there aren't really any stats available. My first stabs at a formula were over-complicated and could never have worked. Slowly but surely, a scoring system began to emerge, which included four basic ingredients - goals, assists, clean sheets and goals conceded. The formula that I settled on back then is still around today, so I suppose it must be pretty good.

If you're new to the game, it works like this. You take on the role of a football manager, and the players you manage are real-life, current professionals in the Premiership. So you could end up managing the likes of Schmeichel, Le Tissier, Shearer and Cole, together unbelievably, in one side. Fantasy indeed, but the performance of this team is based on real events. So if you own Shearer, every time he scores for Blackburn, he scores for you. You get points every time one of your players scores a goal, makes a goal or every time your defenders or goalkeeper keep a clean sheet, but you lose points for every goal they concede. The points are scored as follows :

FOR EVERY GOAL SCORED BY ONE OF YOUR PLAYERS 3 POINTS

FOR EVERY GOAL MADE BY ONE OF YOUR PLAYERS (ASSIST) 2 POINTS

FOR EVERY CLEAN SHEET KEPT BY YOUR GOALKEEPER OR BACK FOUR 3 POINTS

FOR EVERY GOAL CONCEDED BY YOUR GOALKEEPER OR BACK FOUR -1 POINT

The basic game allows for people to set up a league with friends in which each of them own a squad of Premiership players. Each league kicks off with a "Player Auction" at which everyone bids against each other for the likes of Sutton, Giggs, Speed and Jensen. Everyone has a notional budget of £20m to spend on a squad of fifteen, where each player goes to the highest bidder. Once the Auction is complete, your season is underway, and we send you a weekly report showing your league table and a player-by-player breakdown for each manager.

The game was tried on a very small scale the first season. After a few small ads at the start of 1991-92, we'd reached about 30 leagues after a couple of months. A slow start, but promising if you consider that it was a totally alien concept and that we'd spent close to nothing on advertising. Because of the quirky nature of the game, we'd started to attract a little bit of media attention. Robert Pryce in the Guardian's Soccer Diary, October 1991 wrote "It is football without the pain and utterly, of course, fantastic." The Mail on Sunday's IQ section featured Fantasy League in December, proclaiming "You too could be the sheepskin-coated manager with a cool £20m to spend." The biggest article came later on, in February 1992, in Keith Elliot's column in the Independent, where he wrote "Escapism? Absolutely. Welcome to Fantasy League".

It was this escapism and sense of fun that was beginning to capture imaginations of football fans in offices, pubs and clubs up and down the country. Offices that ran a league in 1991-92 were expanding to two divisions in 1992-93. You could now get relegated playing Fantasy League. We began hearing of some weird swap deals, like one league where two flatmates were competing: the deal was Ian Wright for £2m plus one month's washing up. Hmmm. Fantasy League now had a fanzine called "A 30 Point Weekend".

radio 5

Radio 5 even decided to set up a celebrity Fantasy League with us, whose members included the likes of Nick Berry, Shelly Webb, David Baddiel, Frank Skinner and a bloke called Tommy Docherty who reckoned he'd been playing a game similar to Fantasy League in the 1970s!

90 minutes

At the start of the 1993-94 season we set up a league for the readers of the football magazine "90 Minutes". With a circulation of over 70,000, an Auction was pretty much a non-starter. So we came up with a simplified version of the game where players were given fixed prices and readers selected a team of 11 instead of a squad of 15. The competition was a huge success, and attracted over 7000 entries.

the Daily Telegraph

We launched Fantasy League in the Daily Telegraph on Boxing Day, 1993 and as they say, the rest is history. With an entry of over 300,000 it started a revolution in the newspaper industry that has seen countless imitations across a range of different sports.

BBC 2

By mid-January we'd teamed up with BBC2 to launch

'Fantasy Football League' in which fifteen celebrities played Fantasy League. Baddiel and Skinner hosted the programme that was to become cult after-pub viewing on Friday nights.

a strange attraction

So what's the attraction of playing Fantasy League? Ask a dozen Fantasy League managers and you'll probably get a number of different answers. Competitiveness is sure to be high up on everyone's list - beating your friends AND showing that you know more about football. That could be the definition of bliss to a lot of football fans. But there's more to it than beating your friends, isn't there?

The strategy in the game is not to be sniffed at - later on in the book, I'll talk tactics for everything from getting your Auction plan right to timing your substitutions in the run-in. It's not enough to know your football, you have to be sharp to win at this game. There's loads of other reasons to get hooked on Fantasy League. What about power? You, the ordinary football fan, deciding whether Alan Shearer, on a few grand a week, will get a game in your side this weekend. Or, on the train back from work, you're making up your mind whether or not to show Neville Southall the door tomorrow morning. Maybe you play it because it gives you an interest in a meaningless mid-table game because you've got a couple of players appearing in a match that, under normal circumstances, would be about as interesting as counting how many pairs of grey socks you own. Or perhaps Fantasy League's ideal because it gives you the perfect excuse to sit glued to Teletext for hours without being too embarrassed.

what's in the book

The Daily Telegraph and 90 Minutes leagues certainly put Fantasy League on the map, and they are quite possibly the reason you are reading this book. So it seems fitting to start with "The Media Leagues", many managers' introduction to the game. I take a look at some tactics and ideas that might help you pick a better side this time around. It's a simple game but there are many different ways to go about picking a side, and indeed many different types of sides that will do well.

Most of the remainder of the book covers the core format of the game, namely leagues set up between friends - often referred to as "mini leagues". This title distinguishes them from their rather larger counterparts in the media - mini leagues are made up of between 5 and 15 friends and are most commonly run in offices or pubs. This is one of a number of differences from the huge media leagues that will become clear as you get further and further into the book. Another major difference is how teams are picked. Every mini league starts with The Auction, a ritual that could almost be covered in a separate book. It is with this that we kick off our look at mini leagues. Get the right venue, come armed with a short list of stars, bluff, don't bluff, we cover the do's and don'ts of the big day. Having a good Auction is more important than having a good wedding ceremony. You can recover from a bad wedding.

The next chapter gives you tips on the day-to-day management of your side. We're not telling you how to deal with your chairman, talk to the press, or interview a new secretary. We'll leave that to the professionals. Your job's much harder. There's an insight into when and how to buy, getting the most out of your 15 players. We investigate the emotional hedge and attempt to explain the mysterious Fantasy League Triangle.

There's also a chapter on Local Rules, which gives you ideas on how to spice up your league. When you join up, you don't receive a set of complicated or over-elaborate rules; it's up to you to come up with a framework of Local Rules. Because every league is slightly different, Local Rules are a very important aspect of Fantasy League. You might all work together, you might see each other once a week, once a month, you may have loads of time to organise things, you may not. Local Rules give you the opportunity to be practical, but also to be creative and to add extra dimensions to the game. We look at everything from choosing your league's scoring system to setting up budgets for the season, how to operate transfers, mid-season Auctions, excuses for booze-ups, etc. An important chapter once you're into Fantasy League.

We also cover Fantasy Cup competitions, another major part of life in your own league. You can set up your very own head-to-head knockout competition which means you can draw on all those great clichès when your league season is in tatters. Quotes like "We're a Cup side anyway", "Our name is on the Cup", "We can concentrate on the Cup now" are yet more examples of how football imitates Fantasy League.

Talking of real football, the Cup chapter is followed by the Fantasy League Scrapbook, which illustrates how thin the line between Fantasy League and the real football world is. OK, some of the club profiles are a bit over the top, but you can't help noticing how some of these clubs resemble real life clubs. That's certainly the view of The Long Lunchbreak League, or should I say The Principality of Long Lunchbreak? You see, these managers are so involved in the world of Fantasy that they've created a country (sorry, Principality) where all their teams play. There's a map that shows where teams are situated, local derbies, etc. You may say it's sad, I reckon it's what the game's all about.

The last chapter before we launch into the world of stats gives me (more of) an opportunity to make a fool of myself. I put my money where my mouth is and pick the 30 players that are worth going for in 1994-95. I look at all positions, and try to select the dead certs, the probables and the long shots. Whether it's right or wrong, it should make interesting reading as the season unfolds.

The stats section is, as you might expect, comprehensive. It has to be. Like it or not, a good Fantasy League manager needs stats. It's not good for your street cred, but it might help you win your league. Basically, this chapter is split in two. The first half is the Fantasy League Hall of Fame, which covers all the achievements of Fantasy League teams.

There are lots of different tables, but if you've made it into this section it means you can look back with pride on a season of quality management. The second half of the chapter looks in detail at all the Premiership players. We've included a comprehensive guide on everything you need to make decisions on buying and selling players. Points per game ratios, home and away form, favourite pre-match meal, it's all there.

Throughout the book we've tried to include as many contributions as possible, to give readers a flavour of life in a Fantasy League. I can't begin to express my gratitude to everyone who sent in contributions - the quality of material was excellent - it made the selection process very very difficult. Without the contributions the book wouldn't be the same.

Thanks again.

the 'media leagues'

Many people reading this book will have been introduced to Fantasy League by playing it in the Daily Telegraph or 90 Minutes magazine. Because this format is aimed at large audiences, the Auction is removed. Instead, players are given fixed prices and you are given a £20m budget to select your Fantasy team. You pick eleven players in a 4-4-2 formation, with no more than two players from the same Premiership club. Points are scored as follows :

FOR EVERY GOAL SCORED BY ONE OF YOUR PLAYERS	3 Pts
FOR EVERY GOAL MADE BY ONE OF YOUR PLAYERS (ASSIST)	2 Pts
FOR EVERY DEFENDER PLAYING 45 MINUTES OR MORE	1 Pt
FOR EVERY CLEAN SHEET KEPT BY YOUR GOALKEEPER OR BACK FOUR (including 1 point for playing)	3 Pts
FOR EVERY GOAL CONCEDED BY YOUR GOALKEEPER OR BACK FOUR	-1 Pt

The rules are relatively simple, but picking a winning side isn't. I've tried to give you some ideas that might help you pick your side, but you should always remember that there are many different ways to do well - there are many different "winning" sides.

a sample team

Do you go for three or four stars or a side full of solid, consistent performers? Is attack the most important? Or is midfield where the game is won and lost? How important are clean sheets? There really are no easy answers or golden rules, I'm afraid. If you decide your team should be strong in attack, fine - but expect to spend less elsewhere. The side below is what you'd call a well-balanced line-up.

Srnicek	NEWCASTLE	£1.5m	16PTS
Berg	BLACKBURN	£2.1m	30PTS
Kelly	LEEDS	£2.0m	31PTS
Fairclough	LEEDS	£1.6m	32PTS
Peacock	QPR	£1.2m	19PTS
Holden	OLDHAM	£1.3m	24PTS
Earle	WIMBLEDON	£1.7m	30PTS
M Allen	WEST HAM	£0.6m	25PTS
Le Tissier	SOUTHAMPTON	£3.1m	64PTS
Fjortoft	SWINDON	£0.6m	38PTS
Cole	NEWCASTLE	£4.0m	67PTS

Based on last season's prices and points, this side would in fact have won The Daily Telegraph Fantasy League. It has no Arsenal defenders, no players from champions Manchester United, and it has Holden and Fjortoft, two players from relegated clubs. (NB. there aren't three Newcastle players, Peacock was at QPR when the competition started)

This side would have finished on 376 points – four clear of the winning side, Bergholt Wednesday, and with £300,000 and four transfers untouched in the bank.

It's well-balanced because the points were earned evenly from defence (128 pts), midfield (143 pts) and attack (105 pts). The spending is also spread well. £8.4m on defence averages at £1.68m a man, as does the £6.7m spent on midfield. £4.6m on attack comes out at a higher average, but strikers score more points and consequently are more expensive.

If you'd picked Giggs instead of Holden, your midfield would have been stronger, and to afford him you would have had to buy Sutton instead of Cole. The net result - two more points. So by spending more on midfield and less up front, you improve your side. You could have spent less at the back to improve your strikers or less in midfield to improve your defence - the possibilities are endless...

budgeting ideas

I've looked at three methods you can use to pick your side, but you'll probably be best off adapting one of these to suit your team. Its up to you - try to be creative.

You should also bear in mind it might not be worth picking a side that costs exactly £20m. When it comes to transfers, you're likely to want a player that costs more than the player you're releasing. It's advisable therefore to leave a little extra in the bank to allow improvements through transfers.

1. budget by averages

The most simple format works on averages. Eleven players, £20m if you spend £1.8m on each of them your side will cost £19.8m, leaving £0.2m change for transfers.

Obviously, this system over-simplifies things a bit. First of all, decent strikers cost more than £1.8m, and so they should, because they are the highest points scorers. So if you pick your two strikers first, then you can divide out your remaining money across your other nine players to get your new average, or "target" price. You won't spend exactly the same amount on every player, so every time you go over or under your target price, make a note. If you spent £0.3m over the target on one player, you'll need to spend £0.3m less elsewhere. It's not the best of systems, but it should get you a pretty evenly balanced side.

2. budget by position

Everyone has their own theory about what's the most important area to spend on. Some say it's all about having two good strikers, some say all you need is Arsenal defenders, others claim it's won and lost in midfield. In truth, there are many different ways to pick a successful side, it all depends on where you decide to spend your cash. Based on an average of £1.8m per player, you should spend £9m on defence, £7.2 on midfield and £3.6m on attack. In truth, strikers are more valuable, so a well balanced side should cost around 9 - 6.5 - 4.5. This is pretty close to the splits on the side listed above. You might prefer to go for a side that's defence heavy (10.5-6-3.5), midfield heavy (8-8-4) or attack heavy. (8-6-6)

3. budget by price bands

The third option lets you choose players by price. There are masses of permutations available, but I've listed a few that vary from a mix of mid-priced players to a mix of the very expensive and the very cheap. You'll be able to work out many more variations, but the examples below should give you the general idea.

a.	b.	c.	d.	e.
			1x£3.0m	2x£3.0m
4x£2.0m	2x£2.5m	3x£2.5m	4x£1.8m	2x£1.7m
3x£1.8m	2x£1.8m	2x£1.7m	2x£1.6m	1x£1.6m
4x£1.6m	7x£1.6m	6x£1.5m	4x£1.6m	6x£1.6m
£19.8m	**£19.8m**	**£19.9m**	**£20.0m**	**£20.0 m**

picking a solo team

As well as entering the Daily Telegraph or 90 Minutes leagues, many managers choose to subscribe to Fantasy League for a weekly report on their team. You can subscribe in one of two ways. You can either set up a league with 5 to 15 friends, or you can join on your own and we place you in a league with other individual managers. This format is called a "Solo Manager" league. Because Solo Managers can be spread all over the country, the Auction is replaced with a selection from a list of fixed-priced players, as in the Daily Telegraph and 90 Minutes leagues. The only difference is that you are buying a squad of 18 players, so consequently we set the players' prices lower.

Based on this squad size, you should average £1.1m on each player. You can use similar strategies as above, but before you launch into picking your side, you should work out how much you want to spend on your first eleven and how much on your seven subs. A good guide is to aim for 9m on your first eleven and 6m on your subs. This should allow you to get a fairly strong starting line-up and mean that your bench will be useful contributors rather than bottom-of-the-range no-hopers.

things to look out for this season

new scoring system

As you may have noticed from above, we will be operating a slightly different scoring system from last season for the Daily Telegraph. We recommended that they switch to our System B, which we have found to be an improvement on the basic system they operated last season. There is no change to goals or assists; the change only affects defenders. Your goalkeeper and each of your back four will receive a point if they play for 45 minutes or more and a further two points if they keep a clean sheet. One point is deducted for each goal conceded. So if your defender keeps a clean sheet, it's 3 points, one goal conceded is 0 points, two goals is minus 1 point, three goals is minus 2 points, etc.

This new system is a lot fairer to defenders. It has little effect on the top defenders' points, but brings the mid-range defenders a lot closer. So, a player who might have negative points under the old system will almost certainly have positive points on System B. One look at the stats section at the end of the book shows the contrast. Finally, the clean sheet is not as important a factor, and the swing for losing the first goal is not as dramatic. Under the old system a defender drops 5 points from +4 to -1 after conceding the first goal; under System B, the swing is from +3 to 0 – not as soul-destroying!

midfielders' points

Over the course of last season's Daily Telegraph Fantasy League I spoke to a number of people who reckoned that midfield was unimportant to the game.

This is definitely wrong, I think this is how the misunderstanding happened:

With four points for a clean sheet, defenders can race to a very high total in a short time (which can then very easily drop), while midfielders' points will rise slowly but surely.

This was borne out at the end of the season. Sixteen midfielders finished with over 20 points, but just five full backs and three centre backs scored more than 20 points.

The most important point to realise is that the Daily Telegraph league only lasted half a season. For a full season most midfielders' points will double, but many defenders' points won't - they could even go down.

You've been warned: ignore midfield at your peril.

running your own league

You've got the Fantasy League bug. Maybe your team is flying high in a newspaper league and you need a new challenge. Maybe your team is a disaster and you want a fresh start. Maybe you're frustrated because your star striker broke his leg two days after you made your last transfer. Maybe you want the chance to be in a league where you can compete with friends. Maybe you just want to be in a league that you could actually win. If any of the above sound like you, you should consider setting up your own mini league.

A lot of people are under the false impression that Fantasy League started in January 1994 in The Daily Telegraph. While the Telegraph Fantasy League did more than anything else to expose the nation to the game, it was by no means the first Fantasy League. Thousands of Fantasy Leagues, or mini leagues, have been running in offices, pubs and clubs during the last four seasons. This is the game in its original and true form containing many elements that had to be simplified or removed to allow the game to work on a large scale in the media.

So what are the differences? You'll be relieved to learn that the crux of the game - the way points are scored - is exactly the same. I'll try to summarise what's different in the next couple of paragraphs, but really it takes the rest of the book to do some justice to the excitement and enjoyment of competing in your own league.

A league can be made up of 5 to 15 people, so your chances of winning are a lot better than in a league of 300,000. Also, you're allowed to make as many team changes as you like, which means your side need not be crippled just because your star striker gets injured. You'll have a squad of fifteen, so changes can be made strategically; drop a player who's got a tough game on Saturday, bring on a sub who's got a home banker. You can also negotiate swap deals with your friends - over lunch you could be discussing the possibility of Tony Coton plus a million for Ruel Fox...

Another bonus is that you subscribe to Fantasy League, which means we do all the work - you'll get an in-depth weekly report showing your own league table and a player-by-player breakdown for each manager in your league. There's a sample report opposite.

THE MAN WHO BOUGHT DAVE BEASANT FOR £7m.

But by far and away the main reason to run your own league is that everyone's squad is totally unique. This is how it works. At the beginning of your season, you all get together for a "Player Auction", at which you try to outbid each other for each Premiership player. You decide which players go under the hammer, and for how much. This makes for great entertainment, but it also means that each player goes to the highest bidder, so can only be bought once. That means if you managed to outbid everyone for Andy Cole, every time he scores, you're the only one who gets the points. It's that "exclusive hold" on players that's so attractive, and starts to make you feel emotionally attached to the fifteen players in your squad.

> *"Football is no longer something to be enjoyed whoever you are watching as the pressures of football management become apparent. Never before has the number of games played and their distribution across 5 days of the week seemed so important. Weekends in the world of Fantasy League have now been shifted to Thursdays and Fridays. Even then there are the concerns over match fitness and team selection. Who will succumb to the pressure first?"*

(Excerpt from "Get off Don's Sister League" newsletter)

This might seem an exaggerated claim, but if you read on, you'll see that's it's only half the story.

Fantasy League Ltd
PO Box 1977, London N6 4NQ
Tel 081 340 8413 Fax 081 342 9782

9 May 1994

League PIN : 210

Mark Poole
c/o Finlays Lounge Bar
Inverness
IV3 5DD

Collapsing Quiff And Bowl Cut Premiership

LEAGUE TABLE

	GLS (3 PTS)	ASS (2 PTS)	C.S. (4 PTS)	G.A. (-1 PT)	WEEK TOTAL	TOTAL
Two Titleist Golf Balls	68	55	42	144	13	338
Fubar F.C.	57	48	60	174	-1	333
And Thats Jappys Hat-Trick	51	47	49	124	12	319
Barry Bethnels Slimfast Swifts	66	58	44	189	9	301
The Rev Jim Jones Eleven	43	43	57	150	11	293
Henry's Cat All Star XI	47	47	55	179	12	276
M. Burns Radioactive XI	35	45	52	141	25	262
Those Cheeky Chimps You Can't Trust	50	34	42	125	9	261
Almost White Ayrian Mountaineers FC	47	52	49	201	9	240
Ravenscraig Car Park Utd	56	29	52	196	13	238
Malc & Alans Stupid Cockney Gits FC	39	44	49	208	16	193
Dalex Totten F.C.	48	33	37	180	6	178

AND THATS JAPPYS HAT-TRICK
MANAGER : G MACDONALD

TRANSFERS LEFT : 2

		PLAYED	GLS	ASS	C.S	G.A.	WEEK	TOTAL
1	P Srnicek	21	0	0	8	16	4	16
	Hitchcock	0	0	0	0	0	0	0
3	Winterburn	34	0	2	18	23	-2	53
2	Kelly	21	0	2	10	15	6	29
6	Nicol	29	1	3	6	37	-2	-4
5	A Pearce	29	3	4	8	32	-3	17
11	Mcclair	13	1	3	0	0	0	9
8	J Barnes	19	1	2	0	0	0	7
7	Goss	18	3	2	0	0	0	13
4	Flitcroft	20	3	4	0	0	0	17
	Wise	0	0	0	0	0	0	0
10	A Cole	40	34	15	0	0	3	132
9	M Stein	1	2	0	0	0	6	6
	S Barlow	0	0	0	0	0	0	0
	C Maskell	0	0	0	0	0	0	0

the auction

The Auction is the most important day of the Fantasy League season. Apart from being the day you put together your squad, it's also the day that you get to choose your team's name, its image and its identity - will it be a flair side like Manchester United, will you be a Blackburn and bid for everyone in sight, or will you be Arsenal-like in your quest for clean sheets? Two crazy hours filled with hope, despair, tension, deceit and basic arithmetic will decide how the next nine months of your life will develop.

You'll be surprised what a battle of nerves an Auction can be. One mistake can cost you a player that you'll curse all season long, one rush of blood will see you grossly over-paying for a nobody. It's always tense, it's always fun and I guarantee you'll love it.

how does it work?

To make your Auction run smoothly, it's worth getting the organisation right. Get a decent venue, with plenty of room, which you're able to take over for at least two hours. Depending on the size of your league and your Fantasy League experience, you're looking at anything from an hour and a half to three hours. Many leagues prefer to drag things out to add to the sense of drama, others might be short of time - commitments like being home before sunrise or having to get to work to earn a living can sometimes interfere: I'll suggest some short cuts later.

Before you get started, there are a couple of things it's worth being aware of. Firstly, it will help if you get someone who is not in your league to act as an Auctioneer. Your Auction will run more smoothly, they will be neutral in any dispute and it won't give one of the managers two jobs - it's hard enough bidding for a team without trying to chair the whole thing. Also, you may need someone to keep track of everyone's budget, their 4-4-2 and their 2-per-club

quota - this can also be the Auctioneer, or more often than not you can rely on the managers being honest and checking their own sides. Finally, it's worth every manager keeping a clean copy of the starting line-up sheets to fill out after the Auction as your first eleven and subs will often change after the Auction is completed.

THE BID FOR ANDY COLE STANDS AT £20m PLUS THE HOUSE, PLUS THE CAR, PLUS THE DOG AND THE CAT. DO I HEAR A BUDGIE?

Once everything and everyone is present and correct, you're ready to start. The manager who has been nominated to start should raise a player of his choice. This should start at £0, but can start at any reasonable minimum. After the first bid, it's over to the floor, with anyone allowed to raise the bid by your league's chosen amount - most common is £250,000, but anything from £100,000 to £500,000 is fine - it largely depends on time. Bids proceed until the player is sold to the highest bidder, then on to the next manager.

Many leagues choose to go through the player list systematically, i.e. goalkeepers, full backs, centre backs, etc. I would strongly suggest that you raise players in a random order - this adds extra strategy - "who to raise when?" and also avoids some very unrealistic prices e.g. goalkeepers for £8m and strikers for £0.5m.

Whichever order you decide to raise players, the Auction should proceed smoothly until managers start to drop out. This is nothing to do with a physical or mental state, but will happen if managers have spent their £20m or have bought all their fifteen players. Each manager must then sit it out until all managers have "dropped out". Once this has happened, all managers who have not filled their squad resume proceedings with the last stage of the Auction. All players who are still available can be bought for free in rotation. It's important to work out the rotation order for this stage before the Auction - it could be fairest for this to be the order that managers "dropped out", so that those who have sat things out the longest come in first. This stage should move very swiftly but you might need to give managers a time limit for each choice. You must make sure everyone's squad contains at least one goalkeeper, two full backs, two centre backs, four midfielders and two strikers, with no more than 2 players from any one Premiership club.

auction tactics

plan ahead

Like many things in life, a bit of planning can really help. The amount of planning will depend on your personality, but most managers will go into an Auction armed with anything from a scrap of crumpled paper to an A3 columnar accounting spreadsheet... one way or another, it's a plan.

If your tendency is towards columnar spreadsheets, you can look at which teams you want represented at the back, whether your squad will be 5-6-4 or 7-5-3, how to split your £20m between defence, midfield and attack, short lists of midfielders and strikers, which 2 players you want from the top clubs - the possibilities are endless. An fairly serious Auction plan is shown later on.

With Auction plans, bear in mind two golden rules. One, don't over plan - a complicated plan can tie you in knots in the Auction - allow some flexibility. Two, make sure the plan is right.

My 1992-93 Auction went beautifully to plan, I got everyone I wanted and at the price I wanted. Only problem was, the plan was wrong. I'd spent more time devising it than on working out who I wanted. Every player I had bought was awful, and I spent all season recovering from my duff plan. Having a plan is great, but make sure it's right for you - a bit like a mortgage.

don't change your mind

When it comes to having a good Auction, there's one priceless piece of advice: don't change your mind. Players do not transform themselves from donkeys to primadonnas during your Fantasy League Auction. A player cannot, after four pints, become injury prone, move to Barnsley or be on trial with Sampdoria. Check your facts before the Auction and then don't listen to any "honest John" Auction rumours.

don't raise the players you want

One tactic that many managers miss is that you should never raise any players you want. Throw other managers off the scent - it adds a bit of fun. Push up the prices of players you don't want, but be careful not to be left holding the baby - or donkey. Let them bid for anyone else; the later your players come up the less money everyone will have.

squad formations

It's worth giving some thought to the formation of your squad. Some managers quibble that the squad should be sixteen players, so you can have cover in every position. That would be too easy; one of the keys to managing a successful side is getting the balance of your squad right. A common mistake is to buy loads of strikers because they are the biggest points scorers. It's true they score the most points, but it's also true that you can only play two at a time. A month into your season you'll be having a breakdown over all the points you've thrown away by having three free-scoring strikers on your bench!

It's probably best to have three strikers through the season, but because you're bound to get one dud in the Auction, go for four, with a view to selecting the best three after a few weeks. You can use the same approach for midfielders, ie. buy plenty because they're in short supply and you can't be sure who will click. Go for six midfielders, which leaves just five at the back. Having no reserve defenders shouldn't be a problem. If you get three top defenders, the other two can be switched as mid-table Premiership clubs go on good runs - they're relatively easy to pick up because you're buying anyone from the back five.

So the recommended Auction squad is 5 defenders, 6 midfielders and 4 strikers. This is not the best formation to play through the season, but is a good starting platform. For the bulk of the season, go for 6-6-3 or 7-5-3. Three good strikers, with extra midfielders and defenders to switch around for the easy fixtures. Which of these is better is down to where you're stronger and what type of style of football you'd like your team to play.

a sample auction plan

DEFENCE (pick 5)	MIDFIELD (pick 6)	ATTACK (pick 4)
£6m approx	*£6m approx*	*£8m approx*
'TOP' GROUP (3)	'TOP' GROUP (3)	'TOP' GROUP (2)
Arsenal	Giggs/Sharpe	Cole
Man Utd	Lee/Fox	Wright
Blackburn	Speed/McAllister	Cantona
	Wilcox/Ripley	Sutton
	Earle	
	Merson	
	McManaman	
'MID' GROUP (2)	'MID' GROUP (3)	'MID' GROUP (2)
Leeds	Ince/Keane	Rush
Ipswich	Anderton	Stein
Wimbledon	Barnes	Ferdinand
Liverpool	Waddle	Deane/Wallace
QPR	Clark/Sellars	Beardsley
	Roy	Armstrong
		Newell
		Bright

This is just a guide to the sort of plan that's possible; it may be too detailed for many. It's a good idea to split your choices into two groups, so you're sure to end up with a mix of top quality and mid-quality players. Defence has been chosen by clubs, so you're aiming to get anyone from the back 5 of the listed clubs. The budgets for each area are very loose; you should never get too tied to what you plan to spend for a player. I've left out some stupid-money players like Shearer and Le Tissier, but that's because they're generally very pricey - I reckon over about £6m on one player is excessive. That's fairly personal, as is the selection of players.

During the Auction try not to stray from your list, and wait patiently for your players to come up - the later the better.

some short cuts

If you're short of time, here's a few tips that will help speed things up.

i) **Steeper jumps in bids**
Bidding in jumps of £500,000 will mean things move a lot faster than in smaller steps. However, it's not worth moving up in jumps of any more than this.

ii) **Player Limit**
Only bid for 11 players, so all subs are picked up in the rotation stage. There will be no advantage to spending less than £20m on your first eleven. Once you've bought them, you wait until the next stage.

iii) **Time Limit**
Put a time limit on the bidding section of the Auction. If you've got an hour, bid for forty minutes and allow twenty for the rotation stage to fill up squads. There's no benefit in being cautious with your money. If time is up and you've spent £12m, tough. This should be an improvement on (ii), as you will get a more precise cut-off point for the bidding.

iv) **Rotation Only**
This will save the most time, and still maintains much of the excitement and strategy of the Auction. Simply pick players in rotation on a first-come-first-served basis with no budgets. To make sure that this moves quickly, give every manager a time limit for each selection.

if you can't hold an auction

If it's impossible to get everyone together for an Auction, you will need to come up with an alternative. The most popular choice is to run a sealed bid Auction, fairly complicated, but great fun.

Each manager makes a selection of eighteen players, (use extra solo manager subs) accompanied by bids totalling up to £20m, with no more than two players per club. Once all these bids are in, a couple of managers should go through them giving each player to the manager who bids highest. In the event of a tie, the team sheet handed in first should win.

This continues until all team sheets have been checked, crossing off each player as he is bought. After this stage, all managers are given a revised player list and a team sheet showing who they have successfully bought and how much money they have left. From these sheets, they can make bids for their remaining positions. Each selection should also include a second and third reserve player, to come into effect if the first choice is missed.

The value of the main bid transfers to the reserve choices, so there's a lot of skill in deciding who you name as a first, second or third choice player. Reserve bids ensure that virtually all positions are filled in the second stage. If there are any gaps still remaining, they can be filled in the same way, or on a first-come-first-served basis.

....

ONE FOR SORROW

> *Narrowing my eyes, I peered through the gathering smoke. Was she bluffing? A glance down. I was holding two canaries and a minor owl, looking for a magpie to match my pair - but she was after a sharp-shooting gunner with a canonised kicker on the side. Her proposal hung around us like a bad smell. My*

nostrils twitched imperceptibly.

To my right, Lightnin' Jack Lambeth raised a cool mil on a toffee middleman. There was a murmur around the table and Slow Joe Tomlinson doubled the raise. It was a crazy bid - but people were getting desperate. The pool was looking thin, and still there were punters wide open at the back. No amount of money was going to buy a safety net now. It was deal or die.

I needed to clear my head. Picking up the whip, I strolled over to the bar.

"What's it to be, Slim?"

I muttered the usual litany of mathematical comfort. "Three four X's, one half-and-half, two five-year olds and a seven-up, Ned." I was playing with the notion of throwing in a robin to secure the magpie, but I knew she'd push for my pensioner at the least. When it came to trade, she was hard as a hobo's heel.

"How's it going?" Ned asked, nodding towards the menagerie behind me.

"I'm big upfront," I shrugged, "loose behind. I've got a wad you couldn't get your first round, but it's not gonna fill any holes at the rear. The big birds have flown and the little fish in the pool are all dogs and donkeys."

Ned shook his head as he put the drinks on the bar. "It's your old mistake, Slim. You think plenty 'bout scoring, but pay no mind to keeping your sheets clean."

"Mind your goddam business," I snapped - but he was right. Barkeepers usually are.

Back at the meat market, I took a deep breath and looked across at her, grim as a drugstore java. "Okay," I said, "I've got here Smith and Le Tissier for Venison and Parker, but Wise don't make the tape without you throw in Anderton and a million cash."

She smiled thinly, looked to one side, and then snapped her baby-blues back on me, full-beam.

"You must be out of your tiny, befuddled mind," she mocked. "If you can't say something serious, say nothing at all, eh?"

I watched, helpless, as she poached Bright on a two-for-one from Slow Joe. I finished up with a handful of Bassett's Allsorts and a keeper whose name was real short on vowels. I grimaced sulkily.

Wait till I get her home.

M B *March 1994*

GET OFF DON'S SISTER LEAGUE
(Manchester)

AGENDA FOR AUCTION

1) Get beers in

2) Elect Chair

3) Chair gets beers in

4) Choose Auctioneer

5) Auctioneer gets beers in

6) Choose 'accountant' to keep tabs on spending

7) Accountant gets beers in (Georgie get your WAD out!)

8) Choose 'Cup' Organiser

9) Cup organiser gets beers in

10) Elect Disciplinary Committee

11) Managers buy Committee beers (Bribes start now!)

12) Local rules (see attached sheet)

13) AUCTION + lots of beers!

Each manager chooses a player in turn and starts the bidding. When all money is spent or when teams with money left over are completed, managers will take it in turn to pick up 'free transfers' to complete their squads.

14) Get smashed and laugh at Waller's team

BILLY GRANT

The reason why his team is called "Countryman" is because on the day of the 1st Auction he was lured away by a temptress to Brighton for the weekend. Hence he missed the Auction, got all the crap players and stayed rooted to the bottom of the league. The name is a constant reminder that one night of pleasure has cost him nine months of football agony.

IT WAS A WONDERFUL TEAM BUT THE SEASON WOULD BE A DISASTER IF HE COULDN'T THINK OF A DECENT NAME.

managing your side

This is it. The game of Fantasy League is won and lost in the day-to-day management of your side. The auction is important, but a good manager will transform a mediocre auction into a championship, and a bad manager can turn a superb auction into a season of wasted dreams.

It all comes down to team changes. There are two types of team change: substitutions and transfers. At any point in the season, your squad is made up of fifteen players: a first eleven in a 4-4-2 formation and four reserves who can be made up players from any position. When you bring in a reserve, it must be for a player of the same position i.e. you have to keep your 4-4-2 formation intact. This “internal” squad change is imaginatively named a “substitution” and can be done whenever the mood takes you. “Transfers” are altogether more serious. A transfer is an “external” squad change, namely adding or removing a player from your squad. To make a transfer, you can either do a swap deal with another manager or you can buy someone no-one else in you league owns. As far as transfer fees are concerned, this will be down to your league’s Local Rules. Local Rules are explained in the next chapter, and cover budgets, bidding rules, deadlines, etc.

It’s at this point that I’d like to introduce the team at Fantasy League Headquarters. When you call in to make a team change, you’ll talk to either David (a Dagenham & Redbrige fan), Penelope (Leicester City), Mark (West Ham), Jeremy (Wolves) or Suzanne (Manchester United). Over the course of a long hard season they will become the agony aunts and uncles for your Fantasy League team.

A lot of people believe that the more changes you make, the better your side does. A manager who makes a lot of changes will, on average, do better than one who doesn’t. But often it’s quite the opposite. Like good comedy, the secret is timing. You have to choose the right time to make your move - or not to. Remember, it's sometimes easier making a change than resisting making a change...

the early days

The first couple of weeks are the feeling-out period - it will take a few games before you remember all fifteen players without a quick glance at your team sheet. Don't be too quick to judge. You're bound to get some early favourites: the bloke who scores at 3.15 on the first day of the season, your first clean sheet, and your first assist will always give you a warm feeling. Generally, about half your squad are good enough to stay at your club all season; the other half end up being the problem players. Try not to turn on your players too soon - it's not his fault his side let in a goal in the 87th minute, or that you dropped him just before his first goal. Give them time to gel together, give everyone a few games, treat them gently... after all, you fought for these players in the auction. Of course you know all of this, but you'll still be off into the transfer market at the first opportunity, loyalty falling at the first hurdle.

Sure as anything, you'll fall foul of the Fantasy League Triangle; a mysterious cycle of events that makes you prone to violent mood swings towards players in your squad. The Triangle takes anything from two days to two months to navigate; this will depend on how your loyalty stands the test.

transfers

the fantasy league triangle: thinking about buying

If someone's letting you down, chances are you'll have your eye on a replacement. One good game and he's a possibility, but could it be a flash in the pan? Another good game - yes - he's the one. Maybe I should wait one more game.... NO. Many runs only last about four or five games, so buying any later than the second game is often too late. Act fast.

Even better than the "react-mode" transfer is the "anticipate-mode". If you get a feel that a player or a team is about to hit form, that could be the trigger. If you don't fancy yourself as an astrologer, you can flick through the fixture list and have a go on someone who looks like he's in for a run of easy matches. There's nothing more satisfying than buying a player before his first goal, assist or clean sheet. "React-mode" transfers are all about timing, "anticipate-mode" is about inspiration.

Later on in the season, you can buy players for more scientific reasons. If you're locked in a title battle, one tactic is to "shadow" your rival's defence. This means that you buy players so that your defence is made up of the same teams as his. This can also be a frustrating tactic, because you're only competing on six or seven players instead of eleven. Use this if you think your midfield and attack are superior to his, or if you've got a lead you want to protect.

Another good one for the run-in is to buy players from sides that have games in hand. Teams that have had good cup runs will be behind in league fixtures, so picking up their players means you get a few extra games that could be vital.

the fantasy league triangle: now he's yours

There's nothing quite like the buzz you get from a new signing. "This is the player that's gonna win me the league", "Now my squad is perfect - I'm not making any more changes after this". Right. We believe you. Hope springs eternal from every new signing - the sky's the limit. Sometimes, but not that often, the hope is fulfilled. A goal on his debut. Make him captain. Double his wages. Marry him.

OK, so often the first game is quiet. No problem. A goal on his debut would be nice, but that's fairytale stuff. "He needs time to settle in". Three games, no points. No panic. "They've got Oldham at home next week - good for at least a couple of goals..."

Being substituted against Oldham was the final straw. He's got to go.

the fantasy league triangle: thinking about selling

Three games later, that great hope is no more. You can't stand the sight of him on TV, you don't want to read about how he nearly scored, or how he passed to the bloke who got the assist. It's too late, his number's up. First of all, don't do it. As sure as anything, he'll score in the next game. The best bet is to pretend to sell him. Accidentally-on-purpose forget to make that call to Fantasy League. That could do the trick. He's conned into thinking you've sold him, but you haven't.

He scores. 3 points - ha!

Unfortunately, that doesn't always work, so it could be back to the drawing board. Have you given him a couple of games on the trot? Switching a player in and out every week doesn't do anyone any favours - show a bit of loyalty.

Getting back to the world of stats, it's worth checking your player's points per game ratio. You should be looking at 2 points a game for a striker, 1 point a game for a midfielder, 1/2 a point a game for a defender. These should only be looked at if a player has played 5 or more games; any less than that and it's probably too soon to be thinking of selling.

the fantasy league triangle: thinking about buying

If someone's letting you down, chances are you'll have your eye on a replacement. One good game and he's a possibility, but could it be a flash in the pan? Another good game - yes - he's the one. Maybe I should wait one more game.... NO. Many runs only last about four or five games, so buying any later than the second game is often too late. Act fast...

Does all this sound a bit familiar?

substitutions

... AND DEANE ENDS HIS DROUGHT WITH A HAT TRICK.

While the timing of a transfer is critical, timing a substitution is life-or-death. The player is yours, he scores, the points are in the bag, but he's on your bench. So near and yet so far. This is what makes substitutions even more frustrating. To have points scored by your bench on a Saturday is every Fantasy League manager's nightmare. You have to write off 20-30 points a season through ill-timed substitutions, but how can the damage be limited?

home and away

A popular tool for making substitutions is always to play the players that are at home. In truth this over-simplifies the game and is basically cowardly. You remove the weekly decision, and you have a crutch to fall back on whenever it goes wrong - "I decided on this method at the start of the season and I have to stick to it." Nonsense. Be brave. Go on a hunch. Look at away form. Trust your gut feeling. That's what the game's all about.

look at the fixtures

This is the obvious one, but if results were predictable, football and Fantasy League would be very boring. Use the fixture list as a guide, but go on instinct as well.

give players a few games

If you chop and change too often, you run the risk of missing everything. You can be a game behind the clean sheet or a game ahead of it. If someone's just got an assist, the chances are the person you drop for him will get the next assist, not him again. Patience.

striker / defender hedge

This is quite a good one. If you've got a choice between a

couple of strikers and a couple of defenders, it could be worth playing the striker who's playing against the defender. If the striker fails to score, you could get the clean sheet. If the defender concedes a goal, your striker could score it or get the assist. The nightmare scenario is that the defender concedes four goals and the striker's gone AWOL. In any event, this combination will not get you loads of points, but you should get some. Good if you're top of your league, or in a cup competition.

emotional hedge

This one is another old chestnut. Choose your line-up based on the team you support in real life - or rather their rivals. In other words, if your real team is playing a rival team containing one of your players, play him. If the rival team score, you might get some points from him to make up for it. That way, the day won't be a complete disaster. Jim Kilpin illustrates this point with an unwitting emotional hedge against his own side...

....

FANTASY ISLAND

(90MINS ISSUE NO.197 – 19 MARCH)

Dear Kickback

I would like to inform you of a disturbing and sinister aspect to the seemingly fun craze that has swept the nation of late. I refer, of course, to Fantasy Football. I have been a long-standing, long-serving, loyal supporter of Tottenham for many years now and am annoyingly joyous when they win, deeply depressed when they lose or draw.

Last Sunday I watched the live game on Sky against Chelsea. After finally forgiving Andy Gray for his penalty fluff kick, I resigned myself to accepting the inevitable score draw. Alas, I was to be mistaken, for in the 92nd (!) minute Dean Austin clipped a Chelsea player in the penalty area, and the ref awarded appropriately.

Before Fantasy Football came along, you would expect my

natural response to be: throw beer can at telly, scream at ref, kick the dog, etc. But no, I remained unnervingly calm and worryingly non-plussed. The reason?

Mark Stein! Another chance to add three points to my Fantasy League goals tally! Spurs were facing a devastating defeat leaving them on the brink of relegation disaster. Did I care? Did I heck! Stein was about to give me another three points, enough to jump me up 200 places, ever nearer towards that elusive top spot.

Loyal supporter? Pah! Hopeful Fantasist? Maybe!

JIM KILPIN, BIRMINGHAM

COME ON BARMBY, I NEED THE POINTS! LEAVE HIM TONY, LEAVE HIM!
JVC

Where does it end though? A Spurs fan might buy Arsenal players, so that whenever they do well he gets some points - a hedge throughout the season. It's a useful tactic up to a point, but some managers still enforce some real-life loyalty club policy. No Liverpool players for a Man Utd fan, or no Man Utd players for a Man City fan. It's very healthy to retain some real world loyalty. Steve Wood of Preston has got his principles right.

FANTASTIC DAY

(90 MINS ISSUE NO.201 – 16 APRIL)

Dear Kickback

I've become suicidally worried about some of the feelings I've been experiencing recently. I read the letter in KICKBACK which highlighted the effect of owning a Fantasy League team on the undying support of one's own team. I must admit that in recent weeks, the Fantasy League has ruled my life. I have even been comforted by West Ham's recent defeats because of the points I've earned.

However, every so often an unexplainable thought enters my head. At the risk of offending all those "die-hard" Manchester United fans, I'm afraid to say that when United lose, or even draw, I don't give a monkey's about how many Fantasy League points I've won or lost.

Please help me. I feel so callous, for how could I place the importance of Manchester United not winning the League above the performance of my own measly Fantasy League team. Oh, please forgive me! I promise to say ten Alex Fergusons and three Peter Schmeichels every night for a whole week. Save me from the wrath of Eric Cantona's studs, which I know I deserve.

STEVE WOOD, PRESTON

watch him on sky

A Sky dish is a luxury accessory for the serious Fantasy League manager. If your player's going to be on the live match, that can sometimes swing a tough team selection dilemma. It gives you an interest in the game and allows you to get a good ninety-minute look at him.

CHAS NEWKEY-BURDEN

We all know how Graham Taylor was vilified for his constant meddling with our national side. In a nutshell, he used too many different players. But try managing a Fantasy League side and you might find yourself feeling some sympathy for him.

The trick behind a successful side is patience. It's late September and you haven't made the top half of the table yet. Your forward line have managed to both go on a dry patch which would be the envy of the Sahara desert, your midfield have only accumulated a handful of assists and your defence is worringly Swindon-like in its performance. Surely the time is right to give your team a severe upheaval?

Not necessarily. If you were playing last season and Dean Saunders was one of your forwards, you will probably recall his one-man hate campaign against all Fantasy League managers who dared choose him. For weeks, he would have about as much of an idea where the goal is as John Jensen, then suddenly - when the less patient managers had dropped him - he would score a hat-trick and a few assists for good measure.

In January 1994, when Fantasy Football really hit the big-time, the Arsenal back four suddenly took pity on opposing teams and began to leak goals, while Ipswich's sheets were so clean they could have shown them to their mothers-in-law.

Unless your defence is made up of Swindon or Oldham-like players, or you have a John Jensen in midfield, the only time it is necessary to change around your side is when injuries or suspensions affect it. But be warned, if you don't keep a close eye on the progress of injured players, they might just come back to haunt you. I dropped Andy Cole and he came back early from injury and scored a hat-trick. But remember, everything comes to those who wait.

CHAS NEWKEY-BURDEN

After reading this chapter, you're probably more muddled than ever on how to manage your side. Good. It should be tough, and being aware of all of these variables should only make it more difficult, more stressful and more of a nightmare.

THAT ALL IMPORTANT TEAM SELECTION.

a manager's guide to injuries

One thing that unites all Fantasy League managers is the dread of injuries. Worse still, it is being kept in the dark about how long the injury will last. Doesn't the club realise your championship is on the line? Vague reports like "he'll be out for a few weeks" are a manager's nightmare. Is "a few weeks" two weeks or ten weeks? Anyone who owned Teddy Sheringham last season will have suffered umpteen false alarms of "Sheringham back in training" or "Teddy to play in the reserves this week" before chucking the whole thing in and selling him two days before he came on as sub and scored with his first touch against Norwich. Why aren't we told? Don't the press realise that the gory details of John Barnes' knee operations are of vital interest to Fantasy League managers everywhere?

In-depth knowledge of injuries is dispensable, so we've contacted an expert to help out. The Arsenal physio, Gary Lewin, (GradDipPhys MCSP) has very kindly compiled a summary of the ins and outs of the most common football ailments. The survey below is based on a typical football season and shows the frequency and recovery periods for each type of injury.

DIAGNOSIS		Average recovery period (days)	
	%	To full training	To match play
Fractures	4.6	42	51
Operations	9.0	28	35
Back Injuries	6.1	28	41
Head Injuries	3.0	15	25
Muscle & Tendon Injuries			
Hamstring	7.5	8	11
Quadriceps	6.1	7	10
Adductors (Groin)	4.6	11	13
Calf Injuries	6.1	7	9
Tendon	4.6	10	12

DIAGNOSIS	Average recovery period (days)		
	%	To full training	To match play
Joint Injuries			
Knee	12.1	10	14
Ankle	22.7	11	14
Foot	4.6	10	13
Others	3.0	5	7
Skin Lesions	3.0	8	10
Periostitis	3.0	3	5

Gary has also supplied us with a study of when injuries are most likely to occur, so you can plan ahead to the months where you might be worst hit.

JULY	7.6 %
AUGUST	9.1 %
SEPTEMBER	18.2 %
OCTOBER	4.5 %
NOVEMBER	9.1 %
DECEMBER	15.2 %
JANUARY	9.1 %
FEBRUARY	6.1 %
MARCH	3.0 %
APRIL	13.6 %
MAY	4.5 %

A TRAGEDY THERE AS CITY'S PROLIFIC SCORER IS CARRIED OFF...
YESSSS!!

Local Rules is the part of Fantasy League where you get to decide how your league runs. Getting your Local Rules right can streamline your league, add strategy and above all, make it more fun. When forming your Local Rules, take your time. It's difficult to foresee all the angles at the start of the season, so let them evolve slowly. Many leagues' Local Rules only really begin to click after a few weeks of trial and error. Choose what's practical for you, don't over-complicate, but try to be creative.

The first Local Rule you will need to vote on will be which scoring system your league uses. There is a choice of two, imaginatively titled System A and System B.

System A is the original, simpler system that anyone starting from The Daily Telegraph or 90 Minutes leagues will be used to. System B was brought in at the start of 1993-94 and has proved to be a big success.

In any event, it's worth taking a vote on your system before the Auction, because your choice could determine your bidding strategy. Your options are :

scoring system a

Goal : 3 pts

Assist : 2 pts

Clean Sheet : 4 pts

Goal Against : -1 pt

Simple, fair and practical. The swings in points can be huge, so your league will change dramatically from week to week. Beware, with four points for a clean sheet, defence can occasionally become a little too important. Also, in larger leagues, when decent defenders are in short supply, managers are tempted to play absent defenders to avoid losing points.

scoring system b

Goal: 3 pts

Assist: 2 pts

Defender Playing: 1 pt (if on for at least 45 minutes)

Clean Sheet: 3 pts (including 1 for playing)

Goal Against: –1 pt for every goal conceded

System B is designed to protect against managers fielding absent defenders and to avoid too much emphasis on defence. Fielding a defender who does not play gets you no points, which is equivalent to your defender conceding a goal. It is also worth looking at the System B points at the back of the book to see how it makes defenders across all teams more valuable, so you're not in a situation in which only defenders from the top three clubs are worth having. Also, you will notice that the swing for losing a clean sheet in System B is 3 points, whereas in System A the swing is 5 points. Finally, System B should narrow the gap between the top and bottom teams in your league, so your league should be tighter and more exciting through the season.

Below is a step-by-step guide to some of the more popular Local Rule options. You might want to vote on some of these before your Auction, but it should be a case of softly, softly through this chapter. Unless you're pretty confident, don't launch into a million debates before your league's been running a while - you might want to get a feel for what may or may not work for your league before deciding on everything.

do transfers through your chairman

This is a basic that's worth enforcing from day one. If transfers are made direct to Fantasy League, you could end up buying someone another manager owns. If the chairman keeps a master list of everyone's team, things will run a lot smoother. When it comes to substitutions, there should be no problem in making them direct with Fantasy League. In fact, try not to burden your chairman with substitutions at all; it will only be an unnecessary drain on their time.

IT WAS TIME TO BRING ON THE 'SUPERSUB'.

a budget for the season

Most leagues allocate a £5m budget to each team after the auction. This adds an important dimension to the game: risk. It means that you have to think twice before every transfer - "Can I afford him? "Is he worth that?". It's up to you how you allocate your budget.

Some options are :

a) Wipe the slate clean after the auction, so everyone starts with £5m

b) Add £5m to what each manager has left after the auction

c) Make £20m your budget for the season, so you're aiming not to spend it all in the auction

d) Only allocate the £5m after a few months of the season

how do transfers work?

A player's time has come. You want to part company. You have two choices. Either you can do a deal with another manager or you can buy someone no-one else owns - take a dip in the "Free Agent Pool". Deals between managers can be straight swaps, straight cash, player plus cash, loans, options, you name it. For " free agent" transfers, you can set out more standard rules, as explained below. All figures are at your discretion, and these are only suggestions.

flat fee transfers

This is the simplest way of controlling budgets through the season. Give everyone a £5m budget, which can be added to money remaining after the auction. Each week, managers may request players from the pool, notifying the chairman by a Thursday or Friday deadline.

If a request for a player is unopposed, the manager gets him for a flat £250,000. If two or more managers go for the same player, resolve it with a mini-auction, or with sealed bids, or in favour of the lowest team in the league, or by drawing lots. To avoid managers jumping on the bandwagon for a player, requests should be sealed.

sealed bid transfers

This scheme is more sophisticated and should be more fun to run. This also works with a season budget of £5m, where sealed bids are submitted weekly. Each request for a player must include a bid which is at the manager's discretion. Bids start at zero, and should go up in £100,000 jumps. A manager may submit as many requests as he wishes, but the combined value of the bids cannot exceed his current budget. This scheme makes for plenty of strategy and second-guessing, as well as providing an exciting end to each week. Some leagues allow managers alternative choices on a bid, which come into action only if they lose out on their main bid. This can be complicated and perhaps takes some of the pressure off making a bid.

In both of the above, it's assumed that the departing player does not generate you any revenue. In some leagues, managers receive a percentage of the price they paid in the auction for the player that's being sold. It seen as "insurance" money - OK for an injury perhaps, but if the player has a dud season, why be compensated for bidding badly?

....

TO ALL FANTASISTS: TRANSFER NOTICE

Due to a personality clash between the star striker of Foggon's Fighting Flab FC and its manager, it has been agreed by both parties that the player shall leave the club as soon as is practical.

David Hirst has been unhappy at the club since signing

last week. He wants to move to a club that wants him; he does not want to play second fiddle to the in-flavour Gary Penrice or the scum of the earth, Prince of Footballing Darkness, Spawn of all that is wrong with our national game, Dean Saunders.

The club want around £250,000 for this internationally-qualified striker. The club will benefit by then being able to buy a centre back who is not guaranteed to leak at least one goal a week. The buyer will benefit by picking up a striker with huge potential for a fee which is guaranteed to be less than that for which he could be purchased after his return to the pool. The smallest possible bid would be £300,000 to get him back from the pool. There is always the risk that the price would go even higher to be sure of landing the player.

All offers should be made to the team manager by close Wednesday.

mid season auctions

A great way of spicing things up during the season. On a specified date, managers have to sell a fixed number of players back to the pool for all or part of their auction price. All players sold back to the pool (and already in the pool) are then up for auction. If you're short of cash you might have to consider selling an expensive signing to raise finance for new additions.

gate or tv money

This is a variation on the common flat £5m season budget. Let budgets accumulate during the season, say by £500,000 a month. This is realistic and forces managers to pace themselves during the season. The fairest way is to let everyone's budget increase at the same rate (ie. to "share" gate receipts) - this is also how the Premiership TV money works, so it's also the most realistic.

Alternatively, give extra money to teams while they're at the top of the league (realistic but unfair), or give more to those at the bottom (unrealistic but fair).

cash injections

You want to make budgets as volatile as possible, and to provide ways for struggling clubs to raise cash. This rule does just that. If a manager gets the top score at the end of the month, he receives a cash injection of say, £500,000. Second best gets £250,000. A great incentive and an extra interest for end of month scores. Another source of cash can be for a good cup run. If you're running local cups, (see **cup competitions**) why not reward a cup winner with £1m and the runner-up with £500,000? It's worth giving some thought to other ways of providing cash injections.

transfer deadlines

As the season draws to a close, some teams may drop out of your title race. To avoid bottom teams being coerced into selling star players, you may need to enforce an end of season transfer deadline.

carrying money over to next season

THANKS FOR IAN WRIGHT.
YOUR BUNG IS BEHIND THE CISTERN IN TRAP 3 OF THE TOILETS AT WATERLOO.

An extra dimension to budgeting is planning ahead for next season. This should liven up the transfer market towards the end of your season, which is traditionally a quiet period. This can also provide added interest for struggling clubs at the end of the season by allowing them to raise cash for the new campaign. You should be aware that this rule achieves the opposite of transfer deadlines. A struggling club may well be stripped of all its good players by the title challengers, but this will liven up the top of the table race. The most important consideration is HOW the players are sold. As long as managers don't do underhand deals, the rule can be introduced fairly and has definite strengths.

carrying players over to next season

Along the same lines as above, this rule can also add the facet of playing for more than the current season. On an emotional level, managers develop favourites over a nine-month season and can be reduced to tears if they fail to recapture them the following season. Also, it adds a degree of reality and establishes a real-life club "dynasty" for your Fantasy League team. Perhaps most important is the strategy that is involved in choosing who to retain. A player should be retained for all or part of their auction price, or for a flat fee. There should be a limit on how many players you can retain, and the amount you pay to retain a player must come out of your auction budget for next season. Will a player sustain form from one season to the next? How much is it worth investing to retain a few players? How many players are worth keeping? Worth thinking about.

promotion and relegation

If you are able to set up more than one league, promotion and relegation can mean most teams will have something to play for until the final day of the season. It also adds to the reality of your league, which is always a nice touch. With promotion and relegation to play for, it's probably worth introducing transfer deadlines to avoid major controversy. Also, what about giving some thought to promotion play-offs in the last couple of weeks?

sample local rules

We've enclosed a few sample local rules that might be of interest.

....

"GET OFF DON'S SISTER" LEAGUE

All teams are allocated a budget of £5 million on top of the excess from the auction.

Signing players from the pool:

Sealed bids to be submitted to me by Friday of each week, beginning Friday 6th August. Mark envelopes, 'sealed bid' so that I don't open them by mistake.

When all bids are opened if no-one else has bid for your

player then you get him for a flat fee of £250,000. If more than one bid is received, highest bid gets him.

You may put in more than one bid and if you like you can indicate that you only want the 2nd bid to be accepted if your 1st choice goes elsewhere. If you are doing this, please mark against players 1st preference, 2nd preference, etc. No multiple bids for the same player.

Please indicate which player/s you want to release if you get your new player.

You may not sign a player that is not on the Fantasy League list in the hope that they will be joining a Premier League club, as no code will exist for them. Just get in early with those bids when they do sign!

If a side is bottom on 2 successive league print outs from Fantasy League, then they will face a transfer request from one of their players. This player will be chosen out of the hat by myself and will then go into the pool and be subject to bids. If no bids are received, he can be retained. If bids are received, the club selling him gets the fee (remember to make the team change when you lose a player).

Quota of 2 players from each Premier League club will be strictly enforced. If one of your players signs for a club from which you already have 2 players, you must not play him prior to auction.

Private transfers are OK, but remember the disciplinary committee will be looking out for 'service station deals'. Legitimate currency in a transfer deal is a)money, b) a player, c) team changes.

We will have a mini auction mid way through the season. A transfer ban will be imposed 1 month prior to the auction and all teams will be compelled to release 2 players back to the pool on the day of the auction.

The cup draw will be held on the same day as the mini auction. Ian will organise the cup. There will be 6 ties in the first round, with the teams winning each tie (by virtue of getting more points) going through. The 2 losers with the highest points will also progress.

Side which is top on each print out gets £300,000 gate money - side which is 2nd gets £200,000 and side which is 3rd gets £100,000.

The disciplinary committee is Doug (Chairman), myself and Ian. Any info on Brownie's dodgy dealing welcome.

Team changes cannot be made during a programme of games, i.e. You cannot pick one player who is playing on a Tuesday, and then replace him with another who is playing on a Wednesday. Your team must consist of 11 players for an entire weekend and likewise for any weekday programmes. The disciplinary committee will be keeping an eye out for transgressors.

Some great ideas, but I'd be a bit wary about giving extra gate money to the league leaders - isn't this a dangerous case of the rich getting richer? Also, wouldn't it be more skilful to leave the sealed bids up to the manager rather than fixing them at a flat £250,000?

The league I compete in has a simple but very effective set of local rules. If it's not blowing my own trumpet too much, these are the rules of the NCGC Fantasy League :

NCGC Fantasy League

1. *Each manager allocated a budget of £5m after the auction. No money carried forward from the auction.*
2. *Sealed bids can be made every week. All bids must be submitted by Thursday evening. Minimum bid £0, jumps of £250,000. No "alternative" bids if first bid falls through.*
3. *Each bid must also include name of player to be*

released back to the pool. No money is received for him, and he is not available until the following week.

4. *All bids opened on Thursday nights at the Taj Mahal.*
5. *If two managers bid the same amount for a player, revised sealed bids should be submitted by deadlocked managers until a clear winner emerges. Each revised bid can be higher or lower than the previous bid, and there is no limit to the amount of re-bids.*

POSSIBLE REVISIONS :

a. *Looking at the possibility of lowering jumps from £250,000 to £200,000.*
b. *Perhaps introduce a minimum bid of £100,000.*

Although fairly simple, these rules work excellently, but we do have the advantage of all meeting up every Thursday night.

The last word on local rules has to go to the Rockingham Village Stores League :

ROCKINGHAM VILLAGE STORES FANTASY LEAGUE

A1: ROCKINGHAM VILLAGE STORES FANTASY LEAGUE AIMS: THE CHARTER

All those who partake of the piss-take are equally valued. Our success is based upon:

1) a wide framework of piss-taking opportunities.

2) a positive recognition of lack of achievement which undermines self-esteem.

3) no recognition of achievement

4) the celebration of success with lots of alcohol.

B1: MANAGERS' CODE OF CONDUCT

i)Outside the changing room:

Acceptable standards depend upon the example of us all.

All informal contact contributes to standards of behaviour. Expect to:

** deal with any breach of Regulations - to ignore it is to condone it!*

** recognise and use wind-up opportunities.*

Do all you can to:

** humiliate - it breeds resentment*

** victimise - it is fun*

ii)Inside the changing room:

Create and sustain a positive, supportive and secure environment. Well-prepared, stimulating team talks generate very little and earn nothing much.

Expect to:

** be addressed as Boss or Gaffer*

** know and use players' silly nicknames.*

B2: DISCIPLINARY PROCEDURE

Requests for a Disciplinary Hearing can be made by any manager at any time in writing to the League Secretary. The request must:

** name the culprit*

** describe the crime*

** propose a progressive scale of sanctions*

The convened Panel of Peers must select a suitable sanction or any combination thereof.

4Q: GRIEVANCE PROCEDURE

Any manager with a grievance relating to the mismanagement of the RVSFL can SOD OFF.

C1: ASSEMBLIES

(i)Managers' Assemblies

These are to be organised at the Managers' discretion in suitable (ie: Licensed) premises. Normally the Assembly will adjourn to a host managers' house in time for "Match of the Day". The host is to provide food and drink and guest managers are not to abuse the host (for a short while).

(Ii)Success Assembly

The League Champion is to be responsible for this event, at which the trophies are to be presented. Expect it to:

** take part on FA Cup Final Day*

** open at about 1 pm at an agreed (licensed) venue*

** adjourn to the host manager's house in time for the National Anthem at Wembley*

(iii)The MM Cup is to be organised during the season and run by a trustworthy manager (i.e. one who has not yet been caught fiddling the [NC] books). The entry fee is to be a 4-pack. The finalists are to split the loot 60:40.

E1: COMPLAINTS PROCEDURE

See Section 4Q

cup competitions

At the start of season, every side dreams of the championship. Forty two games, week in, week out, it's the true test of quality. It takes real character, a bit of luck, and dogged consistency.

Face it, not all teams are cut out to be champions. You might not have the time to pore into Fantasy League research. Perhaps you work too hard, you might be jinxed with injuries, often your side could be just be crap. In any event, your team might be a cup side. Perhaps it's better suited to the one-off, cut-and-thrust of knockout competition. You might find it's easier to motivate your players for the big occasion than for the forty two week slog of the Premiership.

For the uninitiated, Fantasy Cup football is based on each team's score in a chosen week of Premier League matches. It might seem surprising that it's not based on FA Cup football, but that's because by basing it on league matches all your players are sure to play. Also, it makes it easy to run on any week's report, as you'll be using the "WEEK TOTAL" figure on your league table.

how to organise a fantasy league cup

1. Choose a name for the Cup Competition. Be ingenious.

2. Work out how many rounds you need, taking into account any preliminary rounds or byes which may be necessary.

3. Choose a date for the first round.

4. Draw the matches and any byes.

5. On the chosen week, compare "WEEK TOTAL" on report for the teams paired against each other. The team with the most points progresses. In the event of a draw, the team scoring the most goals goes through.

6. Repeat process until winner emerges.

7. Allow 2-3 hours / days / weeks / months gloating time for the winning manager. Then organise a civic reception with an open-top bus.

possible variations

1. Arrange matches over two legs. (ie. add together two separate WEEK TOTALS)

2. For draws, organise a penalty shoot-out. Each manager has five tosses of a coin, taken one by one, as in a shoot-out. A head is a goal and a tail is a miss. If there is no winner after both managers have completed their five tosses, go to sudden death. Stupid, but realistic.

Many leagues find that cups are so successful that they tend to arrange a few each season. You know you've gone too far when you start calling them silly names like Sherpa Van or Simod.

....

Cup Competitions: This essentially relates to the last sentence. Two fabulous suggestions for names for cup competitions from that man Wilmer. They are "The White Liquid Secreted by Female Animals for the Nourishment of their Young Cup" and "The Lactation Cup." To these I add my own sorry suggestion of "The Fizzy Dirty Water Cup." As you can see, further suggestions would be warmly welcomed. Also, suggestions for prizes are needed. How about free changes for Fantasy League cash to buy yet more players (steady, Mukhtar!)?

We've included contributions from two of the best cup competitions in 1993-94:

....

THE SCUMBUSTING IS AN ART LEAGUE - PIN: 743

This article refers to the Grand Final of the Fantasy

League Cup Qualification Competition.

The Chairman's Free Kick - December 21st 1993

What I want to know is.....Who said football is a funny old game? It's bloody well not! It can ruin your whole day, and put a downer on Christmas and New Year celebrations. It can stop you sleeping and start you drinking - excessively! After what happened on Sunday, you can even start wondering if it's all really worth it, I can tell you.

I don't have Sky T.V., and I'm torn between whether or not I wished I did. Are Yan Rochdale In Disguise versus Three Off The Tee in the SCUMBUSTER CUP came to the wire on Sunday at Old Trafford where representation from Man Utd and Aston Villa fought it out. Saturday night and A.Y.R.I.D. led 3 O.T.T. 9-8, Sunday's statistics were vital.

A.Y.R.I.D.	*3 O.T.T*
P Parker	*R Giggs*
G Pallister	*R Keane*
D Atkinson	*D Saunders*

I listened to Radio 5, tuning in when Keane fed Cantona for Man U.'s 1st! A.Y.R.I.D. 9 - 3 O.T.T. 10! The game was good but I remained confident of a Clean Sheet. That would have given me a win 15-10, enough to allow Saunders to score and Keane to assist. But my confident aura was stressed when Giggs came on and all sorts of sequences went through my mind.

It eased slightly when Saunders went off but Villa got ever closer and I felt that if it was meant to be that they scored, then hopefully it would be Atkinson. Can you follow this?!! I was in mental torture waiting for Mr Barratt to return to the office and call me (does he ever?). Then United scored once and then again and I was jubilant as neither Keane nor Giggs were involved.

One minute left, surely all over, SURELY! ONE

MINUTE! (Singing) "One minute! One minute! One minute!"(Ask David about the tune). I was probably the only person in the entire universe whistling for the end (God my neighbours hate me!). Then it happened, a Villa cross and Cox scored ("Who?" you ask. "The devil in disguise" I say.) My clean sheets gone, Peter Jones wins 2-0 on the day 10-9 for the weekend. Mesmerised, I am - in a daze. Dammit but I never much liked United, so I absolutely detest them now - well done Galatasaray!

My world had ebbed away, the weekend but a damp black hole for memory's sake; Arsenal's lost and Reading only drew. I even called F.L. early the next day to see if Cox's goal had been dramatically disallowed during the after-match drinking session. So I had to concede defeat, down a Scotch or four and call my adversary to offer my congratulations.

Yes, Congratulations Peter Jones and Three Off The Tee, SCUMBUSTER CUP WINNERS 1993 and award ye shall do to the National Competition. Whilst I wish you the very best of luck, I recommend that you consider strengthening your side in readiness. To that end, I'd be very grateful if you would scan the players remaining sheets during Christmas and give me your decision in the first week.

In the meantime, I will hold all changes, changes I know that others wish to make, myself included, quite quickly so the faster the better. I hope that everyone else concurs on them. Remember, only 2 players from any one side and you sell and buy at £300,000. Your swift attention will be much appreciated.

SCUMBUSTER CUP WINNERS 1993,
THREE OFF THE TEE!

THE "THEY DON'T LIKE IT UP 'EM" CHALLENGE CUP 1994

Results:

1) St Albans Hounds 6 : Trotters Athletic 12

2) Polaroid United 14 : Wibble Wibble Lobster Lobster 2

3) AFC Johnners 3 : Galaxy All-Stars 6

Reports:

HOUNDS DUMPED BY TROTTERS

You could see from his face on Friday night that Harry was worried... the way he shifted uneasily from foot to foot...the way he dreaded an Ipswich clean sheet. Even Shearer couldn't save Harry from an embarrassing humbling at the hands of Bacon,s Trotters.

The Ipswich duo of Forrest and Thompson condemned Harry to an Arsenal-like cup exit, and meant a night of wild celebration for Trotters and (of course) some boisterous phone calls on Monday morning. Trotters have undoubtedly peaked in mid-February, and Simon's manager's position looks safe until at least the semis. Could Fee-Orr-Toffed be a Nordic Wembley winner?

As for Harry, Matthew Le Tissier - need I say more?

LOBSTERS SUNK BY POLAROID

In a one sided affair, an upbeat, Upminster performance from Polaroid's ten men accounted for a dispirited Lobster outfit.

Nick was hoping that hitting the barmaid in The Cock would turn out to be a lucky omen - unfortunately it was not to be. He needed a big performance from his Villa striker, and the Villa striker obliged with 3 goals - but the wrong striker as Dean Saunders was sat on Nick's bench. (Another Johnson masterstroke?)

Bosnich, Berg and Beardsley made the game safe for Polaroid. As they strode manfully into the last four, and still harbour hopes of a league and cup double.

For Wibble Wibble there will be no Wembley, Wembley.

GALAXY SCRAPE PAST JOHNNERS

This was the closest fought of the three quarter final ties. Top of the table Galaxy survived an early scare when Robbie Earle bagged early on, but gradually the goals flew past John Beresford, and Galaxy gained a crucial advantage.

Galaxy have been big on assists all season, and Holden and Sutton didn't let Varney down. Sutton's points clinched the win, and worse for Johnners was the inevitable phone call from Galaxy.

AFC Johnners now have to consider where they can go from here (downwards? - ED). Perhaps an assault on the Autoglass Trophy, or even a change of ball colour to claret and blue...

90 MINUTES FROM WEMBLEY

Cup football is upon us again as the 'They Don't Like it up 'em Challenge Cup' reaches the semi-final stage.

POLAROID UTD *vs.* GALAXY ALL-STARS

On paper, this one is hard to call. Polaroid have been consistent if unspectacular in recent weeks, and will fancy their chances of upsetting the long time top of the table, Galaxy All-Stars. Cantona is now fit, and whilst Polaroid will be without Mark Bowen as Norwich don't play, importantly, Galaxy will be without the league's top man, Chris Sutton. Both teams have Blackburn defenders, so Galaxy will be looking to Red Bastards Irwin and Bruce to come up with the goods. Will Ian Marshall be the difference?

GLADSTONE SCREWERS *vs.* TROTTERS ATHLETIC

On paper, this is easy to call. Screwers score plenty of goals, and despite the likely absence of Steino, will also be looking for clean sheets from their two Red Bastards.

But...it has been the year of the underdog, and rumour has it that Simon has been under some real dogs in his time. This season has seen Bolton beat Arsenal, Oxford beat Leeds, Trotters beat the hounds, and West Ham beat Kidderminster, so perhaps the omens are good for Trotters. Will Ipswich defenders be the difference...?

Results next week, when two managers will be getting measured for their suits, and two managers will 'not be taking any calls.'

POLAROID *vs.* SCREWERS

An exciting week of Fantasy Football, saw the celebrations and tears much associated with cup football, and left us with the thrilling Wembley match up of Polaroid Utd. against Gladstone Screwers - Cantona against Cole, Deano against Geordie, Beast against Beauty.

The semi-finals couldn't have been more different - one decided in the last minute, the other a one-sided affair.

RESULTS

1) Galaxy All-Stars 20 - Polaroid United 21

2) Gladstone Screwers 12 - Trotters Athletic 5

Reports:

HOW DO YOU FEEL, VARNEY?

Picture the scene...Hillsborough 5:46pm. Sunday March 20th 1994....Sheffield Wed 1 : Blackburn 1, but more importantly, Galaxy lead Polaroid 20-19, and Ian is already thinking about the Twin Towers. But in the 89th minute, Ripley shoots, Newell bags the rebound, and Deano pockets a last-minute assist to shatter Galaxy's double hopes, and Varney bit the dust.

This was a high scoring contest: Dorigo with 2 clean sheets, goals for Holden and Rush, assists for Gary Speed left Galaxy looking good, but Monsieur Eric's 10 point haul in the 5-0 demolition of Sheffield Wednesday kept Deano afloat, and then Martin Keown shackled Le Big Nose at Le Dell, to give Polaroid via Adams and

Keown two clean sheets. Henning Berg's assist brought Deano closer to Ian, before Ripley delivered the Killer Blow.

Sutton's absence was vital for Galaxy, as was Swindon's double against his Red Bastards. For Deano, Eric's contribution was vital despite his G.B.H. which resulted in his sending off.

So Dean can measure up for his £500 Boss Suit (to be ruined by Nick?...) whilst for Varney.....Robert Lee......if only.

TROTTERS SCREWED BY GOAL KING

Despite their heroics against the hounds in the last round, Trotters were unable to live with a consistent screwers outfit. The major difference was the snip, who moved into the assist market at Upton Park and contributed a decisive 9 points to the screwers.

There had been an earlier scare for Geordie, when Fjortoft scored against the Red Bastards (Schmeichel and Parker), and Ferdinand added an assist, but Winterburn held on for another Arsenal clean sheet and condemned Trotters to their much anticipated cup-exit.

Trotter's defenders were mainly noticeable by their absence (if they don't play, they don't concede!) as Forrest, Thompson, Nicol and Moran were all sidelined. The lacklustre midfield quartet again all flattered to decline, and Trotters, looking at re-election in the league, could also be looking at a new manager.

As for Screwers, dreams of the double persist.......

THE FINAL COUNTDOWN

Deano and Geordie have been measured up for their suits, they've argued about ticket allocation for the big game, Barry Davies has interviewed the managers at the Country Hotel, and Botham beat Beaumont on Cup Final 'Question of Sport'.

The talking is now over as these two big teams face their

final match up at Wembley - where legends are made. (Who writes this crap? - ED)

There's a full league programme for the final. The games are as follows:

Mon 11th April

Blackburn vs. A Villa

Sat 16th April

Arsenal vs. Chelsea

Liverpool vs. Newcastle

Man City vs. Norwich

Oldham vs. West Ham

Wimbledon vs. Man Utd

Sheff Utd vs. A Villa

Southampton vs. Blackburn

Sun 17th April

Leeds vs. Spurs

THE TWO TEAMS

1)POLAROID UNITED

Consistency has been the name of the game for Polaroid, with four players having scored over 35 points. They are handily placed to mount a late title challenge, though they may be affected by the recent loss of Cantona.

In the quarter final, Polaroid had an easy victory over Wibble Wibble, whilst the semi-final will live long in the memory, being decided in the last minute of the final match. Whether Deano's nerves could stand another emotional onslaught is debatable, and Polaroid may have peaked already.

But should Polaroid pull it off, Deano will be dancing in

the streets of Upminster, and Upminster will rightly have earned its place in Fantasy History.

2)GLADSTONE SCREWERS

Previously described as flamboyant, purposeful, exciting and free-scoring, the Screwers have looked to individuals for big performances and Messrs. Cole and Le Tissier have duly obliged.

Screwers have had an easy passage to the Twin Towers, receiving a controversial buy in the Quarter Final and then calmly swotting aside the interesting challenge of Trotters Athletic.

Screwers are currently hard on the trail of league leaders, Galaxy All-Stars, and this could be the first leg of a Famcus Double - I hope so!!!

MATCH ANALYSIS

After Mondays 1-0 win for Blackburn over Aston Villa, Polaroid lead by 3 to 1 due to Berg's clean sheet, so it's fifteen love for Deano, though there's a lot more football to be played.

The big game is at Anfield, where Andy Cole and Neil Ruddock face Beardsley, Fox and Clark. A Ruddock clean sheet would be a real result for Geordie. Similarly, at the Dell, Le Big Nose faces Henning Berg and Stuart Ripley, and again a clean sheet for Berg would be good news for Dean.

Polaroid's 'Jim' Bowen returns to Granada, specifically Maine Road, and will be looking for a rare clean sheet against a rampant City outfit.

The Wimbledon - Man U. Clash sees Schmeichel and Parker face Reg Holdsworth, and Keown, Adams and Winterburn will be looking to snuff out Chelsea (if selected).

Matt Holmes has been on form recently, and the Sunday Match of Leeds vs. Spurs will see White, McAllister and Rosenthal all in the prowl for vital 3 pointers.

So, there you have it - The Bookies have it even and

there's little to choose between the teams.

All that remains is to sing 'Abide with me', and then Boo the National Anthem.

Best Wishes to The Screwers

Geordie

DONKEY DECIDES IT FOR DEANO

Cup Final Result: POLAROID UTD 14 *vs.* GLADSTONE SCREWERS 10

Polaroid Utd dismissed the challenge of the Gladstone Screwers in the Challenge Cup final and picked up the first trophy of the season.

In last week's uncannily accurate cup final preview, Polaroid's consistency was highlighted, as was the flamboyance of Screwers Cole and Le Tissier. In true Arsenal style, consistency beat flamboyance and Deano took the cup.

The deciding factor of the day was George Graham's team selection for Arsenal's home game with Chelsea. Winterburn was injured, and instead of bringing in Linighan, George plumped for Keown and Donkey. They kept a clean sheet scoring 8 points against a Steinless Chelsea attack, for whom the talented Eddie Newton hit a last minute post.

Le Tissier and Cole, Geordie's Mr Reliables, scored 7 and 5 points respectively, but it was the Polaroid midfield which rose to the big occasion. Ripley, Fox and the underrated Matt all picked up points, and at 4:40 on Saturday, the score stood at 14-10. Geordie was desperate for a Man Utd clean sheet against Holdsworth's Wimbledon, but Schmeichel's Teflon hands wisely spilled the ball at the feet of Fash the Bash and Screwers chalked up -2.

At 14-8, Screwers needed miracles on Sunday, but McAllister's late assist was all they could scrape, and Polaroid won the day 14-10.

After the match, both managers were obviously in contrasting moods:

DEANO: *"I can't believe it....I can't believe I've managed to get a trophy on the sideboard....it's unbelievable. When I was a boy, I used to dream about managing a Fantasy League team, and to actually go and win the cup is just brilliant. This has got to be the best day of my life.*

For the match itself, I've been in training for a few weeks, and I was really focused. I knew I would have to be on top-form to beat the Screwers, and all my players performed, especially Donkey. Donkey Adams shows how football should be played, he was magnificent... he's a bit like Beckenbauer in his prime.

It's a great day for Polaroid, and for the whole of Upminster. The town has been gripped by cup-fever, and it's the biggest day for the town since they opened the new ring-road.

We're having a civic reception in the local snooker club tonight, so it should be a great night."

fantasy league scrapbook

This chapter features a small selection of the excellent contributions we regularly receive from leagues all over the country. It's been a very tough task choosing what to include, but we feel that the articles below are a good representation of life in a Fantasy League.

Thanks again to everyone who sent stuff in, we'd have loved to include it all, but the book would have run to five volumes!

long lunchbreak league

When it comes to fertile imaginations, The Long Lunchbreak League are surely the ultimate role models for us all to follow. Not content to merely play in a simple League system, they have concocted The Principality of Long Lunchbreak where all the teams compete in three divisions : Division One, Division Two (South) and Division Two (North). We've published the map which will give you an idea of the regions, local derbies, and basic geography of the Principality. We're not sure whether the place becomes a big tourist trap in the summer.

CLUB - Busy at Work

DIVISION - Two (South)

CHAIRMAN - Craig Hatchard

TOWN - Nocashire, Buumlicker

NICKNAME - Forever Skint

ADDITIONAL INFORMATION

Original member of division Two (South). Colours: Dark & Light Blue/Dark Blue.

A small club that survives by employing a good youth policy. How long they are able to keep Alan Shearer, a home-grown talent, may determine the club's long-term

league future. Complacency in March and April has led to relegation.

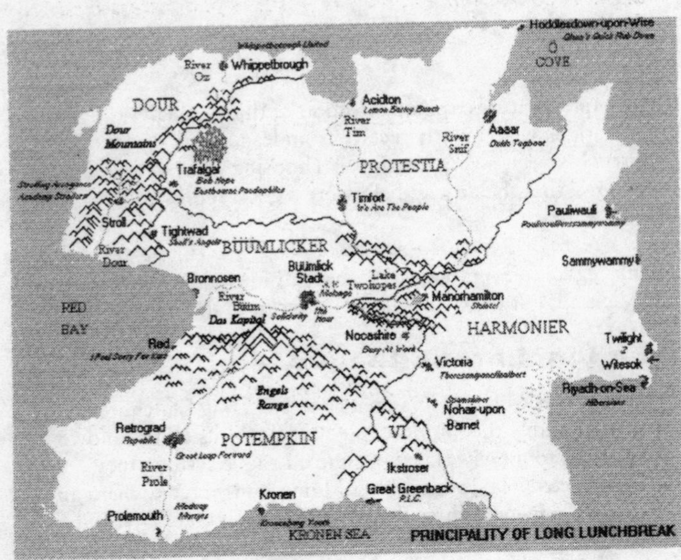

CLUB	*Dukla Tugboat*
DIVISION	*One*
CHAIRMAN	*Andrew Watson*
TOWN	*New Thedesk Park, Aaar, Protestia*
NICKNAME	*Scabs, Blacklegs or Wankers*
HONOURS	*League Champions 1992-93. Smooth Round Bum Shield Winners 1993-94*

ADDITIONAL INFORMATION

Founder member of league. Colours: Red with White Hoops/Red

Founded by refugee dock workers from O, the club won

the inaugural championship. The club now boasts the largest Armchair Supporters Club in the country with the vast majority not living in the Aaaar or Protestia area. A comfortable mid-table position guarantees First Division football next season.

CLUB	*Eastbourne Paedophiles*
DIVISION	*Two (North)*
CHAIRMAN	*Marcus Lyon*
ADDRESS	*School Lane, Trafalgar, Protestia*
NICKNAME	*Little Puppy Dogs*
HONOURS	*Long Lunchbreak League Cup Winners 1993-94. Division Two (North) Champions 1993-94. Protestia County Cup Winners 1994.*

ADDITIONAL INFORMATION

Original member of Division Two (North). Colours: Blue & Red Stripes/Blue.

Club with the largest junior supporters branch in Long Lunchbreak and the only club to provide crëche facilities. A marvellous season has seen the club capture three trophies and they can look forward to their first season in the top division.

CLUB	*Great Leap Forward*
DIVISION	*One*
CHAIRMAN	*Jason Freed*
YEAR FORMED	*1917*
TOWN	*Purges Park, Salt Mine Lane, Retrograd, Potempkin*
NICKNAME	*The Plans or Sickles*
HONOURS	*League Runners-up 1992-93.*

Long Lunchbreak League Cup Finalists 1992-93.

ADDITIONAL INFORMATION

Founder member of league. Colours: Black & Blue Stripes/Black

After finishing runners-up in both league and cup last season, The Plans have struggled to repeat this success. Although the defence has performed admirably, the lack of ability to score goals has cost them dear and the team were relegated, to the heartfelt disappointment of football lovers everywhere. Visiting supporters are guaranteed a warm reception in Retrograd.

CLUB	*Pauliwauliluvssammywammy*
DIVISION	*One*
CHAIRMAN	*Paul Hughes*
YEAR FORMED	*1970*
TOWN	*Highams Park, 666 Lover's Lane, Pauliwali, Harmonier*
NICKNAME	*Westsiders*
HONOURS	*Long Lunchbreak League Cup Finalists 1993-94.* *National Cup semi-finalists 1992-93*

ADDITIONAL INFORMATION:

Founder member of league. Colours: Black/Black

Having made use of the funds provided by the merger with Sammywammy FC to put the club on a firm financial footing, the club has now reverted to playing all its games in Pauliwauli. The jewel in the crown of their first season is Andy Cole and this man, almost totally alone, has secured a First Division berth next season.

CLUB *PLC*

DIVISION *Two (South)*

CHAIRMAN *Jerry Boxall*

TOWN *Prime Development Park, Great Greenback, Vi*

NICKNAME *Satellites*

ADDITIONAL INFORMATION:

Original member of Division Two (South). Colours: White/Navy Blue

Money is the only concern of this club. Their motto is "Profit before Promotion" and only those able to afford executive boxes or satellite dishes are able to watch games. Away fans can watch from a train but are not allowed to disembark.

CLUB *Republic*

DIVISION *One*

CHAIRMAN *Robert Thomas*

YEAR FORMED *1789 as Third Estate F.C., 1972 Republic*

TOWN *Robespierre Park, Durrutti Road, Retrograd, Potempkin*

NICKNAME *Sans Culottes*

HONOURS: *League Champions 1993-94. Long Lunchbreak League Cup Winners 1992-93. Potempkin Cup Winners 1993-94.*

ADDITIONAL INFORMATION:

Founder member of league. Colours: Blue/White

The reconstruction of Robespierre Park during the first half of the season had a detrimental effect on performances. Since the stadium has been back to full capacity of 45,000 (all standing) the team has improved enormously and deservedly took the championship with an impressive run-in. Winning the Potempkin Cup was as important to the club and supporters were overjoyed to see the trophy in Retrograd for the first time. Travel advice for visiting supporters: don't.

CLUB	*Theresonlyonefinalbert*
DIVISION	*Two (South)*
CHAIRMAN	*Alby Westover*
TOWN	*Bumtitty Park, Victoria, Harmonier*
NICKNAME	*The Pervs*
HONOURS	*Division Two (South) Champions 1993-1994*

ADDITIONAL INFORMATION:

Original member of Division Two (South). Colours: White/Black

Commonly regarded as the club with the most whingeing, pessimistic chairman in league. The team has overcome teamtalks such as "We've fucking had it" to claim the Division 2 (S) title, albeit with the most defensive team in the league.

CLUB	*Z*
DIVISION	*Two (South)*
CHAIRMAN	*Mike Tatham*
TOWN	*Tits Oot Lane, Twilight, Harmonier*
NICKNAME	*Zoners*
HONOURS	*Division Two (South) Cup winners 1993-94. Harmonier County Cup Winners 1993-94*

ADDITIONAL INFORMATION:

Original member of Division Two (South).
Colours: White/White

Already Division Two (S) cup winners, Z were in the semi-final of the Long Lunchbreak Cup and ran away with the Harmonier County Cup. Besides this success they gained promotion through the play-offs. The people of Twilight must be very satisfied with their club's performance.

DICKS OUT

Madness and confusion reign at the Wanderers, with May joining Champions Again in exchange for Dicks and Stuart. May was pleased to declare that:

"After a year's struggle at the Wanderers I've decided to move to a club geared for success, playing the kind of football all real fans enjoy. Mark Brown has revitalised the England career of Peter Beardsley and Darren Anderton with others sure to follow, as success breeds success.
P. S. I've also been a lifelong fan."

With players talking that sort of garbage, it's not surprising Wanderers have been so dreadful this season!

CRISIS AT MMC14

Following the recent disastrous start to the new Premiership season and their first round exit to arch rivals OTSTED Offenders FC, rumours of a fierce Boardroom battle are emerging from Hawkwood Lane. An inside source for the club said, "...the lads are pig sick - Brian."

At an emotionally-charged press conference MMC14's manager, the dynamic and highly successful local BMW owner was heard to whimper "It's not fair!"

MMC14's Directors, or should it be Governors (?) have

DUCK NEWS

ISSUE 4

WHAT A PANTOMIME

MANAGER OF THE MONTH

NEXT LEAGUE MEETING

FUTURE EDITIONS

PARSNIP OF THE MONTH

informed their Manager: "make changes, or we will!" The Board have indicated they are unhappy with the recently published league tables, some reports have indicated the source of which is the OFSTED Offenders.

To avert the growing concerns of the Hawkwood Lane faithful, a new Assistant Manager has been brought in to help out the "old man." 16 year old Lee Gartell told the gathered press he was delighted to be involved with such a famous and well-established club.

Let us hope these changes will be the beginning of a new era.

(This weekend's results would seem to indicate that the changes have yet to make an impact - ED.)

....

DYNAMO MATTY LAD

FORMED	*14th Feb 1993*
GROUND	*Full Pamper Park, Bradford*
CAPACITY	*3 Bedrooms*
FACILITIES	*Tea, coffee, and cake on Match Days, one toilet, fitted kitchen*
HONOURS	*None to date*
MANAGER	*Andy Webb*
COACH	*Helen Webb*
CHAIRMAN	*Matthew Webb*
NICKNAME	*'Nappy Boys'*

Formed 6 months after the birth of influential chairman

Matthew "The Lad" Webb, Dynamo are strong contenders for UEFA next season. Initial tactics involved selection of Fanciable Players (by the coach) but lack of pace up front (Lee Chapman) and very leaky defence (Rob Jones and Barry Venison) led to wholesale changes at transfer time. Visitor's facilities for next season will include garden furniture and pre-match entertainment of the chairman crawling and possibly tackling. On the field, defence will be the key, with two proven strikers making each weekend a thirty pointer.

....

I'M A BIT WEAK UP FRONT HITS THE TON

The meteoric rise continues. Another big scoring week for 'I'm a bit weak....', 18 points in total, brings the first Fuzzy Duck centurion. Nick Waters, grizzled Manager of the United team, is "over the moon" at the news. Meanwhile, deep in the basement, there is a little light in the gloom - MMC 14 have reversed the slide with a 16 point weekend that pushes their total up to 37 points. MMC 14 management team say the gap is now only 71 points and there's lots of time yet for a late surge up the table!

....

"YER MAN" JIM McDONALD'S WEE FELLAS LEAGUE

H.Q.	*The Globe Hotel, The Parade, Cowes, Isle of Wight*
FORMED	*August 1993*
PRESIDENT	*Coronation Street's Jim McDonald (Actor Charles Lawson)*
CHAIRMAN	*Steve Brook*
NO. OF TEAMS	*6*

REGULAR MEETINGS: Monday Evenings (coinciding with Sky match)

PRE-SEASON AUCTION: August 1993, involving 7 teams (Beano's Army withdrew before league was finished, after buying 9 defenders and 6 midfielders before running out of money)

WORST TRANSFER DEAL: Candle Brothers - Mark Robins £3.5m

BEST TRANSFER DEAL: Inter Ivorelli - Andy Cole £2.7m

CUP COMPETITION: The 'Newton & Ridley Cup' devised one Monday evening as the end product of a long discussion which started as a simple trivia question, "Who was the Man City supporter in the Dustbin Men?" and ended up as a fully-fledged cup draw.

Current holder 1993/94 season - Oddfellows local 151

Runners up: Inter Ivorelli

END OF SEASON AWARDS EVENING: May 14th

PLANS FOR 1994/1995 SEASON: To expand the League to 8 teams

Interviews for prospective entrants during July (must be a follower of Coronation Street; REM optional). League to be removed: "Yer Man" Jim McDonalds Big Fellas League.

TEAM PROFILES

INTER IVORELLI

Managed by brothers Martin and Paul Ivory, although Paul has been conspicuous by his absence since before the auction. Shrewd tactics and purchases have seen the Ivorellis rarely out of the top two, and look set to win the league. Star players have been Cole and Adams.

ODD FELLOWS LOCAL 151

The management team of Gavin Foster and Mick Stephenson (with spiritual guidance from Michael Stipe) have already secured the Newton and Ridley Cup for the Oddfellows. The goal-scoring ability of Alan Shearer has kept them in contention throughout the season, but have been let down by the defenders, especially the goalkeeper. Allegations of underhand mid-season transfer dealings proved unfounded.

REDWOOD ORIGINALS

Wally Hackling has been the main motivator behind the Redwoods, the name coming from his T-shirt on auction night. Co-manager Alex Higgins has been in hibernation during the winter since pushing for the signing of Jason Cundy, but has recently resurfaced for the end-of-season push. Best players have been David Seaman and Ian Wright.

DINAMO BAKEREST

The Baker Brothers, Richard and Dave Baker have studied player form in fine detail, and have made educated moves in the transfer market. However, they have been plagued by bad luck (having Dean Suanders on the bench while he was scoring regularly, and having Ekouku up front while he was actually abroad playing for his national team). Main points have come from Lee Dixon and Gary McAllister.

THE CANDLE BROTHERS

Drama on the field has been nothing compared with the boardroom ructions at the Candle Brothers. The original management dream team of George Swanson, Justin Choat and Simon Smith were at one stage reduced to the sole leadership of Justin Coat, as romance proved an unavoidable divergence for first, one, then the other, co-manager. However, George Swanson has now been re-instated and can take credit for the signing of Mark Stein (as well as supplying most of the Finances).

ATOM HEART MOTHERWELL

The combination of football romance and Pink Floyd seemed at first a successful idea to co-managers Steve Brook and Richard Hopkins. However there is no place for romance and sentiment in the Fantasy League, and it soon became clear that players like Bryan Robson would not be huge points earners. Long-term injuries to Sherringham and Warhurst saw the signing of Eric Cantona and Peter Beardsley but 'The Crazy Diamonds' have been let down by a generous defence, and an unproductive midfield.

AGENTS – THE CURSE OF THE GAME

Ron 'Flynn' has called for a disciplinary board meeting to be arranged to consider several complaints against Mr Brown. Complaints have been a regular item in previous issues of this newsletter and the following is reported to have happened last week:

Brown phones Thomo and "advises" him to bid for Dave Watson. He states that £400,000 should get him. The following day he calls Clicker and advises a £600,000 bid for the same player and discloses Thomo's interest. Exactly whose interest is the above mentioned Brown acting in?

MMC 14 - CUP SHOCKER!

In the final of the Don Kiddick Trophy last week, MMC 14 finally came good. In a match, which could hardly be called a classic, at the end to the Duck League Cup Competition, MMC 14 emerged as the eventual victors over Yours Darren-Oh! Albion with a score of 2 to -1. The hard-pressed management team from Hawkwood Lane said to the Duck News reporters yesterday that "they were over the moon with the result". The MMC Board are delighted with the news. "We feel that we've now turned the corner and that our indifferent league performance is on the mend." Asked if there was any chance at all of catching the current League leaders, I'm a Bit Weak Up Front United, a mere 115 points ahead in the table, the MMC manager replied: "Football's a funny old game - who knows what's possible? For the moment we're more concerned with preserving our League status and avoiding the drop to worry about the Championship."

GARDENING MISHAPS LEAGUE

Formed : at a barbeque held in a garden somewhere in Bedfordshire

Theme : Gardening mishaps

Member Clubs :

Clothes Line Catastrophe City
Richard Fenn

Birdtable Lobotomy F.C.
Gordie Bluetit

Trod on Hedgehog Barefoot of South
Chimpy Jones

Paraquat Cocktail Academicals
Robert Skilbeck

Percy Thrower's Rake Massacre City
Keith Goatley

Flymo Big Toe Amputees Athletic
Ogee Fenn

Pricked Badly By Sharp Thistle
Steve Hoskins

....

BACK 4 MORE

The manager of Rabid Ron's Raiders ('Ron Flynn') has stated that whilst his team have not made the kind of start he would have liked, he will not be forced into any panic buying ("unlike my compatriots").

"I have built a solid back 4 who have picked up several points and I expect my lacklustre midfield and forward line to gel in the coming weeks." You took the words right out of my mouth, Ron.

....

THE DO I NOT LIKE THAT LEAGUE

CHAIRMAN: BEN NEWTON

The league logo was designed by our Chairman - who should have been working at the time! He also thought up the League's name. The bastardised Latin is supposed to mean 'Through Tailor (a misspelling, perchance?) To The Depths'. If you're interested, that is.

Our bosses would be well peeved at the amount of time we 'waste' on this league if it wasn't for the fact that they are playing too and are almost as bad as we are, anyway.

GEORDIES IN EXILE

That wily little manager from the North East who seems to spend more time out of the country than in it (something to do with tax, I'm led to believe) has signed Devon White.

JAPANESE ARMS LENGTH LEAGUE

Our league of 9 teams, expanding to 14 for next season, is mainly Accountants and Financial people from the Headquarters of Computer Company, ICL.

It is administered by Steve Lumb from Maidenhead, who fitted the job in around his role as Business Review Manager in Bracknell, or was it the other way around!!! He did a superb job throughout - chairing the Auction organising the Cup, chairing the "AGM" and award ceremony as well as the routiness of team changes etc. His own team "Re-election Fever" was so called either because of his life-long support of Halifax Town or having missed many of the big names at the Auction, he knew he would finish in the bottom two - which he did!

The highlight of the season was, after work two weeks ago, when we ran the AGM and Awards Ceremony - Steve arranged inscribed cups for the league and cup competitions we held, a golden boot for the leading scorer (an old boot spray painted on a plinth) which was Andy Cole of Athletico Finchampstead and caricature paintings (produced by an artist in our midst, the non-playing Ian McPherson) for the meanest defence, the best midfield combination. These "paintings" were tremendous. Finally we were all given a sweatshirt with our team name emblazoned and the league and cup winners also received an inscribed cap.

As a football "nut", young Mr Lumb refused to allow any contributions to the cost of these prizes as they are his contribution to what will be, we hope, a long-standing event. We have no hesitation if nominating him as National Chairman of the Year.

....

HAT TRICK HERO

Mr Thompson of Dale has let his team slip badly recently - this is probably due to his tangled love life ("We see him more on the front page than the back!" said one disgruntled fan). Rumour has it that one of these so-called loves is someone involved at Dale, i.e.: he works with her (or him)!!! Let's hope he doesn't follow Tommy Doc. down that slippery slope. Thommo was quoted as saying "It's difficult trying to keep three going at once, but I seem to be managing." (What's that Thommo, three break-ups?)

....

SHOCK TRANSFER NEWS

Chappo for Deano - is this Santa's gift to Ron Knee FC or Ooo Wonky Vonky? Duck News has just discovered that long-term negotiations between mid-table Wonky Vonky and not-so-mid-table Ron Knee FC, to exchange Lee Chapman for Dean Saunders, have been completed in time for the busy holiday league programme. Much-travelled Lee Chapman was said to be delighted by the news after being sidelined by Wonky Vonky's manager, Howard Marshall, all season.

"I've played for nearly every top manager in the game in my career thus far, so the chance to play for David 'Quirky' Whiteside (slimmer of the year) is a real privilege. At least I stand a chance of getting a game - don't I, David?"

Dean Saunders (Ron Knee) was not available for comment yesterday, but was reported to be 'totally gutted' by team mates.

WEMBLEY PARK STATION PUB LEAGUE (ITALY)

In 1991 the present chairman Massimiliano Capuzi came back from a holiday in England where he had come to know about the Fantasy League and soon after a new league was formed in Roma. The league was called 'Proud Lion Pub League' which is the pub where we met every Friday. The league has just completed its third season under the new name "Wembley Park Station Pub League" where we are also regulars.

WPSPL Lifetime Members

GianLuca Vacchio (Amanasta For Ever; Arsenal)

Paolo Carpino (Manchester City; Free Lance FC)

Valerio Aulino (Millwall FC)

Dandolo Fioretti (Old '70 FC)

Cristiano Pasqualini (Everton; Rostock FC; Whiteland)

Oliviero Palermi (Plymount FC)

Andrew Gaddi (A.S. Gaddington; QPR)

Marco Impiglia (M.I.T.; Q.P.R.)

Elio Lechi (Er Gruppetito)

Massimiliano Capuzi (Mods FC)

SCHIZO CORNER

Concern has been expressed that Fantasy Football threatens to undermine the patterns of loyalty and hatred that make football what it is. Mr Crabbe is now an avid follower of Arsenal's defence but hates their attack. Mr Brown has developed a deep affinity for the fortunes of Everton and Mr George has simply given up on Norwich.

UNIVERSITY OF THE DO I NOT LIKE THAT LEAGUE

We are aware that the depth of terrace knowledge among managers in The Do I Not Like That League varies from those who are season ticket holders (albeit at Charlton) to those who take a mild interest in Newcastle's results when they are in the top six of the Premiership.

As a service to our managers therefore, we will be running an occasional series of tutorials on football customs. This week, we address the rules of footballers' nicknames.

It is often supposed that all footballers have nicknames ending in 'y' or 'o', for example Ryan "Giggsy" Giggs and Brian "Robbo" Robson. It is true that these are the most common forms. But there are other variants. Over the page, we set out the nicknames which we consider would be given to The Do I Not Like That League managers, in the unlikely event that any of them were professional footballers. The etymology is given in the more difficult cases. These will be used in future bulletins, or until better monikers are suggested.

Robert ("Robbo") Baird

Steve ("Blobby") Bellerby

Ron ("Big Ron"/"Creedo") Creed

John ("Taffy") Evans

NB: The nickname "Taffy" may be applied to any person with a vaguely Welsh surname. Actual connections with the Principality are not needed)

Craig ("Piggo") Lester [NB: from Lester Pigott]

John ("Macca") McCormick

Mukhtar ("Mucky") Shaikh

Adrian ("Westy") West

John ("Willy") Wilmer

....

THE BUCKS TANDOORI LEAGUE

SUGGESTED PRIZES

Champions: Fully expensed curry at the Bucks Tandoori paid by the other Managers. Also a trophy of some kind.

Runners-up: Main course at the Bucks Tandoori (not inc. side orders)

Bottom: Seven pints of beer to be bought (one for each other manager, plus one for yourself).

Any other suggestions will be considered

THE MASALA CUP

1st round to be played Saturday 5 March '94

Draw to be made at next Managers meeting.

....

PATHETIC FANTASIST

Dale manager Mr Thompson appears undisturbed by his teams placing at the bottom of the table. He was found singing:

"I am bottom of the league, I am bottom of the league", under a table in a Manchester drinking hole this week as he concentrated on 'real football' and celebrated Man United's victory, Liverpool's defeat and Peter Reid's dismissal.

players to watch 1994/95

This is where I put my head on the block and choose the players that I believe will perform in 1994/95. Just how they will perform remains to be seen. It's bound to be a case of hit-and-miss, which only goes to show how tough a job it is to predict Fantasy League form. One look at the stats section will tell you who the big boys are, so I've only briefly highlighted these. I've turned by attention to 30 players who won't attract the huge bids, but who should prove to be fairly solid performers. That's the theory, anyway.

goalkeepers

Break the bank for : **Seaman, Flowers, Schmeichel.**

Three to watch :

1. **Ogrizovic** (Coventry)
   Coventry are an underrated team defensively and Ogrizovic is a consistent performer. Should be able to pick him up pretty cheap at the auction.

2. **Srnicek** (Newcastle)
   Everyone tends to think of Newcastle as very cavalier at the back, but fifteen clean sheets last term mean that who ever is in goal (take any one from three) should be worth having.

3. **Kharin** (Chelsea)
   Third in a set of East Europeans is Chelsea's Dimitri Kharin. The 4-0 drubbing in the Cup Final aside, Kharin, and Chelsea could be tougher opponents this season.

Long Shot : **Southall** (Everton)

full backs

Break the bank for : **Le Saux, Berg, Dixon, Irwin, Winterburn, Parker.**

Five to watch

1. **Kelly** (Leeds)
   It seems Gary Kelly is everyone's favourite full back these days. Leeds are generally good at the back, and Kelly's attacking prowess was good enough for five assists last season.

2. **Breaker** (West Ham)
   If you buy Tim Breaker, you'll have to take the rough with the smooth. West Ham's defence had a couple of good runs last season, but they are prone to leak heavily from time to time. Breaker certainly makes up for it going forward, and anything like his three goals and five assists last season will be very welcome.

3. **Thompson** (Ipswich)
   This might seem a strange choice considering Ipswich are many people's favourites to go down. The strange thing is that, over the last couple of seasons, there seems to be have been an uncanny link between Ipswich struggling and Thompson not being fit. When he plays, they do well, when he doesn't, they plummet. Coincidence? Perhaps. But with Thompson's impressive record from set-pieces, I'd gamble on him.

4. **Barton** (Wimbledon)
   Many people might reckon that the light blond hair alone is enough of a reason to buy Warren, but Wimbledon's resilience and Barton's attacking runs, corners and free-kicks clinch it for me.

5. **Dicks** (Liverpool)
   Much was expected of Dicks when he signed for Liverpool last season, but injuries and transition dogged his, and Liverpool's season. This time around the Reds should be stronger, and if Dicks stays clear of injury he should be worth a punt.

Long Shot : **Kenna** (Southampton)

centre backs

Break the bank for : **Adams, Bould, Bruce, Pallister, May, Hendry, Fairclough.**

Five to watch :

1. **Peacock** (Newcastle)
   With full-backs, your attacking points will come from assists. With centre-backs you're looking for goals from set-pieces. Peacock's got a good goalscoring record, good club and great hairstyle. Could be a top contender in 94-95.

2. **Babb** (Coventry)
   Over the last couple of seasons, the strength of Coventry's defence has been well-kept secret. If they can maintain that consistency, then Babb is your man. Scores his fair share of headers from set-pieces.

3. **Pearce** (Sheff Wed)
   No problem whatsoever with his goalscoring ability, but the problem could be Wednesday's leaky defence. If they can finally kick the habit of letting in last-minute equalisers, Andy Pearce will finally be a leading Fantasy League player.

4. **Vonk** (Man City)
   In terms of Fantasy League points, Man City were the eighth best defence in the Premiership last season - pretty surprising if you consider that they spent much of the season in the relegation zone. Vonk is occasionally drafted in as an emergency centre-forward, which, along with his continental good looks should mean he's your man.

5. **Cooper** (Nottm Forest)
   It might seem a brave and foolish move to recommend a defender from a promoted team, but Nottm Forest are as much a Premiership side as anyone and are sure to settle quickly back into the top flight. Like any centre half who plays Fantasy League, Cooper weighs in with a few goals a term.

Long shot : **Kjeldberg** (Chelsea)

midfielders

Break the bank for: **Le Tissier, Giggs, Fox, Kanchelskis, Earle**

Ten to watch :

1. **Lee** (Newcastle)
   Got better and better as last season continued, particularly after he finally got his first goal. After that, there was no stopping him. Lee, and Newcastle, should be bigger and better this season.

2. **Wilcox** (Blackburn)
   Another midfielder who came good in the second half of the season. 23 of his 34 points came after Christmas, and he's sure to be whipping in those crosses for Shearer and co. again this season.

3. **White** (Leeds)
   Finished the season on a hot streak once he established himself in the first team. A staggering 19 points from his last six games is a return to the form that made him a top player with 64 points in 91-92 and 62 in 92-93.

4. **McManaman** (Liverpool)
   If Liverpool get their act together, McManaman should be supplying a lot of the ammunition and could be a great buy. Beware though, because he tends to score a lot of score points in short bursts. He's scored 10 points in one game in each of the last two seasons. Drop him at your peril.

5. **Salako** (C Palace)
   An old Fantasy League campaigner, Salako was scoring points three seasons ago before people like Andy Cole had even heard of the game. If he stays clear of injury he'll do well.

6. **Bart-Williams** (Sheff Wed)
   6 points in 91-92, 24 points in 92-93 and 36 points last season tell the tale of an improving young prospect. If he keeps up that sort of progress, it could be worth offering the Bart-man a five year deal.

7. **Beagrie** (Man City)
   Before he went to City, Beagrie tried everything (including somersaults) to get Fantasy League points. A change of club and he can't stop assisting. No need for those somersaults now, Peter.

8. **Joachim** (Leicester)
   A bit of a risk as Julian doesn't always get in Leicester's first team. When he does though, he plays very far forward and always proves to be a handful.

9. **Holmes** (West Ham)
   Matthew, or "Matty" to anyone who owns him, is a solid, steady points provider. Pick him up cheap, stick him in your midfield all season and he'll get you 30 points. A nice little earner.

10. **Burley** (Chelsea)
    Scorer of great long-range goals, he should be a regular in Chelsea's side this term. If you think Chelsea will do well, he'll be a good bargain buy.

Long shot : **Caskey** (Spurs)

strikers

Break the bank for **Cole, Shearer, Sutton, Wright, Cantona.**

Eight to watch :

1. **Collymore** (Nottingham Forest)
   If Stan makes the transition from First to Premier as well as Andy Cole last season, you're on to a winner. A goalscorer and a rebel - a tempting cocktail for many a manager.

2. **Holdsworth** (Wimbledon)
   Could really be in the "Break the bank" category, as he's always near the top of the goal charts. Scores points almost every week - a dream buy.

3. **Armstrong** (C Palace)
   Another promising promoted player, Armstrong's a great all-round striker. This means he'll back up plenty of goals with a good assist tally, so even if he's having trouble finding the net, you'll still be getting your fair share of assists.

4. **Newell** (Blackburn)
   Assists play an even bigger part in Newell's game, working as a superb partner to Shearer. A very consistent player with a respectable goalscoring record - play him every week and he'll reward your loyalty.

5. **Walsh** (Man City)
   Often makes a good start at a new club (as he did at City), but then loses his way a bit. If he can keep up his form of last season, he'll be a great buy once again.

6. **Furlong** (Chelsea)
   Chelsea's £2.3m outlay seems steep for a player unproved in the top flight. If you trust Hoddle's judgement or if you can pick him up for less than £2.3m he might be worth a go.

7. **Bright** (Sheff Wed)
   A stalwart centre-forward who you might be able to pick him cheaply. If you do, you'll be getting a great Fantasy League player who is another Mr. Consistency.

8. **Robins** (Norwich)
   Dogged by injury last season but if he can stay fit this season he could be a great buy. A prodigious goalscorer who will probably be overlooked in your Auction. A gamble, but you could pick him up for free.

Long shot : **Watson** (Sheff Wed)

statistics section

HALL OF FAME

FANTASY LEAGUE TOP 50 POINTS SCORERS

All scores are System B

	Team	Manager	Gls	Ass	CS	GA	Pts
1	Athletico Support	Steve Couch	104	85	81	190	658
2	IFK Naked Scuba Diving Hippy Flumps	Robert Cullingworth	95	68	85	148	631
3	Knowledge Is Power	Saul Ainsworth	96	59	87	154	618
4	ACC Milan	Andrew Collery	104	65	71	161	598
5	Brady Bunch	Jon Adams	99	65	70	140	595
6	Ogier's Ogres	Darren	100	66	67	147	592
7	Sheffield Week-on-Thursday	Peter Dadswell	92	80	73	191	591
8	Happy Hammers United	John Steer	85	82	73	158	584
9	Smooth As Silk Utd	Wayne Silk	77	78	81	154	584
10	Persil	Steve Rodgie	99	69	72	185	584
11	Deer Best Player Anagram XI	Mark Colledge	90	72	73	165	583
12	Coton House F.C.	Pat Diggins	92	67	71	144	582
13	Simo's Seagulls	Matthew Sims	108	66	61	164	581
14	Cow's Scud Attackers	Marcus	112	51	64	156	579
15	The Pink Gorillas	Steve Jewhurst	94	58	76	155	577
16	Tulsa Roughnecks	Richard Holden	94	73	67	176	573
17	City Slickers	Peter Lawman	97	65	71	169	573
18	Highbury Heroes	Justin Bickford	108	64	63	203	572
19	Outstandingly United	Mark Hope	96	58	78	183	572
20	The Crazy Gang	Hugh Tohill	91	73	74	192	571
21	Moss Bros Spartak	Chris Asher	83	71	79	170	570
22	Shytehawks	Mick Little	92	70	67	137	569
23	Uncle Monty's Dear Boys	Lee Meister	79	69	78	146	566
24	Scouse Gits	Andy Jackson	91	60	76	160	562

	Team	Manager	Gls	Ass	CS	GA	Pts
25	You Know You Want It Wanderes	Lee Brown / Jason Brown	85	72	66	139	559
26	Sumo City	Mark Brookes	108	63	57	181	558
27	Larry's Leisure Lads	AndyTraynor	93	72	65	167	556
28	H's Leggings	Big Col Bell	95	66	62	141	551
29	Witch Bitter Lemon Teamsters	Val Hines	84	67	73	174	550
30	Toronto Blizzards	PeterWilson	80	81	72	185	550
31	Suntans of Swing	Phil Nicholson	75	72	76	157	548
32	Willie's Warmers	M.Leyland	89	65	68	161	548
33	Great Halibut Of The Seventies	Andrew Wainstein	84	74	67	162	547
34	Somedays You Eat The Bear	I Hart	100	56	70	193	546
35	Lord Rockingham's XI	Donald Rodie / Ray Summers	98	67	65	187	546
36	Senegal Lions	Guy Osborne	74	70	80	162	546
37	Kentish Town Casuals	Goldie	75	86	75	191	545
38	Jurassic Park Rangers	David Warden	86	56	78	174	543
39	Simply The Best	Scott Gearie	103	65	57	192	542
40	Eric Hall's Speech Impediment	Gary Briggs	92	59	68	165	541
41	Swiss Francs For sale	David Halsall	97	73	59	197	541
42	Eleven Merry Men	Mark Sykes	95	72	72	254	539
43	Dynamo Didsbury	Dave Hughes	81	70	75	174	539
44	West Ken Lads	Steve Vickery	93	77	60	194	538
45	Athletico Fob-Yac	Steve Olando/Neil Price	98	62	65	188	538
46	Donkeys Dream Team	Mark Gibson	88	60	70	175	537
47	The Mickey Thomas Bureau De Change	Mark Brockbank	103	65	59	203	536
48	FC Aarau	Michael McDaid	73	66	78	163	534
49	Andy Linighan's School Of Excellence	Neil 'Gooner' Reynolds	78	67	74	159	533
50	Dynamo Battenburg	Steve Barrett / Dave Bowman	88	66	63	156	533

HALL OF FAME

FANTASY LEAGUE TOP 50 AVERAGES

	Team	Manager	Pld	Pts	Ave
1	Mann's Best	David Manns	23	442	19.22
2	Chicken and Beans XI	Gordon Gyaki	10	192	19.20
3	H's Leggings	Big Col Bell	29	551	19.00
4	Athletico Support	Steve Couch	35	658	18.80
5	Nesham Palace	Melvyn Gamblin	10	187	18.70
6	Lilacton Argyle	Nigel Bignell	11	205	18.64
7	King Dick's Star Spangled Spanners	Neil 'Superdome' Thorpe	22	408	18.55
8	Nobby's Stile XI	Stephen Knowles	29	533	18.38
9	Ronnie and Graham's Team That Never	Dom Gin JV	11	200	18.18
10	IFK Naked Scuba Diving Hippy Flumps	Robert Cullingworth	35	631	18.03
11	Jack Hayward's Barmy Army	Paul Reade	10	180	18.00
12	Burning Villas	Jim Culliford / Angela Murphy	13	233	17.92
13	John's Big Pants	John Gibson	10	178	17.80
14	Skipper's Downpatrick Celtic XI	Art Kernan	13	230	17.69
15	West Brom Reserves	Mike Payne	11	194	17.64
16	Duncan McKenzie's Shirts	Michael Brierley	13	229	17.62
17	Chris's Greek Delights	Chris Demetriades	13	229	17.62
18	Dialo Athletico	Chris Gibb	18	316	17.56
19	South Eastern Strollers	Simon Pates	18	312	17.33
20	Fulchester United	Simon Rowson	10	172	17.20
21	Knowledge Is Power	Saul Ainsworth	36	618	17.17
22	The Trevor Sinclair Fan Club	Martin Butterworth	13	223	17.15
23	Rosedale Wanderers	Mark Treacher	13	222	17.08
24	Brady Bunch	Jon Adams	35	595	17.00

	Team	Manager	Pld	Pts	Ave
25	Ian Wright Wright Wright	Daniel Chrisostomou	18	306	17.00
26	Tuffa's Woo Boys	Chris Richards	10	170	17.00
27	A Singularly Stupid Policy	James McElroy	22	373	16.95
28	Ogier's Ogres	Darren Ogier	35	592	16.91
29	Casual Corinthians	Tim Laughton	23	389	16.91
30	Sheffield Week-on-Thursday	Peter Dadswell	35	591	16.89
31	Dulwich Ham Sandwich FC	Jon Doherty	30	505	16.83
32	Oink!	Mike Kennerley	11	185	16.82
33	Bye Bye Barry	Stuart Gould	16	269	16.81
34	Not All Saints	Tony Skinner	13	218	16.77
35	Lolford Utd	Laurence Ford	13	218	16.77
36	Smooth As Silk Utd	Wayne Silk	35	584	16.69
37	Happy Hammers United	John Steer	35	584	16.69
38	Mr Metternich's Mahogany Lime Zester	Mike Van Cresswell	22	367	16.68
39	Deer Best Player Anagram XI	Mark Colledge	35	583	16.66
40	Uncle Monty's Dear Boys	Lee Meister	34	566	16.65
41	ACC Milan	Andrew Collery	36	598	16.61
42	Cows' Scud Attackers	Marcus	35	579	16.54
43	P.S.V. Talking Bolx	Jez Davidson	13	215	16.54
44	The Sunday Hackers	Matthew Turner	21	347	16.52
45	The Pink Gorillas	Steve Jewhurst	35	577	16.49
46	You Know You Want It Wanderes	Lee Brown / Jason Brown	34	559	16.44
47	Barwick Bores	Conal Gridley	22	361	16.41
48	"OO AH CANTONA'	Eamonn Mirner	13	213	16.38
49	Tulsa Roughnecks	Richard Holden	35	573	16.37
50	Mr. Blobby's Flyers	Stephen Smith	20	327	16.35

FANTASY LEAGUE TOP 50 GOALS

	Team	Manager	Goals
1	Cows' Scud Attackers	Marcus	112
2	Sumo City	Mark Brookes	108
3	Pint Of Murphys	P Murphy	108
4	Highbury Heroes	Justin Bickford	108
5	Simo's Seagulls	Matthew Sims	108
6	Terry Conroy's Legs	Nick Hancock	106
7	Red Rose Kings	Nigel Harrison	105
8	Athletico Support	Steve Couch	104
9	ACC Milan	Andrew Collery	104
10	The Mickey Thomas Bureau De Change	Mark Brockbank	103
11	Simply The Best	Scott Gearie	103
12	Rodney Marsh For England	Roger Thomas	102
13	Wallsend Amnesia	Colin Alexander	101
14	Peter's One-Nil Squad	Peter Ciccone	101
15	Mersemagic	Jim Healy	101
16	Somedays You Eat The Bear	I Hart	100
17	XD United On A Friday	John Wilson	100
18	Ogier's Ogres	Darren Ogier	100
19	Beermonsters United	Colin Wafer	99
20	Matty's Nose	Peter & Linda	99
21	Brady Bunch	Jon Adams	99
22	Neasden F.C.	Dave Fowler	99
23	Barnstonworth United	Adrian Thomas	99
24	Persil	Steve Rodgie	99

	Team	Manager	Goals
25	Crown Jules	Dave Harrell	98
26	Lord Rockingham's XI	Donald Rodie & Ray Summers	98
27	68 Guns F.C.	Adrian Luxton	98
28	They're Losing 1-0	David Newman	98
29	Athletico Fob-Yac	Steve Olando Neil Price	98
30	Going Down With Mickey Thomas	Keith Appleton	98
31	The Gatwick 'Irons'	Tony Bull	98
32	Nobby's Stile XI	Stephen Knowles	98
33	Tupton Terriers	Glyn Jones	97
34	0 - 0 AET	Barry Gray	97
35	Redundancy City F.C.	Simon / John Paul / Geoff	97
36	City Slickers	Peter Lawman	97
37	Swiss Francs For sale	David Halsall	97
38	Reg Holdsworth's Devil Horns	Steve Turner	97
39	Harry's Horny Humpers	HarryPhillips	97
40	Russell Athletic	Craig Russell	96
41	Regor	Roger Shaw	96
42	Heavenly Inspired	Tony Head	96
43	Outstandingly United	Mark Hope	96
44	Kitchstone Utd.	N. Cranstone & G. Kitcher	96
45	Knowledge Is Power	Saul Ainsworth	96
46	Bingo Munchengladbach	Ian Booth	96
47	St.Pete'rs Parochials	Dave Leach	95
48	Eleven Merry Men	Mark Sykes	95
49	IFK Naked Scuba Diving Hippy Flumps	Robert Cullingworth	95
50	Check The Hooly Hoolies	Mark Plant	95

FANTASY LEAGUE TOP 50 ASSISTS

	Team	Manager	Assists
1	Kentish Town Casuals	Goldie	86
2	Athletico Support	Steve Couch	85
3	Happy Hammers United	John Steer	82
4	Toronto Blizzards	Peter Wilson	81
5	Sheffield Week-on-Thursday	Peter Dadswell	80
6	Smooth As Silk UTD	Wayne Silk	78
7	Toon South	Liam Collerton	77
8	West Ken Lads	Steve Vickery	77
9	A.C. Kowalski	Simon Mason	76
10	Ramie's Rat Pack	Raymond Brown	76
11	Souness's Hearthrobs	Carl Rogan	76
12	The Northbank Crusaders	Andrew Birch	76
13	Victoria Park Rangers	Richard Huxley	75
14	Lokomotiv Hope Street	Paul Hutton	75
15	Debbie Does Dallas XXVII	Alan Relph	75
16	15 Non Blondes	Stephen Wright	75
17	Great Halibut Of The Seventies	Andrew Wainstein	74
18	Pete's A Toppin'	Peter Hodder	74
19	The Out Of Town Specialities	Stuart Percival	74
20	Teddy Bears	Maria Jane Farrell	74
21	Pointless Rovers	John Woodlock	73
22	The Crazy Gang	Hugh Tohill	73
23	Tulsa Roughnecks	Richard Holden	73
24	Just The Pie	Alan Walles	73

	Team	Manager	Assists
25	Blobby's Boys	Robert King	73
26	Percy & Phyllis United	Peter/Darren	73
27	He shoots...He scores!	Matthew McNamee	73
28	A.F.C. Evil Empire	Mike McEnearney	73
29	Swiss Francs For Sale	David Halsall	73
30	Glen's Garden Shed	Daniel Gold	72
31	K.S. Shish-Kebab	Patrick Barker	72
32	Eleven Merry Men	Mark Sykes	72
33	Suntans of Swing	Phil Nicholson	72
34	Deer Best Player Anagram XI	Mark Colledge	72
35	British Lions	Jon Ostridge	72
36	Roker Rookies on Tour 93/94	John Crabb	72
37	You Know You Want It Wanderers	Lee Brown & Jason Brown	72
38	Larry's Leisure Lads	Andy Traynor	72
39	M.G. Misquotes FC	Brad & John	72
40	Briggersley Rovers	Dave Hattersley & Ian Briggs	72
41	Have I Got News For You	David Goldring	72
42	Cindy Crawford Loves My Pasties	Tony Kay	72
43	Tufnell Park Rangers	David List	72
44	Route 1	Alan Wallen	71
45	The Prima Donna Kebabs	Jim Solan	71
46	Thamesbank Tossers	Steve Gates	71
47	Beermonsters United	Colin Wafer	71
48	Moss Bros Spartak	Chris Asher	71
49	Brown's Allotment XI	Martin Brown	71
50	Le Tissier Was A Bargain At £6.2m	Shaun Windeatt	71

HALL OF FAME

FANTASY LEAGUE TOP 50 CLEAN SHEETS

Team		Manager	Clean Sheets
1	Knowledge Is Power	Saul Ainsworth	87
2	IFK Naked Scuba Diving Hippy Flumps	Robert Cullingworth	85
3	MacNamara's Band	Tony MacNamara	84
4	The Clockend Squatters	Paul Samman	84
5	Gus Caesar's Jabber	Stuart Cass	84
6	"Bell, Summerbee, Lee"	Kieran Conaty	83
7	F.O.A.M. Utd	Stephen Newman	82
8	Athletico Support	Steve Couch	81
9	Chiswick Cosmos	William Shaylor	81
10	Accidents Will Happen IX	Ross Hemsley	81
11	Smooth As Silk UTD	Wayne Silk	81
12	Dursley Destroyers	Dave Hill	81
13	The Tollies	Ian Humphreys	81
14	Spartak Sidney	Phil Hawkins	81
15	Maggie Barstud's Makum Army	George Thomson	80
16	Theresonlyonefinalbert	Albert Westover	80
17	Like A Dog With Two Deans	Gary Hackett	80
18	City Rangers	M. Mullen	80
19	Senegal Lions	Guy Osborne	80
20	One Game At A Time	Philip Eaton	80
21	Fittonroundsschmeichel.....thats 4!	Ian Fitton	79
22	The Ultimate Spinach	Jason Archer	79
23	Moss Bros Spartak	Chris Asher	79
24	Roys Heroes	Roy Bougourd	79

	Team	Manager	Clean Sheets
25	Cowcross Wanderers	Paul Turnbull	79
26	I Once Met Sammy Lee In A Lift F.C.	Dougie Kerr	79
27	Smell's Strollers	Steve Lythgoe	78
28	Heath Hayes Rovers	Andrew Hailwood	78
29	Jurassic Park Rangers	David Warden	78
30	FC Aarau	Michael McDaid	78
31	Raging Tinys	Dina Tolton	78
32	Outstandingly United	Mark Hope	78
33	Vag Forest	Roland Rat	78
34	Uncle Monty's Dear Boys	Lee Meister	78
35	The Dennis Waterman Showbiz XI	Archibald Piehead	78
36	Caversham Academicals	Alan Clinch	78
37	Inter Sarsons	John Nicolas & Steve Astbury	78
38	Sukmiov Dynamos	Peter Green	78
39	White's Diving School	Martin and Mark Green	77
40	Romeo Gray XI (Returns...Again)	Graham Goodkind	77
41	Blue Nose Bastards	Nick Chilcott	77
42	Dynamo Harthill	R McVinnie	77
43	The Chairman's Cheetahs	Nic Patch	77
44	Brechin Wind	Steve Savin	77
45	It's Early Doors	Bryan Riley	77
46	McEwen's Import	Tony McEwen	76
47	Clothes Line Catastrophe City	Richard Fenn	76
48	Bosco's Banshees	Ray Lower	76
49	On Me 'Ead Son Allstars	Chris Thompson	76
50	Lo Milan Quindici	Desmond Belshaw	76

FANTASY LEAGUE BOTTOM 50 LEAKY DEFENCES

	Team	Manager	Goals against
1	Stammer's The II	Tony Ward	271
2	A Gynn With Vengence	David Joyce	260
3	Childwall United	The Northerner	259
4	Highway Select	Jason Doherty	256
5	Don Hutchison Batchelor Of Parts	Pete Stone & Colin Beasley	256
6	Stubborn Staines	Mike Gallagher	255
7	Eleven Merry Men	Mark Sykes	254
8	Brewery Fielders	Andrew Connolly	253
9	Baker's Ball Boys	Clive Baker	252
10	The Likely Lads	Steve Burke	251
11	The Gills	Roger Smith	250
12	Concept AFC	Cliff Collacott	250
13	Mitch's Magic Movers	David MItchell	249
14	The Goons	Sean Richardson	249
15	Linford's Scoring Dong F.C.	Trevor Riches & John McBride	249
16	Taylor 's Turnips	A. Negus	249
17	Saint 'N' Greavsie Allstars	J. White	246
18	Adzio	Adam McCarthy	246
19	Reynolds' Rovers	J Reynolds	246
20	Dukla Penarth	Barry Stock	246
21	The Royle Army	Deborah Roberts	243
22	Jack Walker Junior	Kevin Barrett	243
23	A Team Called Horse	The East End Businesspersons	243
24	The Vomiting Cockatoo's	N. Bateman	243

	Team	Manager	Goals against
25	Split Durex & The Accident F.C.	Robert Nathan	243
26	Beagrie's Acrobatics	Phil Wright	242
27	Nearly Total FC	Pat Amos	242
28	The Boro Party Animals	Andy Weatherhead	242
29	The Cat's Non Stick Gloves	Mark Underwood	242
30	The Frank Large Formation	Steve Jackson	241
31	Trotter United	Steven Field	241
32	Billy's Boots	Gary Beckford	241
33	Para Para Umu Pirates	Terry Smith	241
34	Am I Beige ?	Steve Dudley	241
35	Parma Hammer II (U.N.M.)	Rob Moruzzi & Chris Spragg	240
36	The No Brainers	Christian Smith	240
37	Wally's Wallonia's Army	Mark Peglar	240
38	How Can I Beat Hicksy ???	Ashman and Hanna	240
39	Young Boys Of St Enoch's Toletis	W.C. Condom	240
40	Next Year Definately	Michael 'Tufty' White	240
41	Don't Even Pay When You're Winning	Pav Younis	240
42	Percy Thrower's Rake Massacre City	Keith Goatley	239
43	Frattonenders United	John White	239
44	My Boys	Yvonne Charlton	239
45	W'ere Going To Win The League	Robert Ray	239
46	Canary Yellers	R Gilbert	239
47	The Jim Rose Sideshow	Phil Smith	238
48	Chicago Sting	Martin Clift	238
49	O'Grady's Evil Glare	Stuart Smith	238
50	Bayern Mooey	Dave Clarke	238

HALL OF FAME

AUGUST MANAGER OF THE MONTH

D BJELICA

ROUGH CIGER UTD

POINTS TOTAL	100
Grobbelar	
Jackson	
Staunton	
Adams	
Ruddock	
Ince	
Speed	
Wilkins	
Fox	
Cottee	
Fashanu	

FANTASY TEAM OF THE MONTH

POINTS TOTAL:	146
Seaman	12
Jones	13
Staunton	15
Marshall	17
Ruddock	14
McManaman	12
Giggs	12
Ndlovu	12
Peacock	10
Wegerle	10
Clough	14

SEPTEMBER MANAGER OF THE MONTH

P DADSWELL

SHEFFIELD-WEEK-ON-THURSDAY

POINTS TOTAL :	76
Seaman	
Le Saux	
Staunton	
M Wright	
Bruce	
Merson	
Ndlovu	
Ripley	
Peacock	
Cantona	
Cole	

FANTASY TEAM OF THE MONTH

POINTS TOTAL :	114
Segers	7
Babb	12
Morgan	12
Keown	8
Newsome	8
Sinton	11
Sharpe	9
Flitcroft	7
Lee	6
Sheringham	19
Ekoku	15

OCTOBER MANAGER OF THE MONTH			
D GOLDMAN			
KENTISH TOWN CASUALS		FANTASY TEAM OF THE MONTH	
POINTS TOTAL :	93	POINTS TOTAL :	154
Seaman		Seaman	16
Bowen		Dixon	16
Irwin		Winterburn	16
Adams		Adams	16
Ruddock		Potts	12
Lee		McAllister	13
Waddle		LeTissier	12
Ndlovu		Waddle	10
Ripley		Speed	9
Cantona		Shearer	20
Ferdinand		B Allen	14

NOVEMBER MANAGER OF THE MONTH			
C KANE			
DUKLA PUMPHERSTON		FANTASY TEAM OF THE MONTH	
POINTS TOTAL :	76	POINTS TOTAL :	131
Forrest		Miklosko	9
Bjornbye		Burrows	12
Burrows		Breaker	11
A Linighan		Bould	11
Hendry		A Linighan	10
Sellars		Sellars	15
McAllister		Ryan Jones	12
Ripley		Le Tissier	8
Bart-Williams		M Holmes	7
Cole		Cole	20
Wright		Beardsley	16

HALL OF FAME

DECEMBER MANAGER OF THE MONTH

J GRAY

PEARCE'S BACKPASS F.C.

POINTS TOTAL :	96	POINTS TOTAL :	147
Seaman		Flowers	10
Bardsley		Le Ssaux	15
Berg		Berg	10
Mabbutt		T Adams	13
C Hendry		C Hendry	10
Anderton		Dozzell	15
Giggs		Giggs	13
Townsend		Ince	11
Fox		Holden	11
Wright		Cantona	20
Cantona		Sutton	19

FANTASY TEAM OF THE MONTH

JANUARY MANAGER OF THE MONTH

S AINSWORTH

KNOWLEDGE IS POWER

POINTS TOTAL :	84	POINTS TOTAL :	117
\Seaman		Flowers	10
Parker		Le Saux	15
Berg		Berg	10
Mabbutt		T Adams	13
C Hendry		C Hendry	10
Anderton		Dozzell	15
Giggs		Giggs	13
Townsend		Ince	11
Fox		Holden	11
Wright		Cantona	20
Cantona		Sutton	19

FANTASY TEAM OF THE MONTH

FEBRUARY MANAGER OF THE MONTH

S COUCH

ATHLETICO SUPPORT

POINTS TOTAL :	86
Flowers	
Le Saux	
Barrett	
Adams	
Bruce	
Anderton	
Le Tissier	
Ripley	
Strachan	
Stein	
Cole	

FANTASY TEAM OF THE MONTH

POINTS TOTAL :	117
Bosnich	12
Le Saux	13
Barrett	12
Moran	9
Teale	8
Le Tissier	15
Rennie	9
Goss	7
Merson	6
Sutton	22
Fjortoft	18

MARCH MANAGER OF THE MONTH

C. ASHER

MOSS BROS SPARTAK

POINTS TOTAL :	101
Schmeichel	
Winterburn	
Le Saux	
D Peacock	
Wetherall	
Lee	
Earle	
L Sharpe	
Wilcox	
Sutton	
Cole	

FANTASY TEAM OF THE MONTH

POINTS TOTAL :	147
Srnicek	9
Beresford	10
Kelly	9
Gayle	12
Wetherall	9
Lee	15
Earle	14
Ince	13
Burley	10
Cole	26
Wright	20

APRIL MANAGER OF THE MONTH

M BROCKBANK

M THOMAS BUREAU DE CHANGE

POINTS TOTAL :	114	POINTS TOTAL :	164
Coton		Kharin	9
Barton		Berg	10
Berg		Elkins	15
Fairclough		A Pearce	12
Adams		E Johnsen	12
Sellars		Le Tissier	28
Fox		Ndlovu	14
Le Tissier		Martin Allen	14
Earle		D White	13
Ferdinand		Bright	19
Shearer		Holdsworth	18

POSTN	PTS	AVG
51-100	507-533	15.64-16.34
101-250	475-507	14.53-15.63
251-500	443-475	13.67-14.52
501-1000	404-442	12.69-13.67
1001-2000	359-404	11.41-12.69
2001-3000	322-359	10.51-11.41
3001-4000	288-322	9.69-10.51
4001-5000	247-288	8.86-9.69
5001-6000	193-247	7.91-8.86
6001-7000	129-193	6.29-7.91
7001-8000	66-128	N/A*
8001-END	0-66	N/A*

* MINIMUM 10 WEEKS TO BE ELIGIBLE

HALL OF FAME

League	Champion	Manager	WKS	A	B
"'Yer Man'', Jim McDonalds' Wee Fellas League"	Inter Ivorelli	M & P IVORY	34	421	456
"'20,000 to go!'"	Wizards In The Wet	T SMITH	23	302	337
'Big Ones' International	Portobello Pork	T DELANEY	34	440	476
'Booze at Home League'	Fatzio	A OYEBANJI	9	143	154
'Do I Not Like That' League	Fulchester United	S ROWSON	10	151	172
'Don't Let Starky Win It Again'	Gary's Giant Gonads	G WEST	35	382	444
'England Win World Cup'-What A Fantasy League	Laurel & Hardy	R MOSS	32	404	437
"'He Flicked To Kick, but I Didn't Know'League"	Nesham Palace	M GAMBLIN	10	169	187
'Nick's Shirt & Tie Combination Serie A '	Jel & Tel's Avenging Angels	J DUFFTON	35	485	518
'Qui Mange Tout Les Tarts' Premiership	Simply The Best	A RAE	24	328	350
'Scratch 'N' Sniff'	If Only Ossie Had This XI	L WENZ	9	130	148
'Shearer The Sub' League	Stein Cost Us Hundreds	J COOMBE	7	128	140
'Skinner Normanton Is A Heroe League'	Trad Tornadoes	A WILLIAMS	6	111	120
'Skipper' McMullan Premiership	Skipper's Downpatrick Celtic XI	A KERNAN	13	213	230
'Sorry I Can't Make It' League	Norfolk And Chance XI	S ENGLISH	26	361	392
"'The Ball Bobbles Up, Brian' League"	Mystic Potato	R HARRINGTON	35	454	486
'They Think It's All Over... It Is Now!'	Videocam Rejects	M CRUTCHLEY	35	390	453
'What Are The Rules Again? ' Premier League	Ruggie's Rovers	D RENTON	13	183	208
'You Want It When ?'	West Side Rangers	M FROST	33	362	402
'You're Better Off Talking Bollocks' League	Bayern North End	J LOWES	35	431	478
(Al) Bundy's League	"Win Or Lose, Have A Booze"	N.HAMMER /J.TOMLINSON	30	339	382
"20,000 Leagues Under cc."	Seaman Shoots Into Schmeichels Hand	J WORRALL	35	344	390
"20,000 Leagues Under The Vauxhall Conference"	Fortune's Always Hiding Up The Gary	J CONNOLLY	34	439	459
20000 Leagues Under The Premier	Andy Cole's Sandals	J NAUGHTON	21	306	316
25 Laps Of The String Mobile Workshop	My Spirit Level	S SCOTT	35	458	515

League	Champion	Manager	WKS	A	B
8 Modesty	Persil	S RODGIE	36	538	584
8 Pints And A Curry League	Vindaloo Bottom Burners	R PYGOTT	13	185	195
A.C.&H. Blunderleague	The Dunbar Dribblers	K DUNBAR	35	336	375
AA Premier Chip	Jimmy Greenhoff's Chest F.C.	S LEE	32	393	410
Abbey Life - North London League	Swiss Francs For sale	D HALSALL	36	476	541
Absolutely Fabulous	Winthorpe Wanderers	P HARRIS	9	131	148
Airbus Division One	Forever Blues F.C.	S GRIFFITHS	10	146	162
Albert - Prince Of Leagues	"Who Put Ball In Scousers Net, Alll"	T BOLDEN	16	175	197
Alcoholic Accountants Anonymous	Freezers Fledgelings	R FREEZER	36	410	444
Alcoholics Advertised	Knobrot Rovers	N HILL	9	117	126
Aldershot Cricket Club	Nobby Barnes Eleven	CAPPER & BIRCH	35	368	436
Alec Hunter Ofsted League (AHOL)	Boys From C Floor F.C.	S HAIGH	21	286	313
Alec Hunter Ofsted League (AHOL)	Turnip Strikers	P BUTLER	21	286	310
All I Want For Xmas Is My Dukla Prague Away Kit	Arseold Hamnal	J SYKES	35	389	418
All Saints Kylie Conference	Elgin Marvels	R TULLY	32	289	313
Always Second	Blue Nose Bastards	N CHILCOTT	35	389	430
Andy Cole Went For £8.5 Million	The One-Leggers	J PYER	23	285	313
Andy Whittam Smith's Black And White Army	Friends Of Graham Taylor	O SLOT	23	255	287
Another Disappointing Week For The Midlands	Lard FC	P BOWMAN	35	372	406
Another Excuse To Go To The Globe On A Monday	Golden Fleece 'A' Team	D PRITCHARD	27	331	362
Another League With No Name	Borussia Munichfightback	P GREGSON	18	257	272
Anti - String Vest Wearers Conference	Mine's A Big One Mrs Miggins	S HESSELL	9	137	157
Anti Spam League	Hayleys Babes	L NEWELL	9	122	134
Armchair Mangers League	Walter And Twigs XI	P COLLINS	35	384	447
Armitage Shanks League Division Three (North)	Wednesday Wonders	D JOHN	27	310	333
Armitage Shanks Wednesday League	Super Samp	R JENKINS	20	296	312

HALL OF FAME

League	Champion	Manager	WKS	A	B
Arthur Daley Used Cars Alliance (South)	Goooal Du Brazil!	N DEVEREUX	11	122	143
Arthur Daley Used Cars Alliance (South)	Gaby Roslin Appreciation XI	P JOHNSON	11	122	152
Arthur Montford's Sports Jacket Memorial League	Absolutely Delighted United	S REID/I McCABE	13	178	203
Ashford Super League	Up The Pong	M INSTALL	10	142	157
Asil Nadir Premier League	Douglas Bader Dancing Troupe	B RICHARDSON	35	359	405
ATC MCASS Premier League	ATC Milan	COWIE / MAGUIRE	35	426	458
B. Boys Premier	Ogiers Ogres	D OGIER	35	553	592
B.A.D. Armchair Supporters League	Regor	R SHAW	35	423	499
B.C.A.S. Division One	Lee Chapman Looks Like Don Johnson	K WALKER	29	372	395
B.S.E.Conference (Another Mad Meeting)	Parkway Athletic	A BOND	9	132	149
Back To Basic Instincts League	W.H.A.T. FC	M ROBSON	13	158	175
Bag The Red Mooses	The Bees	B MASON	26	318	363
Balti House Ring - Stingers Conference	Mad Dog Rovers	A MCLEAN	36	453	491
Ban The Blazer Brigade	Deggsy's Drbblers	D RICE	34	443	470
Bank Of Friendship League	Motherwell At Last	A BINNIE	22	248	272
Barclaycard BSD Fantasy Championship	Gayton Giants	C SKINNER	36	448	479
Barnes Keep It On The Carpet Conference	Real Pathetico	P DER PARTHOG	23	334	360
Basildon Council Premiership	Fair E Nuff	P CALLAND	27	364	407
Battered Husbands	Cloughie Likes A Bung	K COTTON	35	480	498
BCAS Premier League	Raggy Arse Rovers	J ENGLAND	32	382	397
Beardy Powell Independent Memorial League	Athletico Support	S COUCH	35	616	658
"Beautiful Game, Ugly Managers League"	Bald Eagles	H GITTLEMAN	32	364	401
Beckenham Premier League	Mala United	F GENDJ	9	136	165
Beer + Curry Premier League	Ron Noades Ate My Hamster	M PITCHES	36	395	452
Beer And Bulimia League	Once Every 26 Years F.C.	M CAMPBELL	36	404	436

League	Champion	Manager	WKS	A	B
Beezer Annual League	You Leeds	R VAUX	35	493	531
Bengal Cuisine Premiership Diamond Formation	Mick Mccarthy's A MCCARTHY	13	170	185	
Benny's Land Registry Loafers	The Crazy Gang	H TOHILL	35	523	571
Benson's Bed Centre Premier League	Bernie's Bruisers	B KELLY	35	388	429
Benwell Hill Cleauseau Neighbourhood Watch League	Geordies Love Lawrie McMenemy Utd	G RICHMOND	17	173	197
Bert Millichip To Draw First League	Team Tentacle	P ROBERTS	34	457	507
Better Late Than Never Combination	Deportive La Pwhelli	R WURSNIP	7	99	118
Bexhill College League	Reliant Magpies	M MALONEY	10	132	144
Bieldside Dernier League	Hutch's Hackers	B HUTCHESON	13	190	201
Big Blue Army League	White's Diving School	GREEN & GREEN	35	519	529
Big Kids League (Keighley)	Aut Vincere Aut Mori	M FANNING	35	399	467
Big Knobs League	Blues Boyz	K WITHERINGTON	17	212	234
Big Lawyers Brief League	Smith Really Did Score F.C.	S TAYLOR	4	71	79
Big Ron's 'Sprint-Sharp' Tourneyment	Outer Milan	P GAUNT	24	300	327
Biochemistry Troubleshooters	Harmans Heroes	D HARMAN	35	383	428
Birmingham Balti Bundeslieger	Basselona	R DRIVER	33	353	406
Blackpool Supporters Club	Larry's Leisure Lads	A TRAYNOR	36	516	556
BLMS Burton League	Sheepshag Army	KERRY & FOX	33	434	480
Block 8 Blockheads	Midfield Maestros	J CRANEY	34	436	483
Blooming Rose Fantasy Football League	Irma Ogden's Husbands	P RAFFERTY	32	377	369
Blueprint Grace Under Pressure	Benskin Bashers	S CRICHTON	34	341	382
Blundersliega	Greenhousemanuir F.C.	G HEATH	21	258	282
Blundersliga Berlin	The Professionals	T HOPCRAFT	27	322	374
Blundeslegia Britvic	Maccas Magicians	S CORMACK	36	416	472
Boags Export Pineapple Lager League	Lilacton Argyle	N BIGNELL	11	186	205

HALL OF FAME

League	Champion	Manager	WKS	A	B
Bobby Charlton Wrapover League	Duncan McKenzie's Shirts	M BRIERLEY	13	213	229
Boot Splashing Muckers-Serie B	SL5 Dealers F.C.	G RAE	25	265	308
Bootsplashing Muckers Serie A	Gotham City	D BROWN	35	418	480
Brady's Blue And White Army League	Bye Bye Barry	S GOULD	16	237	269
Breakfast Serie L	Red Star Parcels	G HOGE	35	448	478
Brewed In Sheffild Div. 1	Tulsa Roughnecks	R HOLDEN	35	520	573
Brewer's Droop Series A	IFK Naked Scuba Diving Hippy Flumps	R CULLINGW'TH	35	613	631
Brian Buxton Memorial League	Rowsell's Prat's	J BOB	35	385	430
Brian Clough Temperance League	Diggers Army	J BARNES	24	287	317
Broken Cheekbone Premiership	Brown's Allotment XI	M BROWN	33	463	503
Brunswick Point Championship	Inurendo Utd.	G WRIGHT	32	366	398
Bubbles League	Ian Wright Wright Wright	D CHRIS'T'MOU	18	290	306
Bunch of Dobbers	West Ken Lads	S VICKERY	35	479	538
Butterflies In The Stomach League	Cheri Lunghi	J JOHNSON	35	383	432
Can Anyone Remember The Auction? Premier Lge	Larbrax Layabouts	B ANDERSON	34	318	383
Can't Think Of A Sodding Name......	Tony Wilsons Suit	G PRESTON	34	374	426
Cannon Blundersleague	Be Like Tim	T REANEY	27	309	351
Captain Birdseyes Fish Finger League	Rug Rats United	D ROBERTSON	9	134	143
Captain Quaffs Drinking League	Not Quite United	G MACKAY	35	442	492
Carling & Blackcurrant Premiership	King Dick's Star Spangled Spanners	NEIL 'SUPERDOME' THORPE	22	388	408
Carling Series A Walkover	Henley Bullets	A ARLETT	27	397	425
Carlton - Television For London	Yorkshire Bores	DAVIDSON & BENNETT	36	364	413
Carpet Capers League	A.C. Mitchum	A EVES	18	251	281
Chill For 2 Hours For Best Results League	Rizla Rovers	M HUTCHINSON	9	120	129

League	Champion	Manager	WKS	A	B
Chippendales	Smooth As Silk UTD	W SILK	35	557	584
Christchurch Premier League	Nicks Nobblers	N SIMPSON	9	117	132
Clapped Out Chemists Serie Z	Bring Back Maggie	P ASHDOWN	35	351	421
Collapsing Quiff And Bowl Cut Premiership	Two Titleist Golf Balls	P ALEXANDER	35	338	381
Collection 2000 Whoops HASL League!	Vomiting Sindy Dolls	A BIRD	24	249	288
Commercially Acceptables Conferemce League	Panthers F.C.	B PATCHING	35	445	491
Completely Obnoxious Developers Association	Inter the Dog	F RANSOM	16	174	198
Compucare Charlies League	Eleven Merry Men	M SYKES	35	463	539
Computer Communications League	Q. P. R.	D PETERS	20	278	300
Computer League	Inter Gasket	G BLESSINGTON	23	286	322
Consort Premier League	Not All Saints	T SKINNER	13	200	218
Contributions Agency Keegan Bunderslager	H's Leggings	BIG COL BELL	29	524	551
Coolmakee Premier	"The Mosh ""N"" Slam Mob"	N O'CALLAGHAN	13	169	180
Coop's Barmy Army Premiership	Jack Army	A RONAN	30	386	408
Coopers Creosote Combination Serie B	"Young, Gifted & Unpleasant"	M FLETCHER	35	445	502
Cornhill Premier League	Lush Athletic F.C.	BARNES/ BRAYBOO/STICK	34	426	483
Corporate Raiders League	The Salad Creamers	N SALUCIDEEN	28	314	355
Coss Premiership	Uncle Jack's Barmy Army	M WHITFORD	34	386	442
Courage Directors Serie A	Athletico Dog Sarah	J HAYWARD	19	220	256
Creme de la Fadge	Fizztafarians World XI	I WHISCOMBE	7	114	128
Crompton Academicals League	Halifaxmen United	J HAWKRIDGE	9	119	134
Cupid Stunts Conference	Eastbury Groovers	J CRYAN	13	180	196
Customs Fund Blunders League	I'm Forever Blowing Titles	S BONDSCHEME	35	399	454
D.P.P.S.	Sporting Chickens In Your Lavatory	M ROBINSON	7	97	111
Dairy Crest Premier Revisited	Athletico Verran	I LOGAN	36	461	496

HALL OF FAME

League	Champion	Manager	WKS	A	B
Dan Air Memorial League	Travis Bickle F.C.	I TURNER	35	410	484
"Darlings,Hearts And Lovies Premier"	Que Bocadillos	A CARRUTHERS	28	381	438
Dav. Dweebdork Premier Division	Andy Linighan Appreciation Society	P FRANCE	33	336	393
Davies Wallis Foyster RBS League	Marseilles	G DAGNALL	27	241	292
Dealadora League	Tuffa's Woo Boys	C RICHARDS	10	151	170
Dear Dora Seaside League (South)	Karl Marx Kickers	P DAVIES	22	237	264
Dear Dora Serie Q	Dynamo Dunnington	P HOLDEN	30	437	470
Derby County Supporters Club London Branch Div 2	Red Barrel Rejects	P PAGE	35	411	458
Diamond Dave Superleague	Dario Gradi Out FC	S WOOD	9	134	152
Didsbury Mowlem Fantasy League	Coleden Wonders	MYDDELTON/ MONTLAKE	28	359	397
Digital Equipment Back To Black Lge (Rightsized)	CPG United	D JONES	11	148	174
Do I Not Like That (West)	Chicken and Beans XI	G GYAKI	10	181	192
Do I Not Like That Premier League	Brassic Lint F. C.	A LES BROWN	7	96	116
Do I Not Like Turnips Memorial League	Whatlings Wanderers	T WHATLING	10	103	128
Do They Expect Us To Drink The Stuff	Frans Thijssen's Mustache	P ALDOUS	28	359	392
Does Everyone Have To Pick Four Full Backs ?	Rodney Marsh For England	R THOMAS	33	465	512
Dog & Partridge Redecoration League	Goal King Cole & Knight Of St.James	D GRUER	36	354	433
Doha & District Anglo-Scottish Alliance League	Jack McGinn And His Biscuit Tin	P SCOTT	35	348	404
Don Morris Rememberance League	Eddies Eagles	G EDWARDS	35	310	388
Drunken Mariners	Turnip Head's Vegetables	P TOWNSEND	36	351	395
Drymen Pottery League?	Rowadennan Ramblers	J BANNERMAN	35	416	446
East End Academicals League	Irresistable Force	H WOODLOCK	35	369	445
East End Academicals League	Pointless Rovers	J WOODLOCK	35	417	445
Eastbourne Easy Lifers League	Chris's Greek Delights	C DEMETRIADES	13	211	229

League	Champion	Manager	WKS	A	B
ECGD Alternative League	George Graham Bagel Co.	S MICHAELSON	35	422	465
ECGD League I	Zampa Road Cool Cats	P LYNCH	35	426	463
Edinburgh Academicals Combination	Lokomotiv Hope Street	P HUTTON	35	452	490
Eight Guys And A Gal Named Moe	Lord Rockinghams XI	SUMMERS & RODIE	35	501	546
Eightacre 'Inta' League	Past The Post Utd	S ASTON	35	476	517
Elbows And Backhanders Premiership	Jordan's Jockstraps	J HARTLEY	13	157	179
Eleven Reasons Why......	Le Team	L UXENBERG	9	105	115
Eleventh Plus Bundesliga	Bayern Mucus	R FORSTER	35	399	451
Elton Welsby's A Tart's Chuff Premiership	Fat Wallet Rovers	P NOBLETT	35	409	453
Elton Welsby's Gymkhana	Melrose FC	SELLARS & ROSE	35	347	417
EMI Music	Jamie's Jokers	J SYKES	13	131	149
Employed Entertaining Virgins	He shoots...He scores!	M MCNAMEE	35	387	450
End Season League	Spike-Tic Thistle FC	M FOX	9	91	104
England's Other Premier League	Trumpton Tacklers	M GREEVES	9	139	148
Eric's Collar Premier League	Banana Skins	R CARD	7	126	136
ERM Virtual Reality	Horsforth Wanderers	R COLLEY	9	119	131
Everybody Do The Ayatollah League	Canton Bluebirds F.C.	G EVANS	36	417	475
Exceedingly Good Pies 3	Shaggy's Superstars	C PAYNE	2	57	63
Exeter Nomads League	Borussia Hotspur	P HOLMES	29	369	421
Extra Time At The Tap League	C.C.C.P.	R SHAW	36	408	469
F. T. M.	Rotterdam '85	J AINSWORTH	35	390	414
F.A. Polack's Premiership	Poor Scouser Tommy	D KAY	16	140	169
F.A. Rickson Premiership	Magic City	I RICKSON	29	349	393
F.A. Sam Smiths Pleasant Premiership	Ashton Villa	J SAYLE	26	266	301
F.W.L.T.F.	Teenage Mutant Amy Turtle	P TEAGUE	36	480	511
FA Royal DutchPremiership	Jan Molby's Diet	T PHILPOT	33	439	474

HALL OF FAME

League	Champion	Manager	WKS	A	B
Farmer's Arms Premiership	Born Loser Utd	M BIDDLE	35	368	437
Fat Beer Swilling Geordie F.C. League	Mr Bean's Team	C WOOD	35	463	498
Fat Rons Champagne League	Uncle Monty's Dear Boys	L MEISTER	34	541	566
Feathered Flight of Fancy Footwork	Burning Villas	J A MURPHY	13	220	233
Featherstall Premier League	"Goon,But Not Forgotten"	P BIRD	35	462	496
Floating Lunch League	Armitage Shanks	M CALLAGHAN	31	447	463
Fly Me To The Moon	Monkey Hangers	M HARVEY	23	283	316
Flying Pig	Barnstonworth United	A THOMAS	36	478	532
Football Kings of Clerkenwell	Kevin Marsh	K MARSH	7	102	114
Fords Premier	The Frods	G CLAYTON	35	353	421
Forest JCR	Marksmen	M SHANNON	19	251	270
Forest JCR	Leyton Orient 2000	T HEWITT	19	251	275
Free Love Legal High League	PSV Fondue	B & Q'S FONDUE'S INC	7	145	157
Freeth Cartwright Fantasy Lge.Div 1	Marching on Together	R BEVERLEY	27	257	290
Frenkel Topping Superleague	Pheasant Pluckers	S ASHCROFT	35	421	464
Frere Chomleley Bischoff League	Dukla Wandsworth	D SYMES	13	150	174
Friends Of King Zog	Three Men Went To Mow	N PITFIELD	35	362	416
Friends of Lutonship	Terry's Vegetables	D ROWLES	28	311	345
Friends Of Natch League	11 Men In Flight	J HILL	17	182	204
Friends Of The Fat Man	Guy's Googlies	N GUY	36	430	482
Fuji Boys	The Blues Brothers	D GIBSON	32	397	428
Fun Alliance Premiership	"""True Blues"""	P SMITH	33	442	482
Fur Coat No Kickers League	Windsmurfers	S WATSON	9	130	146
Fuzzy Duck - Does He? Premiership	Ron Knee FC	D WHITESIDE	22	261	284
G L C Series 'A'	Rusty Nails	T VOSE	18	173	203

League	Champion	Manager	WKS	A	B
G.A. Premier League (North East)	Willies Warmers	M LEYLAND	35	508	548
Get Off Don's Sister League	Rabid Ron's Raiders	R ROONEY	35	446	481
Get The Tarts Off Grandstand League Div. 1	Smell's Strollers	S LYTHGOE	35	494	524
Giggs - Schmiggs !	Moggy Marshall Masters	W BOWER	17	226	243
Give Us A Bung League	Tufnell Park Rangers	D LIST	34	449	489
Godsell Astley Pearce	I Quite Like Dave Walsh	D WALSH	35	353	408
Goeff Boycott Corridor of Uncertainty	Empire Strikes Back	K BUTCHER	9	110	121
Graham Taylor Appreciation Society '93-'94	The Chairman's Cheetah's	N PATCH	35	473	515
Great North Premier League	Ensalada Rusa N.EM.D.	C RICHARDSON	16	216	231
Greig Middleton League	Celwest Cowboys	F BURNS	35	460	505
Guernsey Cricketers Alcoholic League	Rags County T.C.	M POOLE	33	367	419
Guernsey Premiership League	Sylvans - Champions - Not!!!!	T VANCE	32	339	387
Gunnell's Groin Followers Premier Division	The Blackthorn Hackers	G MCDONALD	33	350	397
Guns & Poses	Chipmunks Are Back	C JONES	32	358	400
Gunston 'Felching' Premier League	Fat Blokes' Blunders	C WINSTANLEY	32	337	395
Guppy Paper League	MacNamara's Band	T MACNAMARA	35	453	481
Gwent Community Health Grey Suits Premier Division	Shanks Vitreous China	S HUNTER	5	78	83
H - League	0 - 0 AET	B GRAY	35	485	526
Halas Holte League	Like A Dog With Two Deans	G HACKETT	35	444	479
Half a League	Tupton Terriers	G JONES	35	401	475
Half-Past One In The Golden	Deidre Barlow's Boyfriends	D PRATT	35	440	494
Halifaxitup League	Plymouth Pathetic	A CLARK	34	349	379
Hamble's Plastic Curtains Premier League	Wallsend Amnesia	C ALEXANDER	35	421	487
Hampton Wick Erections Premiership	Petes Mob Alexandra	P WILLIAMSON	13	159	182
Happy Shopper 'Bargains Galore' Premiership	The Mighty Mysterons	P SURTEES	35	409	470
Happy Shopper Premiership	Turnip Soup Stanley	KEVIN & CRAIG			

HALL OF FAME

League	Champion	Manager	WKS	A	B
		MURPHY	33	436	472
Hare & Hounds League	Home Alone (Wimbledon F.C.)	M BURNETT	33	374	418
Harry Dross Premier League	Right Said Ted	T EARL	35	422	448
Heaton & Durham Affiliated League	Frank Worthington All Stars	P WOODHEAD	9	161	173
Heaven or Hull	The Yellow and Green Machine	A & M ALASZEWSKI	7	110	122
Heinz Big Souper League	Inside Traders	DEMAIO & MURWILL	35	366	428
Home Brew Super League	Durkar Dabblers	S OAKES	9	137	150
Home Park Association League	Wimbledon Rangers	J HOLMES	19	216	242
Honey I Shrunk The Premier League	Ken Dodd's Dad's Dog's Dead	I CHAMBERS	36	456	488
Honolulu Baby Sunshine League	Ten-Bellies Utd.	S WILLIAMS	26	327	361
Hot X Bun Super League	The Out Of Town Specialities	S PERCIVAL	36	475	513
Huddersfield & District Couch Potato League	Dean Machine In Full Effect	R DEAN	36	340	422
Huggies 'I Can Wear Big Kid Pants Too' Division 3	Chicken Kiev	J 'JACK FLASH' MOORE	26	296	333
I Think He takes The Penalties	"Bell, Summerbee, Lee"	K CONATY	36	473	497
I'm Not Fussed League	Boing! Boing! Baggies! Baggies!	W PUDDLE	35	466	491
IBIS Fantasy Football Premiership	The Academy	K GOODBODY	17	157	184
If Dixon Plays For Fantasy League	Master Bates United	C LAWSON	16	184	198
If You Hate Gerry McNee Clap Your Hand	Alex's Arabs	A IRVING	35	403	444
Illegitimate Bastards Premier League	11 Tampax Required For This Lot	P TOWNSEND	34	369	428
Ilson Fishy Curtains Association League	Ripley Academical	D MONCRIEFF	36	408	468
Imperial Fantasy Football League	Thatchan Wanderers	T OUGHTON	18	220	237
Imperial Lge	Highbury Heroes	J BICKFORD	35	501	572
INA Linear Fantasy League	Ju Inventus	J RIGBY	30	411	446
Indo House League	Campanologists	E TAYLOR	11	135	153
Indo House League	Sultans Of Ping F.C.	F COUGHLAN	11	135	150

league champions 1993–94

League	Champion	Manager	WKS	A	B
Is Boycott Out Yet ?	Reg Holdsworth Select XI	M PITTS	34	364	414
Is Roy Keane Still Available?	Scuffers Eleven	D BUCKLEY	32	363	402
Is Your Fax Machine Working Premier	Real Sociable	T LANG	35	416	462
It's A Funny Old League	Fanny's Cream Doughnuts	D WATLING	35	448	499
It's A Game Of Seven Half Wits	Early Doors	S MCLEAN	34	427	483
It's All Very Pretty But.....	The Lesley Ash Select Eleven	J POPE	26	340	375
It's Ma Ba' League	Goal King Cole's Barmy Army	M HEYES	13	138	160
It's Not Cricket League	Gooners F.C.	M MORLEY	13	154	186
J D Wetherspoon's Beer Bonanza League	Apparent Madrid	K MICKLEWRIGHT	22	282	305
J.H.R : Sweet F.A. League	Accidents Will Happen IX	R HEMSLEY	35	498	524
Jamesie Cotter's Highland House	Trotters Independant Traders	M DAVIES	20	278	311
Jan Molby Is Fat League	Riggsies Red Noses	S ROSE	35	402	455
Japanese Arm's Length League	Athletico Finchampstead	S CLAYTON	19	232	263
Japanese Arm's Length League	Dunwell Boys	J HIGSON	19	232	255
Jimmy Hill Meets Train Head On (Ha!)	Geordie Wanderers	G WALLAGE	35	349	375
JMP Allstars Premier League	Ludo's Lucky Lads	D BROOKS	9	119	134
John Holmes Meets Mary Poppins Premier	JB Allstars	J BROOMFIELD	13	147	160
John Keister Fair-Play League	Oink!	M KENNERLEY	11	169	185
John Pattens Blunders League	Re-Election Favourites	A LARGE	35	480	521
John Smiths Draught League	IFC Garibaldi	I SMITH	11	156	179
John Thomasons Extra Hot & Juicy League Div 4	Graham Taylor's Rejects	T MANAGERESS	36	399	440
Jolly Bizarre Gardening Mishaps League	Trod on Hedgehog Barefoot of South	C JONES	35	452	498
Jon Mountain Memorial League	Sophie And Kattie	G KERR	32	339	372
Joy Division	Locomotive Light Switch	N MILLAR	27	317	348
Joy Division One	Coton House F.C.	P DIGGINS	36	550	582

HALL OF FAME

League	Champion	Manager	WKS	A	B
Julian & Vinny's School Of Excellence Premier	The Canterbury Panthers	N LEAVES	36	429	456
K. O. R. Premiere League	Winalot	B TAYLOR	35	412	453
Kankaku Superleague	Flying Pigs	G STEINBURG	35	439	493
Kebab King Serie A	Onion Bhaji Utd	J BREWDER	7	113	127
Keogh Ritson	One Andy Walker FC	D JOHNSON	9	124	142
Kernow Combo	Malpas Mudflatners	T BAYLEY	33	350	419
Kettering Post Office Premiership	Blackbeau Breakers	N ANDERSON	17	205	226
Kings Head Flat Lager Superleague	Pompey Stella Ledz	P DOUGLAS	22	262	282
Kirman's Out With Connie League	Spam City	G EVANS	20	240	256
Kleinwort Benson All Share League	Hodds 'n' Sods	M HODDS	30	388	434
Knight Williams Premier League	Buckstoppers	HATCHER / GADD	35	451	483
Koopers Kreosote Blundersleague	Inter Uranus	G DEAN	36	435	502
Kwik Save No Frills Oven Ready CCC Premiership	Kenilworth Kings	D POTTER	36	382	432
L.A. Club Tropicarno	Sully Saints	B O'SULLIVAN	29	307	360
L627 Memorial League	Blanchflower's Blackwater Fever	G KENNEDY	13	182	185
Ladbroke's Fantasy League	Askew Rangers	J FROMENT	32	460	500
Laing and Baing League	Atletico Del Fuego	N BAKER	23	320	346
"Lambeth Beer, Fags and Dirty Slags Premiership"	The Mad Dogs	C MADDOCK	34	421	455
Lancaster Gate Fantasy League	Mario Hedgehogs	H.HANCOCK S.BOOR	34	337	388
Largely Bristols	Mules Kickers	A YUILL	24	281	321
Larling Angel Superleague	Grampas 8 My Hampster	D AUSTIN	35	359	400
Last Orders Please League	No Surrender	D TINK	16	219	236
Latinon Lisdecsia Guaele	Dallam Dynamoes	J DAVY	16	175	195
Laura Ashleys Dangerous Dog League	Inter Sarsons	J.NICOLAS S.ASTBURY	36	409	442
League Of Gentlemen	Canton 'A' Team	P ELWICK	23	265	311

League	Champion	Manager	WKS	A	B
League Of Gentlemen	Old Unpredictables	A MAJOR	23	265	299
League Of Plastic	Bald Prima Donnas	J HUXTABLE	35	436	492
Leasowes League Serie A	Jack Hayward's Barmy Army	P READE	10	162	180
Leather Craftsman	The Run - Out Men	S EVANS	35	392	438
Les Douvres Doughnuts	Where's Me Jumper FC	O GODDARD	28	354	381
Let Your Fingers Do The Strumming	Girlie's Galore Utd.	M WELLS	32	343	390
Levick Goalhangers League	Lokomotiv Longcroft	R GILL	28	371	407
Libby's Umbongo Premier League	Eric Cantona Knows My Wife	M MACCANN	35	468	503
Linacre House Grampus 14	Carl Zeiss Big Boot FC	J MOWBRAY	10	140	152
Lineker - 48 Wright 1 Conference	Dynamo Dazmo	D LEWIS	35	475	523
Live & Exclusive	Half Man Half Donkey	J BENNETT	24	301	328
Lobotomized Newts Premiership	Bobie Boyos	B DAVIES	33	448	485
Long Coffee Break (Downstairs Division)	Mrs. Miggins Tea Shop	M CALLEJA	16	204	218
Long Lunchbreak Div II (South)	Theresonlyonefinalbert	A WESTOVER	35	467	503
Long Lunchbreak League	Republic	R THOMAS	35	424	479
Long Way to Derby League	Bedfont Bees	G KEOGH	35	446	483
Looking Dangerous On Paper League	Ruprik's Rebels	R SAWYER	36	414	460
LP30 Fantasy League	The Mickey Thomas Bureau De Change	M BROCKBANK	36	472	536
LTOM Premier League	Borussia Hair	HARRY	26	293	339
Lunchtime in the Club	Man Treble United	M BARRETT	9	114	133
Lycee Loonies	Boom Shakalaka	B GRIMES-VIORT	5	96	102
Lynne Franks PRemier League	The Joys Of Yiddish	G GOODKIND	36	468	513
Lynne Franks PRemier League	The West Stand Warriors	C BARNES	36	468	513
Lyon Road Super Premier	Collier Row Hotspur	ROGERS & SWEENEY	35	394	445

HALL OF FAME

League	Champion	Manager	WKS	A	B
Magnificent Seven	Charlie Cooke's Corkers	K JARVIS	30	407	435
Major Trauma League	Micks Master Team	M ROUTLEDGE	13	180	199
Make Hay In The Six Yard Box When The Sunshines	The Unbelievers	D WHITEHEAD	35	368	408
Manchester Conflicts	Knowledge Is Power	S AINSWORTH	36	600	618
Mark Almond Stomach Pump League	Going Down With Micky Thomas	K APPLETON	36	432	495
Mary Hinge Memorial League	Pybus United	N PYBUS	10	131	152
Mathesons Toddlers All Star League	Boddingtons	A DAVIES	34	412	470
Maths Classroom League	Wijjit Wanderers	OXBOROUGH MUGGLETON	23	321	347
Max Harleys Haircut Memorial League	The Orchestral Tubular Bells	J GREEN	13	156	173
MCFC 5 MUFC 1 Premier Lge.	Piston Broke	NIVEN & JOHNSON	35	387	437
Megalomaniacs Anonymous	Mile End Misfits	L HORNE	32	358	415
Memories Premier	2 Yrs Now & the Sum Are In Tears	M GOLDING	35	378	421
Mickey Thomas Is Innocent	Reservoir Dogs	R FREEMAN	34	483	533
Midland Off Balance Sheet (MOBS) 93/94	Big Wednesday	T LEONARD	35	394	450
Miles Arms 'Beer Bellies & Hangovers' League	Red Star Blackthorn	S COWARD	9	102	121
Milldon Midland Combination	Sumo City	M BROOKES	35	497	556
Mines A Large One Premier League	Thin Non Athletic	L COOPER	35	356	388
Miserable People In Comfy Chairs League	Sporting Earing	R SYOSS	10	148	161
Monday Night At The Mont	Spar	A MANN	23	249	285
Monkey Hollow Premier Tea - Bag Conference	Bunch Of Wazzocks	P HOLME	33	479	524
Moretons Premiership	Talented Wonderers	A ISMAIL	21	269	294
Morning Wood Division 1	The Huthwaite Cripplers	G TRUMAN	13	158	172
Mostley Harmless	Chissagiuda	M EVANS J GIACON	18	239	252
Motions By Order	Raver's Last XI	D THE RAVE GREEN	13	140	162

League	Champion	Manager	WKS	A	B
Mott MacDonald Premier	Butha Buthe Beauties	M AIREY	36	409	445
Mount Street Premier	Burdett Frenzy	A BULMER	34	454	478
Mrs Tess Tickle's Hairy Ball Fan Club	Piss Poor Performers	P HUNT	36	369	429
Mute Records Premiership	Alex Dawson - Where Are You?	E B NIMAN	13	163	190
N. M. F. L. Div. II	King Brilliant	S TREWARTHA	35	414	437
N.L. Conference	Lodge Rovers	M DAVIES	21	244	269
Nae Mackems Or Smog Monsters	Segedunum	I MACKAY	25	255	298
Nag's Head Eight	Francis Was A Wizard	P SILVERMAN	32	353	399
NCGC SuperGooner League	Great Halibut Of The Seventies	A WAINSTEIN	35	506	547
NCM Fantasy League	He's fast - But He's On the Bench	J WALTON	36	429	492
Neil 'The Drinks Are On Me' Premiership	No Hope Wanderers	C HUTCHINS	7	90	111
Newton & Ridley Premiership	Percy's Poseurs	M SMITH	27	261	302
Nicholson House Premier League	Graham Souness' Pacemaker	D ROWLANDS	32	369	407
Nick Jars Sport Cola Premiership	The Bovvverrred Saabs	C SPYROU	18	193	216
Nixon's Englands No.1 League	Malkin Goal Machine	J ROACH	35	442	459
No Cameras Allowed Combination	J. D. For Yags Not Dags	R POWELL	33	386	438
No Hopers	Nice Holiday Didn't Buy A Hoover	J STEVENSON	36	478	498
No Mean City Serie 'A'	Swindon Pish	C TENNENT	23	349	368
Nonsense League	Stupid Twats	M GRANNELL	29	305	358
North London Gimber Premiership	Edgware Maternity	K BOREHAM	20	230	258
North Manchester Fantasy League Div. 1	Hardly Athletic	J SUTTON	35	410	458
Northern Bank	Matthew's Marvels	M LITTLE	29	351	389
Northern Electric News	TurnipHeads United	I HUTCHINSON	11	126	143
Northern Ireland Serie B	Ian Durrant Blue & White Army	A MCALEER	35	379	432
Northern Ireland's Serie A	Red Star Belfast	M WINTERS	35	407	460
Nortons Late Again League	Swales Out	D WARDLE	20	273	299

HALL OF FAME

League	Champion	Manager	WKS	A	B
Nothing For Second	Bingo Munchengladbach	I BOOTH	34	445	492
Nothing Here Today League	Mr. Blobby's Flyers	S SMITH	20	313	327
Number Of The Beast	Scouse Gits	A JACKSON	35	537	562
NWM - Division 1	Colourford United	C FRYER	36	461	517
NWM - Division 2	Bond F.C.	S HODGE	36	444	487
"Oh, Ah, Leslie Ashe (Allegedly)"	Dialo Athletico	C GIBB	18	289	316
Old Contemptibles	New Spanner Crew	P HASSALL	36	397	439
"On All Fours, Bitch"	Dirtbox Danglers	RAMBO	35	446	494
On The Piste League	One Season Wonders	K LAMB	26	298	335
One For The Road Premier	Large Bacardi Please	B BAILEY	24	322	334
One Pint One Slimmer Federation Div One	Every Wednesday	P ROBSON	13	156	169
One Short of a Dozen	Masterfield	MASTERS	13	147	168
OOH AAH Eric Hamer League	Galatasaray UK Supporters Club	M TAYLOR	24	280	330
Our's !!	Monday Wanderers	O BURKHILL	9	136	151
Out Of Our League	They Think It's All Over	P LANGHAM	33	396	424
Over The Moon	Lolford Utd	L FORD	13	200	218
Over the moon league(aka Lyn's library lge)	Longden Liabilities	M LONGDEN	35	418	474
P.S. Artists	Inter Poll	A LEGGETT	13	124	152
Packet Of Frozen Peas	It's Better Than Tetris FC	J COPE	6	89	93
Paddington Cartel	Bonzo's Bozos	J CROCKER	36	409	474
Panmure Gordon: The Toughest League In The World	Harry's Horny Humpers	H PHILLIPS	36	384	468
Pay The Penalty	The Black Circle	S KEABLE	33	396	429
PBS League	Saltash Strollers	P WHISKER	35	359	384
PDC Memorial League	Unsporting Lisbon	T GILL	9	115	136
PDFM Super League	Sutton's Slammers	M SUTTON	27	278	300
Pedigreezi League	Magpie Direct Norfolk & Longer	T DOBBS	36	342	405

League	Champion	Manager	WKS	A	B
Pennine House Premiership	Fire & Accident Rugby Team (FART)	J SIMMS	7	113	125
Peter Swales Memorial League	"Championis, Championis"	S BOOTH	17	197	218
Peter Symonds Fantasy League	On the Ball City	J BOUGHTON	6	106	116
Phifa League	"Peanuts, Roasted Peanuts"	T BENSON	35	379	426
Piles of Cash Premiership	Jurassic Park Rangers	D WARDEN	35	508	543
Pilgrims Progress	Leaburn Again !	J STICKINGS	36	431	480
Pillow Pants Premier	Gor Seung Lai Hai F.C.	"CON,DAVE & HOVIS"	32	318	401
PJs Pizza Loaf Memorial League	Red Star Balmore	P LILLEY	9	122	140
Portcullis Premier League	Witch Bitter Lemon Teamsters	V HINES	35	504	550
Porter Cottage League	Port Vale's First Team	B O' HAGAN	35	435	489
"Poseurs, Pillocks & Pansies"	I Coglioni Del Cane	R EVANS	35	477	515
Positive Alternative Serie 'A'	Pearce's Backpass F.C.	J GRAY	23	297	324
Post - Teenage Kicks	Yo-Yo F.C.	A DERRY	35	361	413
Postman Pat Premier	Stella Artois F.C.	A O'TOOLE	35	444	483
Postman Pat Premier	Geordie Jocks	H RUSSELL	35	428	483
Prebon Premier Brokers League	Slurper's City	T SUMANA	35	382	430
Premier Catnic	Talking Through Your Arse F.C.	A LAMB	35	372	431
Premier Cru	Friday the 13th	H EASTWOOD	35	405	447
Premier Hot Shots League	Bob's Best XI	R STACK	5	95	108
Premiere Royale	F.O.A.M. Utd	S NEWMAN	35	415	442
Pride Of The South Premier League	Steve Cram's S.O.S.S	S CRANMER	28	380	402
Prima Pasta Serie A	Donna Tartt Fan Club	D MURRAY	35	383	429
Principality Studs League 2	Muffins' Whites	S MULES	32	387	427
Prisoners Cell Block 72	Rugb's Rovers	I CULLIMORE	35	304	376
Pro V.O. League	Vindaloo Utd	C FULSTOW	7	111	122

HALL OF FAME

League	Champion	Manager	WKS	A	B
Profit Related Premiership 'PRP'	110% Effort - 3.5% Cash!	A CAULFIELD	36	461	502
PSV De Hems	Kentish Town Casuals	D GOLDMAN	35	506	545
Punjabi Airways (North East) Super League	David Webb's Cheeekbone	D HAYWARD	34	448	474
Pussers Rum Premier	Al's Irritable Bowel Syndrome	A HAYWARD	35	414	482
Pyjama Tops Nice Spots & Dots	Le Champion Anti Scouse 93 - 94	C BUTLER	33	434	478
QBO Barmy Armani	Champion The Carthorse	T GREEN	27	373	424
Quarrymen	Heavenly Boddies	C TIMMINS	23	231	266
Quarter Pounder Rubbish Serie A	Toz Its Time For Bed F.C.	T WILLIAMS	11	162	176
Queen of England Premiership	Ken Bates Beard F.C.	P MAISSONI	35	422	480
Queen's Memorial League	Arnies Arsekickers	D STOBBART	20	221	246
Racal Premier League	Hook Wanderers	M FREETH	35	452	494
Radio 5 Fantasy League	Terry Conroy's Legs	N HANCOCK	35	428	491
Ram Aurora Southern Comfort League	Glengarry Celtic	A WHITONARCH	13	148	176
Ray Wilkins Square Ball League	Anusol F.C.	A WARDLE	16	158	174
Red Hills 766080	Athletico Wadden 500	NIGEL	36	417	457
Reg Holdsworth Soggy Duvet Premiership	Don Brennan's Left Peg	I RAE	35	496	524
Reg Holdsworth's Better Buy League	Ossie's Nightmare	R CLARKE	27	318	348
Relatives League	Johnnys Giants	J ALLCOCK	18	226	238
Retford & District Fantasy League	Too Good To Go Down	P SEXTON	32	407	448
Richard Keys Jacket Premiership	City Slickers	P LAWMAN	36	536	573
Riddled With Cliche	"Franky, Franky, Franky Worthington"	G KNEESHAW	33	346	396
Right Wingers Premier League	Steve's Athletico Toe	S BOLAND	30	440	463
Robinsons Best Bitter League Division 1	061-226-1191	D IBBOTSON	35	401	458
Rockingham Village Stores Fantasy Football League	Technico Imps	S BERRIDGE	36	426	487
Rocquettes Premier League	City Rangers	M MULLEN	35	456	483

League	Champion	Manager	WKS	A	B
Roding Forost	Cottage Loaf	P AYLOTT	33	432	463
Roedean Rockets Sponsered By Autoglass	Chubsters Cheeks	M C SAYER	13	176	196
Rola - Cola Premiership	FC Aarau	M MCDAID	35	500	534
Ron Booger's Memorial League	Ossie's Dream	E LEVY	36	438	461
Ronnie Radfords Great Left Peg	Special K's	ESPECIAL	36	412	442
Ronseal Premier League	Flagrante Delicto	R COLLINS	35	386	432
Roy Leach	Black Horse Gunners	T COLLISSON	16	126	131
Royal Philharmonic League	The Ganders	T LEAHY	35	439	485
Royal Spank Of Botland League	Tragic Tarts	N MCINNES	7	119	135
RP Sabatier league	Camden Stabbers	A CASSON	29	343	384
Rushden Station Ale Drinkers League	Budgie's Bodgers	S BURGESS	35	417	468
Ruskin Superleague	Dad's Army	D JONES	9	118	138
S & S Pro -Fit 'Roach Super Premiershit	Inter Dick	R HAZELL	33	357	399
S.E.P.D.O Tight Pants Premier League	Seamans 'Babies'	D MAY	10	130	140
S/ton's Last Season In The Premiership	Ask -Em Out FC	P CANTON	28	345	377
Sad Bastards Premier League	Lazy Sods United	R SIMPSON	6	96	106
Saints And Sinners Serie A	Smugglers City	R PROW	34	431	453
Saki Sushi League	Check The Hooly Hoolies	M PLANT	35	497	532
Salford University Fantasy Geography	Sporting Abeergut	A BROOKFIELD	6	81	93
Sandgate League	Athletico Fob-Yac	PRICO / OLANDO	35	490	538
Satsuma League	Cocky Devils	M PORTER	9	156	166
Schofield's Survivors League	Inter Course F.C.	G SPENCER	35	383	427
Scot Amic Fantasise About Being Top Of The League	Son of Sausage	L TYRE	30	387	432
Scott Premier	Roker Rookies on Tour 93/94	J CRABB	35	422	476
Scottish Border League: Brian Clough Division	Coke United	J WILLIAMSON	33	389	414
Scotty's Missing Selection	Tightwod City	J PARTON	10	133	147

HALL OF FAME

League	Champion	Manager	WKS	A	B
Scouts Club League	John's Big Pants	J GIBSON	10	163	178
Seaton Carew Methodist Chapel Table Tennis League	Goat City	R CLARKE	32	337	380
Secret Lemonade Drinkers' League	Atletico Wandsworth	J SALKELP	16	187	213
Sedgwick Energy International Premier Lge	Fat Northern Bastard Exiles	N SMITH	35	400	446
See You Next Tuesday League	Andy Linighans School Of Excellence	N REYNOLDS	35	505	533
Selfridges	No Chancers Utd	R BALASUPIANI	11	144	151
Seria Acacia	Shytehawks	M LITTLE	35	547	569
Seria X	Royle Madrid	M MALONEY	25	358	388
Serie 'Z'	United	G MILLER	9	100	106
Serie BAe	They're Losing 1-0	D NEWMAN	35	411	474
Serie HMV	Janice Fashanu's Porthole Pirates	A PAGE	35	352	382
Serie Us	Inter Tanglefoot	R REYNOLDS	22	277	308
Serie Wasters	The Akash Tandoori FC	C IVEY	21	270	288
Serie Z	Baltic Utd	C WILSON	35	404	461
Serie Z	Armchair Honved	J TAYLOR	35	418	451
Serie Z	Minor Abrasion	T HARPER	35	415	471
Serie Z	Red Star Basildon	P SMYTH	34	322	356
Serie Z	Achilles Last Stand	M BUTTREE	23	258	290
Serie Z	Slackers SOFC	J BENNETT	18	244	260
Serious Steroids Division 1	Caversham Academicals	A CLINCH	36	430	455
She Doesn't Understand	Beeston Boilers	R BRINLEY	24	309	348
Sheldon Premier	D.C.B.M. Milan	B CLEARY	36	445	480
Sherbert Millichip's Crotchless Undies League	Spaten Munchengladbach	M HOLMAN	34	433	475
Shipperley Salmon Paste League Division 6	Timperley United	M PACK	27	379	413
Shirley Cosmos Woodman's Rest Bar Braisers XI	Bargain Basement	J MCMAHON	23	346	369

League	Champion	Manager	WKS	A	B
Sick As A Parrot Serie 'A'	Ten Bellies Utd	BASHFORD & DATE	34	347	395
Sideways for England League	Barney Jams Over Rahno FC	B WALLACE	9	158	170
Sir Alec Adoo Gordons Gin League	South Eastern Strollers	S PATES	18	285	312
Sitting Room Only	Real Socialist Dad	R HEMBREY	23	336	357
Slac Premier League	Amsacs	J MENNELL	36	448	473
Slapdash Hogshead Invitational	Martins Talking Horses	M LEWIS	36	439	488
Smithers Release The Hounds League	Athletico Shirley	S KINGDOM	35	391	433
Smithy's AKA 9 1/2 - 10 1/2 Premiership	Cowcross Wanderers	P TURNBULL	35	442	469
So What Do You Win Then ?	Abitonthe Side	K MACKIE	9	109	123
Social Outcasts Division Six (S.O.D.S.)	A.F.C. Evil Empire	M MCENEARNEY	36	405	471
Soggy's Serie 'A'	Smegs United	A BURNS	7	105	120
Southern Fried Chicken Shakers	Casual Corinthians	T LAUGHTON	23	367	389
Space Alien Lawnmower League	Athletico Toon Army	G BELL	30	399	442
Split Beaver Home League	Two-One	D PRINT	13	168	184
Sports Force	Boro	M BLYTHE	9	126	148
Sportsbra Blundersliga	Clitoris Allsorts	M WATERHOUSE	32	373	408
St Dennis The Menace League	Dynamo Drecklys	I BICKNELL	7	93	109
St Gregorys Premiership	Wilman Wanderers	J HUNT	27	372	380
St Johns Toun League PLC	Mark United	M STURGESS	9	110	126
St. Andrew's College Fantasy League	FC First Year	T LADS	6	86	95
Stagedoor Hardcore Premiership	Toon Army Exiles	A ROSS	25	329	373
"Stand Up, Stand Up, Stand Up League"	C. Below	L HAYCROFT	35	454	490
Star Soccer	Mannion Knighted	T MANNION	35	366	424
Stars On Sunday Serie 'A'	Inswinging Yorkers FC	S SADIQ	36	389	434
Sticky Belly League	Wait Another 26yrs Red Scum B'strds	A JAMES	36	412	438

HALL OF FAME

League	Champion	Manager	WKS	A	B
Stowmarket Bundesliga	Kingston Rovers	A KING	34	421	443
Suburban Housewives' Dinner Party	Lombardyonians	N BYNE	13	164	182
Sullivan's Sunday Sport Whips & Leather League	"Bobby Gould's ""Barmy Army"""	I PATTERN	35	431	473
Summerhouse League	Ian's Idols	I ACHURCH	29	358	393
Supplementary League	Blues 4 Swindon 6	K BAYLISS	13	163	195
Swales Out League 93 - 94	Stan Bowles Ate My Hamster	P.RUANE/R.SMITH	34	419	451
T Woodley's Trainspotter's Guide To The Galaxy	Go Ahead Spaniels	B PAYNE	13	183	201
T.W.I.A.T.	Sweet Enough	G JOINT	34	380	424
Taff Bluebird	Ricky Wright Blues	M DAVIS	35	437	464
Tampax Free-Flowing Football League	Mann's Best	D MANNS	23	412	442
Tangerine Joy Jelly Premier League (Members Only)	We'll Run Rings Around Uranus	KEV AND MIKE	35	437	482
Teenage Kicks Premier	68 Guns F.C.	A LUXTON	35	446	498
"Ten Blokes,Two Girlfriends,One Wife"	Franz Kafka Homicide XI	M PURKISS	24	332	350
Terry McDermott Looks Like Harry Enfields Scousers	Dynamo Jarreau	A CAMERON	32	335	385
Terry McDermott's Remarkable Moustache	P.S.V. Talking Bolx	J DAVIDSON	13	195	215
Terry Venables Business School League	Ianford	I SALE	29	330	379
Tesco Country Club	The Gunners	K CARROLL	13	120	137
Thames Water wet Dreamers Conference	Surreal madrid	T SMITH	30	328	379
That's Litho Div. 1	A.F.C.Salmon	L FARREN	32	434	461
The '10 Quid For This' Premiership	Cider Army	A SIMPSON	18	259	273
The 'Almost 7 Up' League	Wagon Wheel XI	A WRAGG	18	252	276
The 'Chinny' Hill League	Lynham's Overdraft First XI	K SIMMONDS	35	395	463
"The 'Come Back Terry Cooper' League, Division 1"	Shambles City	J TURNER	6	100	110
"The 'Do I Like That, Or What?' League"	Dynamo Madras	J GOBBI/J PORTON	13	151	162
The 'Do I Not Like That' League	West Brom Reserves	M PAYNE	11	170	194
The 'Do I Not Like That' League	The Graeme Souness XI	W PATON	9	140	151

League	Champion	Manager	WKS	A	B
The 'Grosvenok' Table Croquet League	The Villiboard Cluck Swingtet	M PRYKE	36	434	478
The 'Hand Of God' Serie 'A'	Sao Paulo Stanklifters	S EL YOUNGO	35	369	431
The 'Henry Staplehurst Memorial' League	Dirty Northern Bastards	A GARTSIDE	9	112	128
The 'Investigations R Us' League	Dynamo Belsize Park	N WARDEN	30	305	348
The 'Just One Cornetto' Serie 'A'	Outstandingly United	M HOPE	35	533	572
The 'Lenscrafters' League Of Notions	Thalassic Park	R BENNETT	9	112	128
The 'Not The Premier League' League	Fittonroundsschmeichel.....thats 4!	I FITTON	35	424	452
The 'Oh No He's Injured/A Substitute' League	The Sunday Hackers	M TURNER	21	318	347
The 'Over The Hill' Mob	2 of the best(L'pool)9 of the rest	P KOPITE	35	393	456
The 'Scumbusting Is An Art' League	Widdicambe Wallop	D BARRATT	23	311	331
The 'What Goes On At Afternoon' Conference	Wicked Wanderers	I BYRNE	25	268	304
The 'Who ate all the pies?' Superleague	Dukla Pumpherston	C KANE	35	437	453
The 'Why Aren't Nottingham Forest In It?' League	Fair Isle Pharoahs	M SHEEHY	34	478	521
The 'Will Mike Buckley-Stanton Ever Pay League'	Ian Marshall's Sideburns	G THURLOW	30	413	450
"The 20,000th League Under The Sea"	Typos Untied	M SALTER	35	394	425
The 30 Miles East Of England Premiership	Springhead Regulars	G PARTIS	29	382	415
The 5/8 - 1/2 WHMU League	Lees United	R LEES	35	344	399
The Academy	Fulham R's	J WATKINS	36	389	427
The Albanian Premier	Pausing To Pee Against The Goalpost	S FIELD	35	374	406
The Albert Smith Memorial League	Where's Beardsley ?	K BURN	35	436	479
The Alex Archer Memorial League	Almost Foreign	G WATKINS	23	245	288
"The And, And !, And League"	Filbert's Fighters	J TAYLOR	33	432	484
The Angel League	Dynamo Battenburg	BARRETT & BOWMAN	35	492	533
The Anglo - Irish Superleague	9th May 1987 F.C.	N SWINBANK	36	378	443
The Annette Waugh Memorial League	Chigley RMI	M JONES	25	323	354

HALL OF FAME

League	Champion	Manager	WKS	A	B
The Anonymous Envelope League	Eric Hall's Speech Impediment	G BRIGGS	36	501	541
The Anti Rifle League	Rusty's Cakey Pigs	R BARNES-HEATH	9	139	154
The Appaling Premier	They Suck (Don't They)	D LOYNES	36	394	462
The Artful Bodgers Serie A	Stonkin Good Shooters	G HARPER	18	262	271
The Arthur Guinness Supporters Club Division 3	Sarah's Eleven	I BARNETT	27	373	403
The Artichoke & Associated Vegetables League	AFC Chigley	K SANDERS	33	316	353
The B.C.C.I. Credit League	The Man With The Huge Teeth	S TAYLOR	36	408	482
The Baker Street Volunteers	Somedays You Eat The Bear	I HART	35	499	546
The Balham Premiership	The Emanuelle Beart Crazed Stalkers	M VASEY	35	486	525
The Balmoral Beer Bellies Superleague	Le Tissier Was A Bargain At £6.2m	S WINDEATT	35	414	475
The Beleagured League	The D Hirst Serie XXXX	P GRAHAM	36	408	455
The Bentley's Bitter Premiership	Cymru Crusaders	N ASPINALL	27	329	357
The Bernard Tapie 'Slip Us A Fifa' League	Olympique Bribery	J LOWE	36	386	452
The Best Advice League	Mr Metternichs Mahogany Lime Zester	M VAN CRESSWELL	22	341	367
The Better of The Two Lytham Leagues	Ooh Bully Bully 2 - Legend Lives On	J SILVANI	35	312	385
The Betty Swollox Conference	Nobby's Stile XI	S KNOWLES	29	512	533
The Big & Bouncy Midlands League	Simo's Seagulls	M SIMS	36	536	581
The Big Bung League	Clapham Northerners	J HULME	36	419	477
The Big Durex Premier League	XX127	J PARSONS	16	166	181
The Big P3 Single Crystal X-Ray Diffraction League	Blunderland	D RICHARDS	7	107	117
The Big Stiff One	Tess Tickles Utd	K GRAYLING	36	426	482
The Bill Werbenuik Beer Drinkers Premier Lge	Pogue Mahoneys	J DRINKWATER	35	418	465
The Billy The Fish Ate Aquarian League	Lincoln Loiterers	N BRANT	36	448	483
The Blenheim Conference	The Pink Gorillas	S JEWHURST	35	547	577

League	Champion	Manager	WKS	A	B
The Boddies Premiership	Running Down The Wing F.C.	I GABBIE	32	359	410
The Boys Done Good	The Dogs Bollix	M WAY	30	328	362
The Bring Back Bobby Robson Premiership	Ian Marshall's Barber	A RUDGE	34	465	493
"The Buck, Guisborough"	Acklam Boro Branch	P ROONEY	29	290	350
The Bucks Tandoori League	Athletico Chiswick	M DIBSDALL	17	194	221
The Budweiser Zeebraship	Hood Academicals	M CHESHIRE	9	128	150
The Bull Conference	Barwick Bores	C GRIDLEY	22	345	361
The Bunker League	Senegal Lions	G OSBORNE	36	520	546
The Butchers Arms League	Fawsley Falcons	T SAUNDERS	17	208	240
The Capital Premiership	And Smith Must Score	D BACON	32	347	384
The Capstan Full Strength Football League	Drop The Dead Donkey	P MURPHY	28	296	323
The Cedar Street Euro League	Walthamstow Rangers	LES VENABLES DYER	26	367	420
The Charles Charlie Charles Champions League	Flemhousemanure	K G WEIGHILL	17	208	235
The Chase	West Scan United	B HANLON	2	65	68
The Chef & Brewer Fantasy League	Wileys Strong Lager XI	N WILEY	33	365	412
The Childish Squabbling League	Boggart Hole Clough	C SHAW	36	462	519
The Chuck Wimbledon Out of the League - League	I Hope Someone Signs Tim Flowers FC	T DEAKIN	34	418	470
The Conference Pear Conference	1862 Donna Summers Afternoon	R HOWORTH	36	471	505
The Cool For Cats Premiership	Alexanders XI	A CHRISTIE	34	482	507
The Coopers Premiership	The Red & White Kops	A GOURLEY	17	210	241
The Crash And Burn Premier League	Real Madras FC	M BARRETT	35	429	482
The Croydon Pro-Ratas	Top Of The League	PAUL & PAUL	30	410	449
The Cubie Challenge League	The Walnuts	A WYMAN	25	227	270
The Dandelion & Burdock Premiership	Randy Vanwarmer Athletic	P CASWELL	13	158	175
The David Simpson Invitational	You Waht United	D BRITTON	34	501	526

HALL OF FAME

League	Champion	Manager	WKS	A	B
The Deep Pan Steeplechase League	Scooby Doo's Allstar XI	A POWERS	9	123	141
The Devonshire Drinkers Superleague	Woodshed Utd	P THOMAS	22	245	281
The Dim Sum Combination	Australia's A Long Way To Go For A	K MURPHY	35	372	428
The Dirty Dozen	Ontheball City	R BOOTY	26	295	348
The Do I Not Like That League	AC Bilbao	T CONNAUGHTON	9	127	144
The Do I Not Like That League	Charlton Reserves	R CREED	9	118	125
The Dodgy Excuse For A Meeting Premiership	Week 14 Club	M RICHMOND	21	216	254
The Doner Escargot After The Wine Bar League	Laro United	G R. RANIERI	32	337	376
The Downfall Of Liverpool F.C. Memorial League	The Firm	C MURRAY	22	278	304
The Dream Combination	Leiceseverton	P MARTIN/E JONES	25	261	312
The Dreamers and Schemers	A.C. Milamb	P LAMBERT	35	408	472
The Dripping Tap League	Simply The Best	S GEARIE	34	475	542
The Dynamo Premiership	The Bothered Boleyn Boys	I LLEWELYN	33	375	437
The Earie Robins Sterland Serie A	Marching All Together	N HODGSON	27	369	390
The Easton Avenue League	Emulators Of Les Cobb	D EAST	36	440	491
The Eddie The Eagle Premiership	Dream Team United	C NAGINTON	9	129	144
The Edwards Veeder Premier	Red Rose Kings	N HARRISON	36	423	494
The Eleven Lagers And Twenty-Two Popadums	Herbert Chapman Commemorative XI	D LUSH	36	379	432
The Elvis Presley Memorial League	Mackem Haters United	G JOHNSTON	36	457	470
The Entertainers Say ' Who The F*** Are Man Utd?'	Peter's Pansies	P GRIEVES	18	246	265
The Euroshell Extra-Terrestrial Egg Butty League	Hamish's Hotshots	J GIBB	23	281	325
The Exiles Central League	Nightmare On Filbert Street	C BELL	17	221	244
The F.A. 'Bodyform' League	Alan Little's Barmy Army	J STEVENS	29	390	441
The F.A. Premier League	Tottenham Hotspur	J GOLASZEWSKI	19	243	276
The F.L.C. League	Dicks Dicks We All Love Dicks	T TURTLE	27	327	359

League	Champion	Manager	WKS	A	B
The Fantasy To Reality League	Fulchester Rovers	J BROWNSDON	24	267	304
The Fanzine Fantasy League	Till The World Stops	P VALE	30	359	371
The Far And Wide League	Heroes	T TALON	35	415	448
The Firkin Legless League	Pete's A Toppin'	P HODDER	35	460	488
The Fisher Drinking Premiership	The Flying Foxes	G GREGORY	16	197	217
The Flap Cock League	Calmdown Calmdown United	"PAUL, NICK & DAVID"	36	398	438
The Founder Members Bung Free League	Joey Is Our King	B BENTON	19	232	263
The Fourth Division	The Irrational Jingoists	P HARTSHORN	32	339	407
The Fourth Division	One Team in London	N SHORTALL	32	379	407
The Freddie Starr Ate My Football League	Newcastle II (The Second Coming)	J MCFADYEN	35	413	452
The Friends Of Nancy Premiership	Guacamole Globetrotters	J LIDDLE/T KISSANE	13	170	187
The Game of Two Halves Cliche League	Cradley Heathens	A RAYBOULD	35	392	432
The Geordie Luvvies League	Red Star Falmouth Dynamo	S CHAMBERS S HAMIL	13	175	190
The George Best Liver & Kidneys Memorial League	Newcastle Dreamers	J JARVIS	36	397	447
The Gillian Taylforth B.J. Premiership	Get Motivated	EUGENE	9	131	146
The Good Jugs Premiership	Arthur C's Mysterious Eleven	P BOSHER	32	439	476
The Good Mixer	Kevin Peter Hall	MUDDY	35	402	445
The Good The Bad And The Hopeless League	Pint Of Murphys	P MURPHY	35	435	511
The Graham Kelly Depreciation Society League	Gulls Galore	R COOMBES	22	270	307
The Grolsch League	Medway Town FC	P WHARTON	23	226	264
The Group 4 Security Conference	Club Tropicana	A BEST	23	309	335
The Guildford/Reading Premiership	Stamford Bridge Stormtroopers	R CLAESSENS	20	214	244
The H B Lincoln Wednesday League	Eleven-Non-Blondes	C DELANEY	10	119	130
The Handy Don't You Think League	Steaming Dump Returns	R MASTROPIERRO	25	327	366
The Harry Secombe's Highway to Hell League	The Welsh Leakers	R MALIK	33	379	419

HALL OF FAME

League	Champion	Manager	WKS	A	B
The Harvey Floor Bangers	Go Ahead Emus	J BURKE	34	397	472
The Heather Locklear Babewatch Schwing! Ship	John Motson's Cliches	D LEACH	3	62	71
The Heineken Schmeineken League	I Once Met Sammy Lee In A Lift F.C.	D KERR	36	467	495
The High Pedigree Content League	Too Blue To Be True	A TODD	22	310	353
The Hillingdon League	Rosedale Wanderers	M TREACHER	13	201	222
The Horse for Breakfast League	Restar Titanic	A DANIELS	5	81	91
The Howdy-Doody Homer League	Totally Wondrous Wanderers	N MCKINNON	13	139	169
The Human League	Nigel's left Me	J BEWLEY	30	396	432
The Human League	Bud-Max United	S MORRISON	9	129	146
The Human League (Don't You Want Me JB)	Inter Milan Kundera	M THOMAS	35	445	480
The Inn League	Jan Molby's Eleven And A Half	A GELLION	36	292	381
The J & C Moores League	The Number Ones	N WREST	35	347	399
The Jack Shit Memorial League	Ooh! Roger Palmer	B WILLIAMS	27	275	306
The James Alexander Gordon Championship	Peter's One-Nil Squad	P CICCONE	35	466	515
The John Sharp Memorial Drinker's Elbow League	Mandy Van Den Hauwe's First XI	N READ	32	378	418
The Jojodororoowmaga League	Ronnie and Graham's Team That Never	DOM/GIN/JV	11	189	200
The Krafty Dreamwhip Premier League	The Best XI	C PILLING	34	414	462
The Larfin' Bru League Of Holsten Experts Serie A	Kipper Skipper's Cheeky Chappies	J DE LORD	24	353	385
The Late Starting But Total Quality Management Lge	Joe Longthorne's Pianist's XI	P WILSON	18	246	268
The Leach Ale Gut League	Surreal Madrid	J OVENS	23	314	333
The League Against Bad Sports	Dodgy Desperados	P KONOPKA	35	378	440
The League Of Brian	Lee One Pen	G WILSON	16	165	188
The League Of Gobble	Inter 'Me' Birds Twat	D CHALKER	21	252	283
The League Of Leagues	Lick It & Like It !	M ENRIGHT	32	319	350
The League Of Mortimer	Nottingham Florist	D PERKINS	17	205	226

League	Champion	Manager	WKS	A	B
The League With No Name	Raving Irons	A BAUGH	33	286	339
The League With No Name	The Totty Posse	I STRINGFELLOW	33	335	402
The League With No Name	Classy Clowns	J OVERTON	22	271	296
The League With No Name	Horns Of The Buffallo	J BIRTWISTLE	22	235	254
The Leeds Y-Frontals Premier League	Scoop City	C BENSON	9	132	150
The Legal And General Hyper League	Clarkey's Champions ('92)	B CLARKE	35	437	489
The Legless Virgin's League	Windsor Wovals	G FLACK	28	377	398
The Lesley 'Ooh-Aah' Cantona Conferance	Guns 'N' Poses	D ASHBEE	35	477	512
The Linford 9.87 Sunday League	Kevin Beattie XI	S WARDE	34	451	496
The Long Lunchbreak Division 2 (North)	Eastbourne Paedophiles F.C.	M LYON	36	404	463
The Lumpington League	V.Singletons Sticky Flap Plastic XI	CRANSTONE & BALTROP	34	429	475
The Magnificent Seven	Suavey Harveys Barmy Army	R HARVEY	23	337	358
The Magnificent Seven Plus One	Rusty Bullet Holes	I STILL/S BARTLETT	13	177	200
The Magpie Mackem Serie A	Deer Best Player Anagram XI	M COLLEDGE	35	541	583
The Makem Muddler's	Up Where We Belong	J PEARSON	35	452	473
The Mania League	Donkeys Dream Team	M GIBSON	36	489	537
The Mary Hinge League	Peraguin Farquar Celebrity Allstars	C JENKINS	35	428	477
The Maurice Flitcroft Premiership Conference	Reg Holdsworth Appreciation Society	J DAWSON	36	357	420
The Maximum Protection Shield	Woolwich Heath 1893	D THORNE	30	320	355
The Michael Jackson Allegedly U-13 Boys League	Pace At The Back	BAUMBER & SEAMAN	32	415	470
The Michael Jackson U-11s League	Graham Taylor Select XI	A ASLAM	32	382	413
The Midland Superleague	Under Pressure Premiership XI	B RANDHAWA	13	193	212
The Misery League	The Lemon Popsicles	S SYMONS	32	465	502
The Mother Of All Leagues	Sporting Bras	M SHAPTER	36	335	406

HALL OF FAME

League	Champion	Manager	WKS	A	B
The Mullerd And Ratarsed League	The Elite Eleven	S REED	18	229	243
The Muscat Premiership	The Linford Christie Lunch Box XI	P NESS	13	150	167
The Naris Fizz Premier	Wolfie Hampton Wanderers FC	G WOLFE	13	166	188
The Nash Arms Jolly Boys	Moss Bros Spartak	C ASHER	35	537	570
The Nearly Done League	Beermonsters United	C WAFER	35	462	519
The NME Serie Eh ?	Dynamo Ben Nevis	K CAMERON	23	268	303
The Nod's Memorial Old F.L.	Dynamo Monks	R SUTCLIFFE	16	231	243
The Norfolk and Good League	Jenny Taylors All Stars	I.SCOTT T HULLOCK	28	307	362
The North East Hot Bed Of Soccer League	Fatsio	A GRAHAM	24	257	306
The Northwood Hills Beaver League	Donosti	J DINGLE	32	336	402
The Oak And Academics Premier	The Avenging Angels	R BORMAN	28	343	376
The Official Body Organ League	Flushing Red Cheeks	S COOK	36	368	424
The Old Red Lion League	Toon Army	T DOUGLASS	36	425	453
The Penguin Premiership	Class Act	P FOXWELL	22	292	316
The Pennywise Allo Luv Northern Alliance	E. A. Barmy Army	D HUMPHREYS	10	128	145
The Persil Premiership	Ohnoingoalagain F.C.	J WALSH	13	163	182
The Peter Swales Haircut Appreciation Society	Ian's Inadequates Unathletic	M BELL	18	231	246
The Portwall Premiership	The James Gang	R JAMES	30	367	386
The Poxy Little Cup League	Diamond Geezer	S JONES	13	167	185
The Prince Of Orange League	Armitage Shanks All Stars	K HOBBS	19	199	231
The Professor Yaffle Premiership	Portway Magic	M CROSS	11	135	158
The PW Memorial League	Dynamo Didsbury	D HUGHES	35	509	539
The Queens Hotel Premiership	Cows's Scud Attackers	MARCUS	35	538	579
The Rainbow Inn	Mix & Match	C EWAN	2	41	43
The Rathbones League	Saturn V	S BILBAO	35	440	494

League	Champion	Manager	WKS	A	B
The Rebels Without A Clue	Highway Select	J DOHERTY	36	344	433
The Red Cow Richmond	Dances Through Wolves	S ROBINSON	32	420	455
The Red Dwarf Intergallactic Premiership	Inter Tivoli	P NAUGHTON	35	395	446
The Right Sized League	Are Arsenal Wimbledon in Disguise	P PETLEY	28	293	350
The Rolf Harris Stylophone Premier League	You Know You Want It Wanderes	L & J BROWN	34	524	559
The Ronald Koeman Appreciation Society	Piping Sheep Thistle	M DEAR	18	265	276
The Royal League Of London	Dynamo Semtex	CALVIN MANLEY	27	315	363
The Russ Mould League	Frank Worthington F.C.	M BEILBY	19	207	244
The Sack Graham Taylor League	"Crystal Palace F.C. , In Disguise"	M ASHENDEN	36	425	464
The Sack Graham Taylor League	Thunderbird 1	S EDWARDS	36	363	415
The Shambles Premiership	A Wasted Saturday Afternoon	N TONGUE	29	342	365
The Sharon Onions League	Eric The Red Card	N PARKES	25	299	327
The Shuttleworth's Premiership	Honest It's True AFC	J BROWN	30	450	486
The Silky And Dazz Premier League	Suntans of Swing	P NICHOLSON	35	516	548
The Silverwood Fantsy League	Surreal Fish	M MILNER	10	112	125
The Slightly Silly League	ACC Milan	A COLLERY	36	565	598
The Sly Bastard Wayne Piggott League	West Brom Wankers	MR.PRIVACY	36	369	432
The Southern Shandy - Drinking Poofters League	Highland Haggis Chasers	D SHORT	7	125	145
The Sportsmans Premier League	Wilky's Michael Jackson	R JACKSON	35	389	439
The Square Ball League	Briggersley Rovers	HATTERSLEY BRIGGS	36	426	484
The Stanley League	Big Jugs United	I BASSETT	4	97	101
The Stubborn Staines Championship	The Gooners Army	N GALATIN	9	109	121
The Sweet F.A. Premier League	K.Y.F.C.	N PICKFORD	35	418	471
The Sweet F.A. Retirement League	Fish Fingers	K FINDLATER	9	109	132
The Sweet FA League	Real Mapperley	C VINES	35	425	471

HALL OF FAME

League	Champion	Manager	WKS	A	B
The Tampax Flowing Football League	One Season Wonders	K CHIK	35	395	429
The Tesco's Value Premiership	Iain Dowies Uglier Sisters	J REUBERSON	25	361	395
The Tetley League	East Stand Bondholders	N STALLWORTHY	35	371	424
The Tim Read & Brian Sutton Great Mates League	Money Inc.	L GREAVES	35	464	514
The Tommy Ticklers	Rineker Returns	C MANNS	35	369	415
The Tony Brook Strategy League	Piddle Plodders	L GARRATT	28	332	360
The Tottenham Hotspur Haters League	The Italian Stallion XI	M ZANELLI	3	57	65
The Towers Perrin Premier	Veni Vidi Vici	M BORGHELLO	36	403	448
The Trocadero Fantasy League	Lucky Seven	I YAPP	36	443	471
The Uninspired	With The POPPER For The Poppers FC	M ROBINS	27	297	319
The Up Yours Gary Newbon League	Duchess of Argyle's Eleven	J BRAIN	35	332	358
The Vera Duckworth Manchester 2000 League	Sugar Is A Bastard	A PENNOCK	36	486	527
The Victoria Flat And Cloudy Premier League	A.F.C. Santos	B RICHBELL	35	427	455
The Vinny Jones Fair Play League	Owl Town	O COSKER	30	368	416
The Virginia Bottomley Twinset League	Dynamo Chicken Kiev	A PARKIN	23	329	359
The Vision	Nil Satis Nisi Optimum	A RIGG	35	403	445
The Vision 2000 Absolute Fantasy League	Shitehawks	S PEGGS	9	141	154
The Voice of The Beehive	Gresty Rovers	A LATHAM	35	419	478
The Wannabees	Twenty One - Twelve (21:12)	K TRACY	34	452	502
The We Hate Flashman League	Kevin Keegans Kurlers	A KESHWANI	35	472	498
The Wear Sport Superleague	Mann United	L MANN	7	81	100
The Whatsagoodtitle ? League	Thunderball	D GILL	35	468	521
The White Hart Premiership	Will's Winners UTD	W WORSDELL	6	72	88
The White Hart Premiership	Sheriff's All Star	P SHERIFF	6	72	86
The Wide As A Gate League	A Singularly Stupid Policy	J MCELROY	22	359	373

League	Champion	Manager	WKS	A	B
The Willie Gettagame Fantasy League	On Me 'Ead Son Allstars	C THOMPSON	35	480	518
The Windmill Road Premiership	If Only I Had The Donkey	K PEGG (EL PEGO)	35	343	371
The WM Business Systems Premier League	Copland Falcons	G BELL	30	327	389
The Wucking Fankers Premier	The Trevor Sinclair Fan Club	M BUTTERWORTH	13	196	223
The XRM It'll Be Alright On The Night League	Mango Munchers	T BURTON	20	272	293
The Young Turnips	Marvelous Great Tremendous	M TAYLOR	25	297	320
The'Don Redmond'Memorial League	Geefax All Stars	G DAVIES	35	414	467
Theaksons Old Pec	Wippet Wanderers	A JOHNSON	35	365	400
There Must Be More To Life Than This League	You Get Nowt For Coming Second	M JACOBS	13	195	210
There's No 'F' In Ekoku League	Hale Winos	J BUCKLEY	19	217	246
They Don't Like It Up 'Em	Gladstone Screwers	S FORT	20	254	289
They Think It's All Over 'USA 94'	Happy Hammers United	J STEER	35	553	584
This Table Is Reserved From 6 Premiership	Ganglands Gits	T LAWLOR	35	433	482
This Took A Lot Of Bloody Organising !	Polly Anna And The Raggedy Men	J WALKER	36	467	530
Thomson's Holidays Computer Services	XD United On A Friday	J WILSON	35	388	448
Time Gentlemen Please	Edmund's Leather Codpiece	P BENNETT	23	305	326
Tired And Emotional League Div.3	Sheer Class Rovers	J LEBETKIN	27	332	347
Tofik Bakhramov Premier League	K.S. Shish-Kebab	P BARKER	35	409	477
Top Deck Shandy League (South)	Men In Wool Clothing	D GIBSON	36	420	468
"Towers Perrin, Newbury"	Palmers Wizards	R PALMER	35	475	489
Trabant Turbo	110% Tooting	P BARTLETT	33	408	440
Tram Slam	Mr Clough's Overdraft	J MCGUINESS	27	357	376
Treppauf Und Treppab League	Noeffingunners United	D NISBET	6	133	137
Trevor Francis Is The Devil Premiership	Beerfica	D SLEVIN	33	411	447
Trevors Snug 8 Premier	Rifa United	A BARR	34	350	396
Truly International Team Syndicate	Torpedo Belgrano	R GREEN	35	335	389

HALL OF FAME

League	Champion	Manager	WKS	A	B
TSB Supreme Combination League	Fulchest United	J DAWN	36	385	448
Turnip Tel Must Go Division	Red Devils Utd	D SMITH	13	159	183
Turnip Tel Must Go Division	Jacob Rovers	C ORMOROD	13	159	173
Turnips In Abundance	Wally & The Wing Backs	M CARR	36	456	515
TV New Era League	Tricky Trees	S UDDIN	9	111	125
Tynesiders At Rosies	S.B.S.	T DORKIN	19	221	254
UHU Adventurers League	Manufique	C POWELL	35	337	356
US. ED. Sani-Towels	The Lost Boys	K SCOTT	33	378	413
Usan with Class	I Can Exclusively Reveal	J REID	35	459	500
Van Den Bergh Foods Ltd	The Dog Pollocks	J WALTERS	30	385	425
Ventnor Veterans	Martin's Magicians	M OSBOURNE	27	349	390
Vera Cerri's Underpaid Army Serie D	We Only Hate Glasgow Rangers FC	R SHIPLEY	9	115	128
Vic Callow Works Here	The Mick Coop Appreciation Society	J HARDING	34	467	504
Vidal Sassoon Wash 'n Go League	Toon South	L COLLERTON	35	406	465
Viv Nicholson Memorial League	Thora Hird's A1 Chubby Buffalo XI	A BRUTY	35	336	374
W + S Premier League	Bolton Abbey Monks	M RYDE	35	371	420
W + S Premier League	The Big Girls Blouses	P STEPHENSON	35	371	425
Wacko Jacko Under 12s League	Steve Bull's A Tatta	D MATTHEWS	32	386	410
Wally Milner Body Slam League	Bankupt And Hove Albion	R HIGGINS	18	269	287
Warren Fantasy Football League (Waffle)	A.C. Kowalski	S MASON	35	404	474
We Are Top Of The League League	You Know That AC Milan	I LOOSEMOORE	34	348	400
We Don't Work For A Living League	Barnaby's Bunglers	B WYNTER	35	382	449
We Hate Tottenham Celtic Prem Div	Back To The Valley	S BARRETT	35	384	438
We Know F.A. About Football League	Brady Bunch	J ADAMS	35	567	595
We Now Have A Nominal Interest In The Premier Lge	Cathays Academicals	P STEAD	28	367	389

League	Champion	Manager	WKS	A	B
We Took The Coke Machine End	Embra Untied	J COOPER	32	362	390
We'll Think Of A Name Later League	Dodgy Hip Athletic	S DAVIS	22	278	307
We've Got The Silliest Name In The League Lge	Toon Army	BREVE	35	415	468
Well Red	Dulwich Ham Sandwich FC	J DOHERTY	30	471	505
Wellington Premier League	Sycophants Corner B	A HICKS	35	375	413
Wembley Park Station Pub League	Plymouth FC	O PALERMI	24	281	302
West 8 Sports League	Luton 'R's	N MARSHAL	34	335	372
West End Premier	"""OO AH CANTONA"""	E MIRNER	13	201	213
Whassisfantasyleaguelarkthen	Pete's Pirates Argyle	P BLACKMAN	11	121	138
What The Hell Does Mike Dent Do League?	Athletico Tanglefoot	A PENNYCOOK	9	114	127
When Saturday Comes	Old Fallopians	C SILK	34	414	440
When Thursday Comes	For Fox Sake	L MIDDLETON	35	432	481
Where's The Head On That Pint Northern Premier	Dynamo Chicken Kiev	A FOGG	19	209	242
White Horse Premier	Stating Albion	M PHILPOTT	32	346	385
White Rankers League	Moss & Co Dynamoes	K MOSS	35	360	419
Willis Carroon All Stars	So You Tried To Ban Us Mr Croker	J DAVIDSON	35	404	438
Worker's Playtime Div. 1	Creatures From The Black Lagoon	R.EDWARDS M.WIGGIN	29	351	421
World Cup '94 - Sheffield Play-off Group	Sheffield Week-on-Thursday	P DADSWELL	35	537	591
Wot No Coffee Conference League	Darwen End Soup Eaters	G YOUNG	7	102	124
Wot? No Geoff Thomas League - Take Two	Old Speckled Men	L O'HARA	35	355	422
Wretched Road Premier	Inter Bed	TOON & BALL	35	485	501
Wrexham Pheasant Pluckers League	The Dongers	C HOWARD	22	227	265
Wunch Of Bankers Premiership	Radders United	S WHITTLE	35	335	398
Yellow Pages Premiership	International Rescue	J HALLETT	35	445	489
Zambian Memorial League	Someone Else Got Hoddle	MARION	26	360	381

HALL OF FAME

FANTASY LEAGUE TOP 50 POINTS SCORERS – SOLO MANAGERS

	Team	Manager	GLS	ASS	CS	GA	TOT
1	Hearts Of Thistle	Anthony Lewis	113	78	72	172	611
2	Bexhill Boyz F.C.	Gerard Aherne	105	60	86	170	594
3	AC Rep. Of Yorkshire Villa Reserves	Chris Jameson	114	65	66	153	583
4	Increasingly Less Athletic F.C.	John Strongman	100	53	74	137	565
5	Knighton's Crusaders	Ross Armstrong	100	70	72	163	565
6	F.C. Pele' Dynamos	Paul Heron	109	70	71	186	565
7	The Dickie Davis Decorating Kit	Bryn Williams	113	61	72	186	563
8	Bobby Wibnit's Living Legend	Flis & April Taylor	89	71	77	155	562
9	Eintracht Fanny-Magnets	David Hughes	112	69	69	169	551
10	Fortuna Fish Sandwich	Fraser Smalley	100	69	68	165	545
11	Glorplay United	Iain Cairns	82	76	71	140	542
12	3 Men And A Team	Mick Derbyshire	86	69	71	153	527
13	Dazza's Dazzlers	Darren Hillard	98	58	71	167	527
14	Gerry Atrik's Dribblers	Declan Conaty	98	64	66	159	527
15	Maine Road's Muddy Marvels	Joshua Langton	97	72	63	162	525
16	Ron's Boys	R A Jacobs	106	66	65	187	523
17	Rod Hull Kingston Rovers	A. M. Green	93	77	61	155	522
18	Seaman Shoots In Schmeichel's Box	Russell Packford	102	71	63	181	519
19	Sad Bunch Of Losers	Tony Small	99	65	65	170	517
20	Melchester Rovers	Keith Wilson	75	61	82	159	516
21	Confussion Personified	Tony French	109	72	57	182	513
22	Sons Of Tottering GrotSpur	David Hancock	94	72	63	167	511
23	Barnselona	P Toll	103	70	56	163	510
24	The Ralph Milne Fan Club	Jon Mather	97	63	67	175	510

	Team	Manager	GLS	ASS	CS	GA	TOT
25	Evenley Park Rangers	Brian Howells	79	65	73	149	510
26	Toon Army 2	Robin Elliot	80	71	75	173	509
27	Ttnhm HtSpr (Oh No! Already Used!)	Les Camp	105	67	64	198	507
28	Saints March On	Carl Haworth	95	64	62	154	507
29	Whitestick Tappers	Colin Campbell	88	64	69	163	505
30	Bristol City	Andrew Marshfield	77	61	73	140	505
31	Dynamo Zimmers	Frederick & J. Munn	86	68	65	150	504
32	You'll Always Beat Des Walker	Terry Prett	76	58	82	168	504
33	Carling's Darlings	David Brewster	83	60	70	145	504
34	Hartcliffe F.C.	Jeffrey Payne	68	68	78	149	503
35	Rifle Volunteer Rovers	Sue Braithwait	77	69	78	181	500
36	Netherton Wanderers	P Hillard	92	69	63	166	500
37	Homeley's HotSpurs	Clare Jacobs	88	66	74	193	499
38	Crew Cut Alexandra	Adam Hosking	97	60	62	163	496
39	Paynters Pilgrims	Sean Jones	89	66	71	187	496
40	W.T.F. Flip Le Flem	Andrew Davies	100	59	58	154	496
41	Cooper's Creosote XI	Kenneth Walsh	87	65	71	181	494
42	We're The Left Side	Bridget Atkinson	94	65	49	114	494
43	F.C. Dago Love Machine	Pete Miller	87	59	70	166	493
44	Stanley Bowles/ Betting Slips	Tony Jameson-Allen	56	80	86	179	493
45	Which Broom Will Albion	Roland Gayner	100	66	56	164	492
46	Mickey Thomas Goes Down F.C.	Daniel Marshall	85	61	64	142	491
47	Vapid Vedra	Peter Laing	76	64	70	147	489
48	Bodgit And Scarper	S J Campbell	86	74	63	172	486
49	Saint Alan's Ball Boys	Mike Prince	80	52	77	166	486
50	Leicester City? Only Joachim	Glynn Marshall	92	58	64	153	485

HALL OF FAME

FANTASY LEAGUE TOP 50 AVERAGES – SOLO MANAGERS

	Team	Manager	Pts	Pld	Ave
1	Chopper Harris FC	Tristan Long	202	10	20.20
2	Casual Free Thinkers FC	John Dewar	261	13	20.08
3	Redfearn Three Two	Dave Schofield	198	10	19.80
4	Harley's Tigers	Crispin Leyser	214	11	19.45
5	Latchford Toffees F.C.	Ian Thomas	250	13	19.23
6	Newburt Park rovers	Gary Brown	439	23	19.09
7	Done Up Like A Kipper !	Jerry De Lord	381	20	19.05
8	The Monkey Is In The Tree	Nick Hemmings & Marc Joyce	414	22	18.82
9	Tottering Hotspuds	Mark Lynch	188	10	18.80
10	Arguably Their Best Side	Brian Carrick	356	19	18.74
11	Cruzcampo La Coruna	Rob Oliver	373	20	18.65
12	We're The Left Side	Bridget Atkinson	494	27	18.30
13	Paul McGrath's Fitness Instructor	Martin Kay	236	13	18.15
14	My Left Foot	Jochen Tree	481	27	17.81
15	Michael Jackson's Under 13's	Kieron Smith	354	20	17.70
16	Nobby's Heroes	Ian Judd	419	24	17.46
17	Hearts Of Thistle	Anthony Lewis	611	35	17.46
18	The Sad Financial Analysts	Ian Woolley	349	20	17.45
19	Charles Charlie Charles XI	Bob Drinkall	348	20	17.40
20	Leicester Fosse '94	Neil Stretton	226	13	17.38
21	P.S.V. Superspecs	Rob Wiles	226	13	17.38
22	Kwesi's Fantasy Kings FC	Kwesi Cairns	346	20	17.30
23	P. S. V. Bristol	Jonathan Munn	224	13	17.23
24	Ormondroyd's Nose	Matthew Brown	430	25	17.20

	Team	Manager	ts	Pld	Ave
25	B.R.F.C.	Graham Norman	445	26	17.12
26	Chris's Dream Team	Chris Broadfoot	171	10	17.10
27	Bexhill Boyz F.C.	Gerard Aherne	594	35	16.97
28	Garam Masala	Marc Jaffrey	441	26	16.96
29	Early Doors	Robert Andrews	474	28	16.93
30	La La Celtic	David Anton	186	11	16.91
31	Toon Town	Michael Brodie	219	13	16.85
32	Porters South	Lee Smith & Martin Marshall	387	23	16.83
33	Red Star Bell End	Jon Stone	185	11	16.82
34	Ndlovu Train	Graham Evans	184	11	16.73
35	Adrian Heath Is God	James Bradshaw	217	13	16.69
36	AC Rep. Of Yorkshire Villa Reserves	Chris Jameson	583	35	16.66
37	Just One Good Season	Samuel Rush	449	27	16.63
38	Knighton's Crusaders	Ross Armstrong	565	34	16.62
39	F.C. Pele' Dynamos	Paul Heron	565	34	16.62
40	Wallace Road Glory Boys	Jethro Curtis	216	13	16.62
41	Jordan's Highflyers	Jordan & Julie Kemp	447	27	16.56
42	Depreciating Beavers	Marc Landsberg	331	20	16.55
43	Holtenders in the Sky	Stewart Knott	215	13	16.54
44	The Brooking Brief	Brendan Buggy	214	13	16.46
45	The Newcomers	Manish Thakrar	411	25	16.44
46	The Grecians	Robert Isaac	164	10	16.40
47	Porticus Kerb Crawlers	Martin Drake	377	23	16.39
48	Camberwick Green	Ian Ridley	180	11	16.36
49	The Beautiful Gameboys	Terry Cooney	375	23	16.30
50	Here We Go Again	Andi Charalambides	309	19	16.26

FANTASY LEAGUE TOP 50 GOALS – SOLO MANAGERS

	Team	Manager	Goals
1	AC Rep. Of Yorkshire Villa Reserves	Chris Jameson	114
2	Hearts Of Thistle	Anthony Lewis	113
3	The Dickie Davis Decorating Kit	Bryn Williams	113
4	Eintracht Fanny-Magnets	David Hughes	112
5	Confussion Personified	Tony French	109
6	F.C. Pele Dynamos	Paul Heron	109
7	Ron's Boys	R A Jacobs	106
8	Ttnhm HtSpr (Oh No! Already Used!)	Les Camp	105
9	Bexhill Boyz F.C.	Gerard Aherne	105
10	Barnselona	P Toll	103
11	Seaman Shoots In Schmeichels Box	Russell Packford	102
12	Terry Duckworth's Innocent	Alf Vaughan	102
13	Increasingly Less Athletic F.C.	John Strongman	100
14	Greasy Chip Butty	Jacqui Cryan	100
15	Which Broom Will Albeon	Roland Gayner	100
16	Fortuna FishSandwich	Fraser Smalley	100
17	Knighton's Crusaders	Ross Armstrong	100
18	W.T.F. Flip Le Flem	Andrew Davies	100
19	Sad Bunch Of Losers	Tony Small	99
20	Dynamo Blarpstain	Jason John	99
21	Dazza's Dazzlers	Darren Hillard	98
22	Gerry Atrik's Dribblers	Declan Conaty	98
23	Milton Abbas Parish Council	Mark Alman	98
24	Early Doors	Robert Andrews	98

	Team	Manager	Goals
25	Dukla Dumptruck	Jim Duggan	97
26	The Ralph Milne Fan Club	Jon Mather	97
27	Maine Road's Muddy Marvels	Joshua Langton	97
28	Sugar & Spite F.C.	Jo Palmer	97
29	Crew Cut Alexandra	Adam Hosking	97
30	Magic Sponge Panacea	Mike Kazer	96
31	Melfort Meanies	Craig Elam	96
32	A Fairytale Season - Grimm	Dave Foulger	96
33	Ally McCoist's Lucky Troll	Shane Dorrian	95
34	Saints March On	Carl Haworth	95
35	ATP Athletic	Stephen Davey	95
36	Garam Masala	Marc Jaffrey	95
37	Julian Must Stay	Alan Stables	95
38	Well It Was A Bonus	Ben Cranfield	94
39	Sons Of Tottering GrotSpur	David Hancock	94
40	We're The Left Side	Bridget Atkinson	94
41	Alf Tupper Comebacks	Katharine Crossley	93
42	The Blind School	Alex Houghton	93
43	Rod Hull Kingston Rovers	A. M. Green	93
44	Haven Green Pirates	Phil Richardson	92
45	Lanark K-Standers	Stuart Craig	92
46	Tai Bach Monsters	Wayne Holder	92
47	Netherton Wanderers	P Hillard	92
48	Leicester City ? Only Joachim	Glynn Marshall	92
49	Bristol Nomads	Richard Waller	91
50	Look At His Face	I Evans & S Fletcher	90

FANTASY LEAGUE TOP 50 ASSISTS – SOLO MANAGERS

	Team	Manager	Assists
1	Brooklands Bigshorts	Martin Connolly	84
2	Stanley Bowles' Betting Slips	Tony Jameson-Allen	80
3	Lee 1 (Pen.)	Anthony Smith	79
4	The Blue And White Army	Paul Bown	78
5	Asic's Aces	Anthony Maddox	78
6	The Bombay Ducks	Andrew Bryan	78
7	Hearts Of Thistle	Anthony Lewis	78
8	Rod Hull Kingston Rovers	A. M. Green	77
9	Glorplay United	Iain Cairns	76
10	Stoke MadDogs	Wayne Manning	75
11	Greasy Chip Butty	Jacqui Cryan	74
12	Bodgit And Scarper	S J Campbell	74
13	The Blind School	Alex Houghton	74
14	Billy Whitehurst Is God	Mark Williams	73
15	Maine Roads Muddy Marvels	Joshua Langton	72
16	Sons Of Tottering GrotSpur	David Hancock	72
17	Toon Army 2	Robin Elliot	71
18	Seaman Shoots In Schmeichels Box	Russell Packford	71
19	Shank's Red Army	Simon Girling	71
20	Thamesdown Rovers	Mark Fry	71
21	Bobby Wibnit's Living Legend	Flis & April Taylor	71
22	Razorblades XI	Nigel Fox	71
23	The Invisible Men	Robert Woodhouse	71
24	Hare & Tortoise Rangers	Garry Lloyd	71

	Team	Manager	Assists
25	Barnselona	P Toll	70
26	Huyton Baddies In Exile	Bryan Tyrer	70
27	Red Star Balmullo	Peter Thommeny	70
28	Dream 4500 FC	Rex Lowther	70
29	ATP Athletic	Stephen Davey	70
30	Mickey Thomas Bust Fund	Conrad Lee Harris	70
31	Confussion Personified	Tony French	70
32	St Etienne	Michael Hydes	70
33	Widdringtoon Army	Terry Arkle	70
34	Knighton's Crusaders	Ross Armstrong	70
35	F.C. Pele' Dynamos	Paul Heron	70
36	A Fairytale Season - Grimm	Dave Foulger	70
37	Sky Blue Army	Simon Lynch	70
38	Cranny's Crapshots F.C.	Stephen Cranshaw	70
39	Eddie May's Barmy Army	Stuart Reed	70
40	Bobby Moore Heavens XI	Steve Keyes	69
41	3 Men And A Team	Mick Derbyshire	69
42	Ironopolis Exiles	Peter Drew	69
43	The West Standers	John Langford	69
44	Rifle Volunteer Rovers	Sue Braithwait	69
45	Eintracht Fanny-Magnets	David Hughes	69
46	Netherton Wanderers	P Hillard	69
47	Fortuna Fish Sandwich	Fraser Smalley	69
48	Julian Dicks Appreciation Society X	Tony Hamilton	69
49	Bruisya Crunchnpassbach	Pat Whymer	69
50	BillanBenFICA	Toni & Guy	68

FANTASY LEAGUE TOP 50 CLEAN SHEETS – SOLO MANAGERS

	Team	Manager	Clean Sheets
1	Stanley Bowles' Betting Slips	Tony Jameson-Allen	86
2	Bexhill Boyz F.C.	Gerard Aherne	86
3	Bankers F.C.	Tony Walton	84
4	Melchester Rovers	Keith Wilson	82
5	You'll Always Beat Des Walker	Terry Prett	82
6	Europa Town	Sean McFadden	81
7	Smudger's Heroes	Dave Smith	80
8	Dynamo Barnet	R G Coleman	78
9	Rifle Volunteer Rovers	Sue Braithwait	78
10	Hartcliffe F.C.	Jeffrey Payne	78
11	Bobby Wibnit's Living Legend	Flis & April Taylor	77
12	Saint Alan's Ball Boys	Mike Prince	77
13	County Club	C B Kilkhams	77
14	Uncle Tony's Donkey Ride	Bruce Pagram	76
15	Toon Army 2	Robin Elliot	75
16	Simply Reds	Ben Goad	75
17	Harry's Boys	P Crozier	75
18	Increasingly Less Athletic F.C.	John Strongman	74
19	Homeley's HotSpurs	Clare Jacobs	74
20	Ecclespo Hibs	Ian Wilson	73
21	The Nearly Men	Richard Newey	73
22	Reservoir Owls	Craig Thompson	73
23	Evenley Park Rangers	Brian Howells	73
24	Bristol City	Andrew Marshfield	73

	Team	Manager	Clean Sheets
25	Merson's Magic Men	Stephen Ballard	73
26	Boddie's Best	John Tindall	73
27	Early Doors Utd.	T Jopson	73
28	Rifle Volunteer United	David Braithwait	72
29	I've Set My Stall Out	Dave Foulger	72
30	Hearts Of Thistle	Anthony Lewis	72
31	The Dickie Davis Decorating Kit	Bryn Williams	72
32	Temple Bar 4th XI	Simon Carr	72
33	Knighton's Crusaders	Ross Armstrong	72
34	Reg Holdsworth's Eyeballs	Tony Maggs	72
35	Glorplay United	Iain Cairns	71
36	BillanBenFICA	Toni & Guy	71
37	Cooper's Creosote XI	Kenneth Walsh	71
38	3 Men And A Team	Mick Derbyshire	71
39	Parma Ham United	Stephen Peck	71
40	FA Cup Winners X 8	Dawn Povey	71
41	Dazza's Dazzlers	Darren Hillard	71
42	Paynter's Pilgrims	Sean Jones	71
43	F.C. Pele' Dynamos	Paul Heron	71
44	Cranny's Crapshots F.C.	Stephen Cranshaw	71
45	Athletico Lee Chapman	Terry Sparks	70
46	Pathetic Athletic	Tony Smith	70
47	F.C. Dago Love Machine	Pete Miller	70
48	Vapid Vedra	Peter Laing	70
49	The Blue And White Army	Paul Bown	70
50	He Must Do... And Does	Richard Brazier	70

FANTASY LEAGUE BOTTOM 50 LEAKY DEFENCES – SOLO MANAGERS

	Team	Manager	Goals against
1	Bob Dylan's Clarets	Danny West	239
2	Wal's All Stars	Ian Wassell	224
3	Stoned Soccer Team	Andrew Stone	224
4	Exeter City F.F.C.	Roger Wellman	220
5	Brooklands Bigshorts	Martin Connolly	219
6	Worldwide Wamblers	Russell Codger	217
7	Huyton Baddies In Exile	Bryan Tyrer	216
8	Eastbourne Gunners	Pete Hodkinson	216
9	Greasy Chip Butty	Jacqui Cryan	214
10	Make Mine A Julian Dicks	Jane Beattie	210
11	Sugar & Spite F.C.	Jo Palmer	210
12	Another Wasted Corner	James Stanton (Jnr)	210
13	Red Star Norwich	Martin Higgs	209
14	Norwich Nutters	James Adlam	209
15	XI Ruby Murrays	Roy Murray	208
16	Rifle Volunteer United	David Braithwait	208
17	Looking For A Sponsor	Adam Redhouse	208
18	The Sticky Toffees	Neil Wolstenholme	207
19	Two Nil Lead	Steve Ham	205
20	Ayrshire & Galloway Dy-Drm Believrs	Douglas Greenwood	205
21	St Etienne's Greens	Gilles Pelard	205
22	The Footballng Talents Of Brisingamen	Ian Bagley	204
23	Lascelles Federation	Damien Stock	204
24	Torpedo Monkton	Keith Pettitt	203

	Team	Manager	Goals against
25	Joseph's Giants	Mark Joseph	203
26	Roydon Town	Kevin Coaker	203
27	The Bulging JockStraps	Philip Bearman	203
28	Ally McCoist's Lucky Troll	Shane Dorrian	202
29	Dream 4500 FC	Rex Lowther	202
30	Sporting Cricklewood	Lino Nunes	201
31	Parma Ham United	Stephen Peck	201
32	What A Squad!	Mark Fox	201
33	The Pitch Dwellers	David Norris	200
34	Magic Sponge Panacea	Mike Kazer	200
35	Namrog's Backward XI	Paul Gorman	200
36	BillanBenFICA	Toni & Guy	199
37	The Star-Inn Sulgrave	Andy Willerton	199
38	Garibaldi Stags	Roger Hall	199
39	ATP Athletic	Stephen Davey	199
40	The Undecided	Lee Spencer	199
41	Ttnhm HtSpr (Oh No! Already Used!)	Les Camp	198
42	Spurs 'R' Hot	Jerry Ryder	198
43	Bristol Nomads	Richard Waller	198
44	Piglet Pants United	Russell Deane	198
45	Micky Stockwell's 4 Foot XI	Dave Hassell	197
46	Produced By Fred Quimby	Stuart Ellis	197
47	Blyth Spirits F.C.	Peter Blyth	197
48	Ironopolis Exiles	Peter Drew	196
49	Hendo's Heroes	Darren Hendersen	196
50	Eintracht Eastry	John Brazier	196

HALL OF FAME

FANTASY LEAGUE TOP 50 – DAILY TELEGRAPH LEAGUE

	Team	Manager	Pts
1	Bergholt Wednesday	D W Beck	372
2	Bjork United	C J Dew	369
3	Eeza Goode FC	J C Hooper	364
4	Hassocks United F C	B R Stubbs	360
4	Eril and the Reds	J A Durno	360
6	Coppice Rangers	F Glyhnn	359
7	The Greengers	R Prill	358
8	Locomotive Crewe FC	J R Timmins	357
9	Liberty 1888	A Rampaul	355
9	Balreick Srai - my son	S K Srai	355
9	Surreal Madrid	G H Wildman	355
12	Dalesman F C Leeds	M L Bramfitt	354
12	Tennyson Rovers	J A Ellis	354
14	Berkhamsted Bears	P S Hinson	353
14	Yellowstone Rangers	G D Rankine	353
14	Willy's Wanderers	W Platts	353
17	Best of the Best	I B Kaye	352
17	Sick Parrots	R I Jones	352
19	Rosies Rascals	R C A Clements	351
20	Traumatic Town	H S Winch	350
21	Elite Fleet	T E Hutchings	349
21	Spa Action Force	S C Keys	349
21	Hummelton Academicals	M Ewens	349
21	Chinwig Old Boys	R Bailey	349

	Team	Manager	Pts
21	Mean Machine	M C Jackson	349
21	Hounsdown We R We R	P Rundell	349
27	Fly Fishing by	D M Thornton	348
27	Bardsey Rovers F C	N J Lofthouse	348
29	The Canaries	P Griffin	347
29	Selly Oak Wanderers	P G A Hickman	347
29	You're Sacked Wadman	J Graebe	347
29	Super Johns Army	M Bartlett	347
29	Mattchester United	M J Hatton	347
34	Gods United	V E Edmondson	346
34	Toffee Bhoys XI	L H Harris	346
34	Meats United	J C P Parikh	346
34	Birminghamisa City	R K Jepson	346
34	St Reatham Red Heads	S M Firman	346
34	Young Ones	R Young	346
34	Bristol Bent Shooters	J A Stok	346
34	Elegant Mess	L M Frost	346
42	MMMMMM Utd	M M Miller	345
42	Torpedo Westhay AFC	P J Adlam	345
44	Hutton Village Unt	T E Eccleshall	344
44	Matt's Lads	M J Easton	344
44	British Beef FC	J LIpscombe	344
44	Chickenrun Supreme	S Ward	344
44	Chaspatval United	P L Fernandez	344
49	Samuel Peadoria	P I Davies	343
49	Pinmorelorinthians	P R Dawson	343

HALL OF FAME

FANTASY LEAGUE TOP 50 – 90 MINUTES LEAGUE

	Team	Manager	GLS	ASS	CS	GA	TOT
1	Phoenix Rovers	Nick Pallis	104	55	63	127	547
2	Timperley Small Shorts	Richard English	104	52	59	112	540
3	Rowcroft's Rejects	Brian Rowcroft	88	68	67	129	539
4	Dynamo Hampstead	Tom Moore	93	62	66	129	538
5	CIty Slickers	Howard Martin	100	66	58	127	537
6	Dawns Delights	Gavin Crossley	96	65	53	93	537
7	Skins and Angels	Ian Warner	88	68	66	128	536
8	Vile Utd	Mark Summerville	90	56	68	119	535
9	Rose Winfield Star XI	Stephen Rose	103	58	63	144	533
10	EFC'S Yam Yam Scallies	Paul Hale	99	57	62	127	532
11	Houchen's Header 1987	Scott Pittam	96	59	64	131	531
12	Sharpe Shuffle XI	Lance Thomas	105	60	59	142	529
13	Dave Todd's Ho6 Rod	David Todd	93	75	61	146	527
14	Gonnawintheleague	Julian Gregory	96	57	66	140	526
15	Court's Culprits	Adrian Court	101	57	65	152	525
16	"Blood, Sweat and Tears"	Derek Baxton	97	63	58	124	525
17	Frank's Second XI	Steve Miles	88	65	64	128	522
18	Canaanranliansanlane	David Noble	91	55	68	133	522
19	Shades of Andy Hunt	James Dodd	102	59	59	144	516
20	Rev's Holy Rollers	Keith le Cheminant	102	57	55	125	515
21	Newscored	A P	101	60	55	131	512
22	FC Utd	William Bishop	93	55	62	125	512
23	Fairbanks United	Michael Fairbanks	100	58	57	132	512
24	Mine`s a Quiche	Kevin Downs	95	60	56	118	511

	Team	Manager	GLS	ASS	CS	GA	TOT
25	We Reek of Chic XXX	Jamie Stuart	90	60	61	124	510
26	Tyrannic Wingers	Colin Walford	103	62	52	134	507
27	The Team with No Name	Neil Powell	92	65	56	123	507
28	West Ham I wish FC	Marc Joyce	105	60	54	144	507
29	Kavos `92	Edward Holman	82	74	61	132	506
30	Dearne Destroyers	Natalie Trickett	106	61	55	154	506
31	The De Niro Boys	Sue Golay	97	67	57	147	506
32	Inspiration F.C.	John Mock	100	60	55	136	504
33	K.J.S.E. United	C Davis	99	54	51	106	503
34	Rampant Rovers	Nicholas RImmer	90	57	63	134	502
35	Dynamo SCO	John Schofield	105	57	55	149	500
36	AC Parker	S.P. Parker	108	48	56	145	499
37	Middlesbrough's Missing Millions	John Kay	92	60	59	133	499
38	Are you sure Shreeves?	Daniel Macklin	94	52	62	135	499
39	Jim's Crazy Addicks	James Sawkins	98	62	54	135	499
40	Dukla Orange	Graeme Burnett	102	53	60	154	498
41	HMS Full Of It	Seamus Leavey	92	63	58	136	498
42	AFC Redcar	Gavin Othick	92	55	58	120	498
43	Max's Cumbrians	Paul Mcneill	82	53	68	126	498
44	Trawden Tornadoes	Peter Anslow	107	48	56	143	498
45	Club Shandy '63	Sharon Puxty	101	55	56	140	497
46	Don Kiddick XI	Kieran Conaty	94	51	62	137	495
47	West Lode town AFC	O.J. Whitling	86	62	59	123	495
48	Willingham Wildebeests	Lucas Green	102	60	55	151	495
49	Bewick Rangers	Ian Bewick	86	63	60	133	491
50	Eve Kennedy Lesbian XI	Paul J Parker	95	58	60	150	491

THE DAILY TELEGRAPH LEAGUE – BOTTOM 25

295800	Graham Taylor XI	S Ebsworth	-147
295801	Barely Athletic	G Tailor	-148
295801	Gibbos Pyramid Tours	S R Gibson	-148
295803	Killer Shark Thistle	H Haddock	-149
295803	Englands Choice	A S MacGabhann	-149
295805	Brian Stack you Turnip!	L A Walsh	-151
295805	Taylors Turnips	MJ Green	-151
295807	El Tel for Presidento	R J Hansell	-152
295807	Cheap n Cheerful	J A Allan	-152
295809	Qwerty B	O G Passey	-153
295810	Irish Blue Jays	A N Kjeldsen	-154
295810	Where Palace Belong	M A Church	-154
295812	Cheap But Cheerful	T Thorp	-156
295812	Tippy Utd USA Branch	M A Dovaston	-156
295814	Not Quite Athletic	M Tierney	-157
295814	The Laggards	D P S Powell	-157
295816	Enfield Super Losers	E G Calver	-158
295816	The Blunderers	D G Towers	-158
295816	Kevins Connectors	A Hunter	-158
295819	Back down to the GM	M ONeill	-160
295820	Last but not least	K M Seagrave	-161
295821	Drummonds Demons	M Drummond	-163
295822	Forward with Franny	M J Leigh	-164
295823	Woodenspooners 11	S F T Wood	-170
295824	Greenjob FC	M P Simpson	-171

THE 90 MINUTES LEAGUE – BOTTOM 25

7186	Selhurst Park Rangers	Colin Darnell	25	35	37	185	108
7187	Dynamo Southport	Paul L6	27	28	33	162	107
7188	Hotspurs Cousin	Jim Tant	29	37	31	178	107
7189	Russel Osmans Red Army	Jason Donovan	37	23	27	160	105
7190	Pat Nevin`s Still Here	Chris Byrne	29	31	35	185	104
7191	Something Imaginative	P J Watters	33	32	10	104	99
7192	Athletico Square Inn	Brain O`Connor	34	28	23	151	99
7193	F.C. Woodstock	Alistair Salmon	21	26	34	153	98
7194	The Mighty Morses	Mrs J Bafico	14	13	32	99	97
7195	Kingswood Rovers	James Wright	22	16	32	129	97
7196	Wimbledon FC	Wayne Harbar	26	40	24	163	91
7197	Russell Athletic	Russell Eglen	21	41	18	127	90
7198	The Hulk FC	Per-Mikael Stude	22	25	21	112	88
7199	Rinhold Cowboys	Tim Blightman	26	25	26	147	85
7200	Majorca 93	Rob Hindley	34	32	32	215	79
7201	Millfield Raiders	Julie Cooper	27	28	26	164	77
7202	Stevie`s Wanderers	Steve Brodie	16	13	14	59	71
7203	My Team XI	Michael Cribbs	39	42	18	206	67
7204	The Anfield Bias	Steve Brown	31	24	22	167	62
7205	Dynamo Battery	Paul Craig	27	32	27	199	54
7206	Fantasy League XI	Ben Saxon	12	25	32	163	51
7207	Wigan Pie Eaters XI	David 5oberts	23	30	25	178	51
7208	Roachford Select	Mark Shelton	18	17	28	167	33
7209	United Ireland United	Mark Ellis	13	19	22	136	29
7210	Windos Ninowt	Matthew P Smith	30	30	14	188	18

HALL OF FAME

RADIO FIVE LEAGUE FINAL TABLE

Team	Manager	GLS	ASS	CS	GA	TOT
Terry Conroy's Legs	Nick Hancock	106	58	47	194	491
Ruddles County	Rick Johansen	79	49	55	204	419
Skunk City	Matt Miles	57	66	65	213	416
Bonetti's Belles	Shelly Webb	49	57	61	187	379
The Outsiders	Pat Nevin	55	38	64	197	361
Dynamo Stratford	Danny Kelly	68	46	37	158	344
Universal Love Team	Clare Grogan	48	52	44	154	325
Cram's Crusaders	Steve Cram	37	50	51	146	313
Osgood Isgood	Nigel Clark	53	48	46	207	307
Doc's Devils	Tommy Docherty	50	33	48	196	287
God Bless Lou Macari	Dominik Diamond	33	35	51	150	266
Buy 90 Minutes	Paul Hawksbee	39	45	38	234	221

THOSE TEAM LINE-UPS IN FULL

Buy 90 Minutes	Terry Conroy's Legs	Doc's Devils	Bonetti's Belles
PaulHawksbee	**Nick Hancock**	**Tommy Docherty**	**Shelly Webb**
Gunn	Bosnich	Flowers	Seaman
Elkins	Thompson	E Barrett	Irwin
Burrows	J Dicks	Pointon	Barton
D Walker	Marshall	Scales	Kjeldberg
S Potts	Fairclough	K Moran	Wetherall
Wise	Dozzell	D White	Ndlovu
Sinclair	Le Tissier	G McAllister	R Holden
R Keane	R Lee	Lomas	Goss
Anderton	Beagrie	Speed	T Sinclair
T Morley	M Stein	Sheron	Rod Wallace
Fowler	A Cole	Fashanu	Atkinson

Cram's Crusaders

Steve Cram

D James
R Nilsson
P Parker
Teale
A Linighan
Houghton
Ripley
Sinton
McManaman
M Hughes
Sheringham

Universal Love Team

Clare Grogan

C Woods
L Dixon
J Beresford
Ruddock
Bould
Stuart
Ince
L Clark
G Hodges
Rush
Ferdinand

The Outsiders

Pat Nevin

Segers
Dorigo
Le Saux
Bruce
Watson
Caskey
Mcclair
G Parker
Barker
Bright
Beardsley

Ruddles County

Rick Johansen

Lukic
Staunton
Venison
McGrath
Hendry
Sharpe
Barnes
Fox
Maddison
Cantona
Shearer

Skunk City

Matt Miles

pressman
winterburn
breaker
adams
d linighan
g peacock
giggs
sellars
holmes
deane
newell

Osgood Isgood

Nigel Clark

Thorstvedt
may
culverouse
pallister
m wright
wilkins
townsend
earle
burley
sutton
campbell

Dynamo Stratford

Danny Kelly

Srnicek
Bardlsey
R Jones
Hall
D Peacock
Wilcox
Bart-Williams
Redknapp
Merson
Holdsworth
Wright

God Bless Lou Macari

Dominik Diamond

Schmeichel
Berg
Kelly
Nielson
Fitzgerald
Waddle
Kanchelskis
Sherwood
Strachan
Saunders
Fjortoft

HALL OF FAME

League	Club	Manger	Pts
Beds/ Herts Super League	Whitestick Tappers	C CAMPBELL	505
Berks/ Bucks Super League	Ttnhm HtSpr (Oh No! Already Used!)	L CAMP	507
Bristol & West Super League	Dynamo Zimmers	F & J MUNN	504
East Anglia Super League	Bodgit And Scarper	S CAMPBELL	486
East Midlands Super League	Rifle Volunteer Rovers	S BRAITHWAIT	500
Essex Super League	Which Broom Will Albeon	R GAYNER	492
Ireland Super League	Melchester Rovers	K WILSON	516
Kent & City Of London Super League	Eintracht Fanny-Magnets	D HUGHES	551
North & West London	Sad Bunch Of Losers	T SMALL	517
North East SuperLeague	Glorplay United	I CAIRNS	542
North West Super League	Increasingly Less Athletic F.C.	J STRONGMAN	565
Scotland Superleague	Cooper's Creosote XI	K WALSH	494
South Coast (East) Super League	Bexhill Boyz F.C.	G AHERNE	594
South Coast (West) Super League	Saints March On	C HAWORTH	507
South London/ Surrey/ Kent Super League	Seaman Shoots In Schmeichels Box	R PACKFORD	519
West Midlands Super League	AC Rep. Of Yorkshire Villa Reserves	C JAMESON	583
Yorkshire Superleague	3 Men And A Team	M DERBYSHIRE	527
Fantasy Superleague A	Bristol City	A MARSHFIELD	505
Fantasy Superleague B	Boddie's Best	J TINDALL	472
Fantasy Superleague C	Hearts Of Thistle	A LEWIS	611
Fantasy Superleague D	Confussion Personified	T FRENCH	513
Fantasy Superleague E	Gerbils Utd	M ELAM	469
Fantasy Superleague F	F.C. Pele' Dynamos	P HERON	565
Fantasy Superleague F	Knightons Crusaders	R ARMSTRONG	565
Fantasy Superleague G	Leicester City ? Only Joachim	G MARSHALL	485
Fantasy Superleague H	Carlings Darlings	D BREWSTER	504

League	Club	Manger	Pts
Fantasy Superleague J	Osgoods Allstars	M MCKEOWN	472
Fantasy Superleague L	Barnselona	P TOLL	510
Fantasy Superleague M	Atletico East Brom.	M JONES	427
Fantasy Superleague M	Ooh Aah The Manager !	M WILLIAMS	421
Fantasy Superleague N	Four Pints Of Bitter & A Lager Top	D TIMM	474
Fantasy Superleague P	Claires Handbag	S SMALL	407
Fantasy Superleague R	Early Doors	R ANDREWS	474
Fantasy Superleague S	My Left Foot	J TREE	481
Fantasy Superleague T	We're The Left Side	B ATKINSON	494
Fantasy Superleague U	B.R.F.C.	G NORMAN	445
Fantasy Superleague V	Garam Masala	M JAFFREY	441
Fantasy Superleague W	Ormondroyd's Nose	M BROWN	430
Fantasy Superleague X	Potteries Dream Team	A PATE	383
Fantasy Superleague Y	Nobby's Heroes	I JUDD	419
Fantasy Superleague AA	Porters South	L SMITH/.M MARSHALL	387
Fantasy Superleague BB	Newburt Park rovers	G BROWN	439
Fantasy Superleague CC	The Monkey Is In The Tree	N HEMMINGS/M JOYCE	414
Fantasy Superleague DD	Pilsbury Dough Boys	P MAXWELL	311
Fantasy Superleague EE	Pat Stanton Lives !!!	P MCCOMBIE	339
Fantasy Superleague FF	Michael Jackson's Under 13's	K SMITH	354
Fantasy Superleague GG	Arguably Their Best Side	B CARRICK	356
Fantasy Superleague HH	AC Cults	A CLARK	287
Fantasy Superleague II	Macca's Knees	L MILLER	276
Fantasy Superleague JJ	Total Football XI	M ADAMS	212
Fantasy Superleague KK	Leicester Fosse '94	N STRETTON	226
Fantasy Superleague LL	Casual Free Thinkers FC	J DEWAR	261

HALL OF FAME

League	Club	Manger	PtsFantasy
Superleague MM	Latchford Toffees F.C.	I THOMAS	250
Fantasy Superleague NN	Toon Town	M BRODIE	219
Fantasy Superleague OO	Paul McGrath's Fitness Instructor	M KAY	236
Fantasy Superleague PP	La La Celtic	D ANTON	186
Fantasy Superleague QQ	Camberwick Green	I RIDLEY	180
Fantasy Superleague RR	Harley's Tigers	C LEYSER	214
Fantasy Superleague SS	Chopper Harris FC	T LONG	202
Fantasy Superleague TT	Redfearn Three Two	D SCHOFIELD	198
Fantasy Superleague UU	Tottering Hotspuds	M LYNCH	188
Fantasy Superleague VV	Raymond Carver's Shorts	M GODLIMAN	171
Fantasy Superleague WW	United All Stars	A SUFRONIOU	166
Fantasy Superleague XX	Fashanu's Elbow !	T MEISELS	177
Fantasy Superleague YY	Bag Of Flour Split	J DAVE	166
Fantasy Superleague ZZ	Wear Casuals	D KEELER	180
Fantasy Superleague AAA	The Muppet Show F.C.	L ASLAM	165
Fantasy Superleague BBB	Hamster County	D FISHER	169
Fantasy Superleague CCC	Roving Wanderers	C WRIGHT	144
Fantasy Superleague DDD	Vermillion United	G HARPER	137
Fantasy Superleague EEE	Barlow's Barbarian's	M C BARLOW	157
Fantasy Superleague FFF	Baltasound Sporting Aardwark	M G PENNINGTON	144
Fantasy Superleague GGG	PSV Glens	T LOMAS	129
Fantasy Superleague HHH	Elasti City	L TOWNSEND	135
Fantasy Superleague III	Glentoran	S GRAHAM	116
Fantasy Superleague JJJ	Jimmy Hills Musical Underpants	S KNAPPER	89
Fantasy Superleague LLL	Bigger and Better	F GUNDERSEN	97
Fantasy Superleague MMM	The Work Shy Fops	T PEARCE	49

League	Club	Manger	Pts
Fantasy Superleague NNN	K - Billy's Supersounds	C CLARK	66
Fantasy Superleague PPP	The Dream Team	R EDWARDS	34
A Hundred Quid Weekend	Done Up Like A Kipper !	JERRY DE LORD	381
The Fruit Bowl	David Laub's Team	D LAUB	376
The Betta Buys Supermarket Premier	A Fairytale Season - Grimm	D FOULGER	470

solo/media league spreads

POSTN	90 MINUTES LEAGUE	PTS
51-100		468-491
101-250		442-468
251-500		417-442
501-1000		389-417
1001-2000		351-388
2001-3000		322-351
3001-4000		296-322
4001-5000		267-296
5001-6000		231-267
6001-7000		165-231
7001-END		18-165

POSTN	THE DAILY TELEGRAPH LEAGUE	PTS
TOP 21%		OVER 235
NEXT 21.8%		203-234
NEXT 21.1%		168-202
NEXT 21.1%		126-167
BOTTOM 15%		UNDER 126

POSTN	SOLO MANAGERS	PTS	AVG
51-100		501-527	15.09-16.24
101-250		422-501	13.31-15.06
251-500		291-420	11.00-13.31
501-750		147-291	4.00-11.00
751-END		0-147	N/A*

* MINIMUM 10 WEEKS TO BE ELIGIBLE

key to the listings

what the symbols mean

RANK	RANKING WITHIN POSITION (ACCORDING TO SYSTEM B POINTS)
TEL £	TELEGRAPH PRICE
SOL £	SOLO PRICE
PLD	PLAYED
G	GOALS
A	ASSISTS
CS	CLEAN SHEETS
GA	GOALS AGAINST
A	TOTAL POINTS (SYSTEM A)
B	TOTAL POINTS (SYSTEM B)
94A	TOTAL POINTS IN 1994 (SYSTEM A)
94B	TOTAL POINTS IN 1994 (SYSTEM B)
P/G	POINTS PER GAME (SYSTEM B)
HG	GOALS CORED (HOME)
HA	ASSISTS (HOME)
AG	GOALS CORED (AWAY)
AA	ASSISTS (AWAY)
9192	TOTAL 1991-92 SEASON
9293	TOTAL 1992-93 SEASON

BOLD CODE NUMBER – INDICATES A PENALTY TAKER

UNDERSCORED CODE NUMBER – INDICATES A CORNER TAKER

BOLD & UNDERSCORED - INDICATES CORNER AND PENALTY TAKER

*	CHANGED CLASSIFICATION FROM MIDFIELD TO FULL BACK (PTS ARE NOT APPLICABLE)

goalkeepers

CODE	NAME	CLUB	RANK	TEL £	SOL £	PLD	G	A	CS	GA	A	B	94A	94B	P/G	HG	HA	AG	AA	9192	9293
101	Spink	A V	20	1.5	0.7	14	0	0	4	21	-5	1	-11	-7	0.07	0	0	0	0	11	2
139	Bosnich	A V	8	2	1.3	28	0	0	9	28	8	18	9	14	0.64	0	0	0	0	0	21
102	Seaman	ARS	1	2.7	2	39	0	4	20	24	64	63	29	30	1.62	0	3	0	1	-4	28
103	Mimms	BLA	13	1.2	0.5	13	0	0	5	13	7	10	0	0	0.77	0	0	0	0	0	30
127	Flowers	BLA	5	2.5	1.8	41	0	0	13	45	7	22	21	23	0.54	0	0	0	0	1	-17
124	N Martyn	C P	-	1.5	0.7	46	0	-	-	-	-	-	-	-	-	-	-	-	-	2	-17
105	Hitchcock	CHE	24	1.3	0.5	2	0	0	0	5	-5	-3	0	0	-1.5	0	0	0	0	-9	5
137	Kharin	CHE	10	1.6	0.7	40	0	1	11	48	-2	16	-1	8	0.4	0	1	0	0	-	-9
107	Ogrizovic	COV	3	1.8	1.1	33	0	1	11	32	14	25	10	17	0.76	0	1	0	0	18	-5
140	Gould	COV	23	1.2	0.5	9	0	0	2	13	-5	0	-1	0	0	0	0	0	0	0	-5
109	Southall	EVE	20	1.6	0.7	42	0	0	11	63	-19	1	-21	-8	0.02	0	0	0	0	1	-1
110	Forrest	IPS	9	1.6	0.8	29	0	0	10	32	8	17	-1	4	0.59	0	0	0	0	0	-6
135	Baker	IPS	24	1.6	0.5	15	0	0	4	26	-10	-3	-13	-7	-0.2	0	0	0	0	-	-11
111	Lukic	LEE	7	2	1.3	20	0	0	9	19	17	19	22	21	0.95	0	0	0	0	43	-8
115	Beeney	LEE	4	2	1.3	22	0	1	9	20	18	22	4	5	1	0	0	0	1	-	0

CODE	NAME	CLUB	RANK	TEL £	SOL £	PLD	G	A	CS	GA	A	B	94A	94B	P/G	HG	HA	AG	AA	9192	9293
104	K Poole	LEI	-	1.4	0.6	16	-	-	-	-	-	-	-	-	-	-	-	-	-	-	-
125	G Ward	LEI	-	1.4	0.6	37	-	-	-	-	-	-	-	-	-	-	-	-	-	-	-
118	M Stensgard	LIV	-	1.7	0.8	-	-	-	-	-	-	-	-	-	-	-	-	-	-	-	-
131	D James	LIV	19	1.7	0.8	13	0	0	2	15	-7	2	-7	2	0.15	0	0	0	0	0	2
114	Coton	M C	10	1.6	0.7	31	0	1	10	37	5	16	11	12	0.52	0	0	0	1	17	0
141	Dibble	M C	18	1.2	0.5	8	0	0	2	9	-1	3	-1	3	0.38	0	0	0	0	-	-
116	Schmeichel	M U	2	2.5	1.8	39	0	1	15	38	24	33	9	13	0.85	0	0	0	1	38	43
142	G Walsh	M U	16	1.2	0.5	2	0	0	2		8	6	8	6	3	0	0	0	0	-	-
112	Hooper	NEW	10	1.8	1.1	19	0	1	7	19	11	16	-5	-1	0.84	0	0	0	1	7	-3
120	P Srnicek	NEW	6	1.8	1.1	20	0	0	8	16	16	20	16	17	1	0	0	0	0	-	0
119	Gunn	NOR	14	1.5	0.6	41	0	3	10	58	-12	9	-17	-3	0.22	0	2	0	1	-6	-21
122	M Crossley	NOT	-	1.4	0.6	-	-	-	-	-	-	-	-	-	-	-	-	-	-	-12	-25
123	Steyskal	QPR	15	1.5	0.7	26	0	0	8	34	-2	8	-4	1	0.31	0	0	0	0	15	-7
134	Roberts	QPR	29	1.5	0.5	16	0	0	2	30	-22	-10	-9	-2	-0.63	0	0	0	0	-	-18
126	C Woods	S W	24	1.6	0.8	10	0	0	2	17	-9	-3	0	0	-0.3	0	0	0	0	11	-12
136	Pressman	S W	10	1.6	0.8	28	0	1	8	30	4	16	-3	8	0.57	0	1	0	0	-	-

CODE	NAME	CLUB	RANK	TEL £	SOL £	PLD	G	A	CS	GA	A	B	94A	94B	P/G	HG	HA	AG	AA	9192	9293
106	Beasant	SOT	27	1.4	0.6	25	0	0	4	38	-22	-5	-17	-4	-0.2	0	0	0	0	-16	1
117	Andrews	SOT	20	1.2	0.5	3	0	0	1	4	0	1	0	0	0.33	0	0	0	0	0	0
128	I Walker	TOT	28	1.4	0.6	11	0	0	2	21	-13	-6	-17	-8	-0.55	0	0	0	0	-10	-21
129	Thorstvedt	TOT	17	1.5	0.6	31	0	0	6	38	-14	5	-6	0	0.16	0	0	0	0	-25	-5
133	L Miklosko	W H	11	1.5	0.7	42	0	1	14	58	0	14	-13	-2	0.33	0	0	0	1	-	0
130	Segers	WIM	12	1.7	1	41	0	0	11	51	-7	12	-9	4	0.29	0	0	0	0	8	3

full backs

CODE	NAME	CLUB	RANK	TEL £	SOL £	PLD	G	A	CS	GA	A	B	94A	94B	P/G	HG	HA	AG	AA	9192	9293
201	Kubicki	A V	48	1.2	0.5	1	0	0	0	2	-2	-1	0	0	-1	0	0	0	0	6	0
202	E Barrett	A V	22	1.8	0.8	39	0	0	12	47	1	16	-3	6	0.41	0	0	0	0	-13	25
203	**Staunton**	A V	22	2	1.1	24	2	2	6	30	4	16	-13	-3	0.67	2	0	0	2	23	46
277	B Small	A V	43	1.3	0.6	9	0	0	2	10	-2	3	2	2	0.33	0	0	0	0	-	-12
204	L Dixon	ARS	6	2.7	2	32	0	2	16	22	46	46	28	29	1.44	0	1	0	1	9	26
205	Winterburn	ARS	4	2.7	2	34	0	2	18	23	53	51	19	20	1.5	0	1	0	1	10	20
209	A Wright	BLA	37	2	1.2	8	0	1	2	8	2	6	-3	0	0.75	0	1	0	0	0	24
212	Le Saux	BLA	1	2.7	2	41	2	8	17	34	56	63	34	36	1.54	1	5	1	3	17	6
281	Berg	BLA	3	2.7	2	38	1	3	18	30	51	53	31	32	1.39	0	1	1	2	0	7

CODE	NAME	CLUB	RANK	TEL £	SOL £	PLD	G	A	CS	GA	A	B	94A	94B	P/G	HG	HA	AG	AA	9192	9293
254	J Humphrey	C P	-	1.5	0.6	32	1	-	-	-	-	-	-	-	-	-	-	-	-	-5	-5
256	**D Gordon**	C P	-	1.6	0.8	39	5	-	-	-	-	-	-	-	-	-	-	-	-	-	-
258	R Shaw	C P	-	1.5	0.6	30	2	-	-	-	-	-	-	-	-	-	-	-	-	-9	-10
213	F Sinclair	CHE	24	1.5	0.6	35	0	3	9	44	-2	15	4	11	0.43	0	1	0	2	-4	-2
214	S Clarke	CHE	16	1.5	0.7	39	0	2	11	45	3	20	-2	7	0.51	0	2	0	0	-10	-12
215	G Hall	CHE	55	1.5	0.6	4	0	0	0	8	-8	-4	-3	-2	-1	0	0	0	0	-4	-4
217	Barnard	CHE	-	1.5	0.6	9	1	2	0	0	-	-	-	-	-	-	-	-	-	-	5
218	S Minto	CHE	-	1.6	0.7	-	-	-	-	-	-	-	-	-	-	-	-	-	-	-	-
216	Borrows	COV	25	1.6	0.8	29	0	1	8	33	1	14	3	13	0.48	0	1	0	0	4	-3
221	S Morgan	COV	9	1.6	0.9	36	2	1	12	36	20	32	13	20	0.89	1	0	1	1	-	-
219	I Snodin	EVE	51	1.5	0.6	28	0	0	6	42	-18	-2	-25	-11	-0.07	0	0	0	0	0	-6
220	M Jackson	EVE	32	1.5	0.6	37	0	2	10	54	-10	7	-13	-2	0.19	0	2	0	0	10	18
223	Hinchcliffe	EVE	27	1.5	0.6	25	0	3	6	34	-4	9	0	5	0.36	0	2	0	1	30	9
284	Holmes	EVE	40	1.5	0.6	15	0	1	5	22	0	5	-5	-3	0.33	0	0	0	1	-	0
222	Stockwell*	IPS	-	1.5	0.7	42	1	2	0	0	-	-	-	-	-	0	1	1	1	0	20
224	**N Thompson**	IPS	10	1.8	0.9	32	0	5	12	37	21	29	7	10	0.91	0	4	0	1	0	31

CODE	NAME	CLUB	RANK	TEL £	SOL £	PLD	G	A	CS	GA	A	B	94A	94B	P/G	HG	HA	AG	AA	9192	9293
225	Yallop	IPS	54	1.2	0.5	3	0	0	0	6	-6	-3	-3	-2	-1	0	0	0	0	0	3
226	G Kelly	LEE	5	2.5	1.8	39	0	5	17	34	44	49	30	30	1.26	0	3	0	2	0	0
227	Dorigo	LEE	7	2.2	1.5	37	0	3	14	35	27	36	16	19	0.97	0	1	0	2	56	-1
228	K Sharp*	LEE	-	1.5	0.6	7	0	0	0	0	-	-	-	-	-	0	0	0	0	0	0
229	Ray Wallace	LEE	46	1.2	0.5	0	0	0	0	0	0	0	0	0	-	0	0	0	0	0	-6
264	Worthington*	LEE	-	1.9	1	30	1	5	0	0	-	-	-	-	-	1	4	0	1	25	13
244	G Coatsworth	LEI	-	1.3	0.6	17	2	-	-	-	-	-	-	-	-	-	-	-	-	-	-
245	M Whitlow	LEI	-	1.4	0.6	34	3	-	-	-	-	-	-	-	-	-	-	-	-	-	-
246	S Grayson	LEI	-	1.4	0.6	46	1	-	-	-	-	-	-	-	-	-	-	-	-	-	-
267	G Mills	LEI	-	1.3	0.6	22	-	-	-	-	-	-	-	-	-	-	-	-	-	-	-
211	**J Dicks**	LIV	21	1.8	1	31	3	2	7	41	0	17	2	14	0.55	1	1	2	1	-	0
230	Rob Jones	LIV	17	1.8	1	37	0	7	8	48	-2	19	-8	5	0.51	0	3	0	4	12	9
232	Bjornbye	LIV	30	1.4	0.7	7	0	2	1	5	3	8	3	4	1.14	0	1	0	1	0	10
234	A Hill	M C	30	1.5	0.7	14	0	0	4	14	2	8	6	9	0.57	0	0	0	0	31	3
240	Edgehill	M C	44	1.5	0.7	17	0	2	3	25	-9	2	0	7	0.12	0	2	0	0	0	0
268	I Brightwell*	M C	-	1.5	0.7	6	0	2	0	0	-	-	-	-	-	0	1	0	1	14	11

CODE	NAME	CLUB	RANK	TEL £	SOL £	PLD	G	A	CS	GA	A	B	94A	94B	P/G	HG	HA	AG	AA	9192	9293
272	T Phelan	M C	26	1.6	0.7	30	1	0	7	37	-6	10	3	9	0.33	1	0	0	0	22	4
236	Irwin	M U	2	2.7	2	42	2	6	17	38	48	56	24	27	1.33	0	1	2	5	54	67
237	P Parker	M U	8	2.5	1.8	39	0	0	15	35	25	34	14	17	0.87	0	0	0	0	28	28
238	B Venison	NEW	19	2	1.3	36	0	0	11	40	4	18	-4	3	0.5	0	0	0	0	-	0
239	J Beresford	NEW	10	2	1.3	34	0	3	11	33	17	29	10	17	0.85	0	2	0	1	-	0
247	R Elliot	NEW	32	1.7	0.9	12	0	1	3	13	1	7	-3	1	0.58	0	0	0	1	0	0
241	Woodthorpe	NOR	56	1.4	0.6	19	0	1	3	33	-19	-6	-14	-4	-0.32	0	0	0	1	-9	6
242	Bowen	NOR	14	1.6	0.8	41	5	5	10	60	5	26	-13	2	0.63	3	1	2	4	-10	-12
243	Culverhouse	NOR	41	1.4	0.6	42	1	0	10	61	-18	4	-21	-6	0.1	1	0	0	0	-15	-16
235	Haaland	NOT	-	1.4	0.6	-	-	-	-	-	-	-	-	-	-	-	-	-	-	-	-
248	D Lyttle	NOT	-	1.4	0.6	-	-	-	-	-	-	-	-	-	-	-	-	-	-	-	-
249	**S Pearce**	NOT	-	1.8	1	-	-	-	-	-	-	-	-	-	-	-	-	-	-	18	3
250	B Laws	NOT	-	1.4	0.6	-	-	-	-	-	-	-	-	-	-	-	-	-	-	-7	-31
251	**C Wilson**	QPR	27	1.6	0.7	42	3	1	10	64	-13	9	-10	2	0.21	3	0	0	1	10	-4
252	Bardsley	QPR	24	1.6	0.8	32	0	6	8	45	-1	15	-8	2	0.47	0	5	0	1	14	6
253	Brevett	QPR	51	1.2	0.5	4	0	0	0	6	-6	-2	-3	0	-0.5	0	0	0	0	0	-4

CODE	NAME	CLUB	RANK	TEL £	SOL £	PLD	G	A	CS	GA	A	B	94A	94B	P/G	HG	HA	AG	AA	9192	9293
259	King	S W	57	1.6	0.7	8	0	0	1	17	-13	-7	-9	-6	-0.88	0	0	0	0	16	5
261	Atherton	S W	17	1.6	0.7	40	0	1	11	45	1	19	29	29	0.48	0	1	0	1	22	-14
275	Coleman	S W	51	1.6	0.7	7	1	1	0	14	-9	-2	-9	-3	-0.29	0	1	1	0	0	0
260	S Charlton	SOT	48	1.4	0.6	30	1	1	5	46	-21	-1	-14	-4	-0.03	0	0	1	1	-	-
262	Kenna	SOT	32	1.6	0.8	40	2	6	6	63	-21	7	-4	7	0.18	2	1	0	5	10	-6
263	Dodd	SOT	45	1.3	0.6	5	0	0	1	6	-2	1	0	1	0.2	0	0	0	0	-2	-7
265	Benali	SOT	57	1.4	0.6	35	0	1	5	54	-32	-7	-13	-2	-0.2	0	1	0	0	14	4
255	S Campbell	TOT	46	1.4	0.6	25	0	3	2	35	-21	0	-18	-9	0	0	1	0	2	0	0
266	Austin	TOT	32	1.5	0.6	20	0	2	5	27	-3	7	-7	0	0.35	0	0	0	2	0	-11
270	Edinburgh	TOT	48	1.5	0.6	23	0	1	3	32	-18	-1	-13	-3	-0.04	0	0	0	1	-9	-3
283	Kerslake	TOT	41	1.3	0.6	16	0	4	2	24	-8	4	-6	1	0.25	0	2	0	2	-	2
208	Breacker	W H	10	1.7	1	40	3	5	13	56	15	29	-3	8	0.73	2	3	1	2	-	0
210	K Brown	W H	37	1.2	0.5	6	0	0	3	6	6	6	7	6	1	0	0	0	0	-	0
231	Burrows	W H	15	1.7	0.8	27	1	1	11	30	19	24	1	5	0.89	1	0	0	1	45	5
233	Rowland	W H	37	1.2	0.5	13	0	2	4	19	1	6	-8	-2	0.46	0	0	0	2	0	0
271	Elkins	WIM	19	1.6	0.9	18	1	6	4	23	8	18	8	18	1	1	3	0	3	-3	14

CODE	NAME	CLUB	RANK	TEL £	SOL £	PLD	G	A	CS	GA	A	B	94A	94B	P/G	HG	HA	AG	AA	9192	9293
273	Joseph	WIM	27	1.6	0.8	13	0	0	5	14	6	9	1	1	0.69	0	0	0	0	4	9
274	Barton	WIM	13	1.8	1.1	36	2	4	11	44	14	28	-2	10	0.78	2	2	0	2	18	8
278	Kimble	WIM	32	1.3	0.5	14	0	2	4	19	1	7	0	0	0.5	0	1	0	1	0	0

centre backs

CODE	NAME	CLUB	RANK	TEL £	SOL £	PLD	G	A	CS	GA	A	B	94A	94B	P/G	HG	HA	AG	AA	9192	9293
301	Ehiogu	A V	46	1.7	0.7	14	0	0	5	19	1	5	-2	2	0.36	0	0	0	0	0	-2
302	P McGrath	A V	22	1.8	0.8	30	1	1	8	34	3	17	-4	3	0.57	0	1	1	0	13	39
303	Teale	A V	17	1.8	1	36	1	0	12	40	11	23	1	7	0.64	0	0	1	0	12	24
305	Bould	ARS	9	2.7	2	23	1	2	10	17	30	33	18	21	1.43	1	2	0	0	1	16
307	T Adams	ARS	1	2.7	2	35	0	2	20	21	63	58	29	29	1.66	0	1	0	1	5	28
308	A Linighan	ARS	7	2.3	1.5	20	0	2	12	11	41	37	3	4	1.85	0	0	0	2	-8	25
322	Keown	ARS	9	2.3	1.6	23	0	2	10	14	30	33	6	8	1.43	0	1	0	1	11	7
310	C Hendry	BLA	13	2.6	1.9	23	0	0	10	15	25	28	16	18	1.22	0	0	0	0	0	42
311	K Moran	BLA	26	2.4	1.7	19	1	0	5	19	4	13	1	6	0.68	1	0	0	0	0	43
378	Marker	BLA	21	2.2	1.3	18	0	0	7	14	14	18	10	9	1	0	0	0	0	-	-7
355	E Young	C P	-	1.7	0.8	46	5	-	-	-	-	-	-	-	-	-	-	-	-	6	16
357	A Thorn	C P	-	1.5	0.6	10	-	-	-	-	-	-	-	-	-	-	-	-	-	-8	-6

CODE	NAME	CLUB	RANK	TEL £	SOL £	PLD	G	A	CS	GA	A	B	94A	94B	P/G	HG	HA	AG	AA	9192	9293
359	C Coleman	C P	-	1.6	0.8	46	3	-	-	-	-	-	-	-	-	-	-	-	-	23	18
365	D Patterson	C P	-	1.5	0.6	-	-	-	-	-	-	-	-	-	-	-	-	-	-	-	-
382	E Smith	C P	-	1.5	0.6	-	-	-	-	-	-	-	-	-	-	-	-	-	-	-	-
316	E Johnsen	CHE	34	1.5	0.6	27	1	0	8	36	-1	10	8	13	0.37	1	0	0	0	0	-11
340	Donaghy	CHE	49	1.4	0.6	24	1	0	4	31	-12	4	-7	-2	0.17	1	0	0	0	19	4
351	G Hoddle	CHE	37	1.4	0.6	16	1	2	3	20	-1	9	1	3	0.56	1	1	0	1	-	0
377	D Lee	CHE	46	1.4	0.6	4	1	0	1	4	3	5	-1	0	1.25	1	0	0	0	-	6
379	Kjeldberg	CHE	20	1.6	0.7	27	1	1	9	31	10	19	11	14	0.7	1	1	0	0	-	-
320	Babb	COV	6	1.8	1.1	40	3	2	13	39	26	40	2	14	1	1	1	2	1	-	0
381	Busst	COV	64	1.4	0.5	3	0	0	0	6	-6	-3	-4	-3	-1	0	0	0	0	0	1
323	Ablett	EVE	39	1.5	0.6	32	1	2	8	47	-8	8	-14	-5	0.25	1	1	0	1	11	-15
324	D Watson	EVE	39	1.5	0.6	26	1	0	7	35	-4	8	-8	-1	0.31	0	0	1	0	27	4
325	**Wark**	IPS	13	1.6	0.8	38	3	1	13	47	16	28	-5	4	0.74	1	1	2	0	0	10
326	P Whelan	IPS	25	1.5	0.6	28	0	0	10	34	6	14	-14	-5	0.5	0	0	0	0	0	-11
327	Youds	IPS	29	1.2	0.5	20	1	0	6	23	4	12	-9	-1	0.6	1	0	0	0	0	-12
328	D Linighan	IPS	17	1.6	0.7	38	3	0	13	50	11	23	-4	6	0.61	3	0	0	0	0	-2

CODE	NAME	CLUB	RANK	TEL £	SOL £	PLD	G	A	CS	GA	A	B	94A	94B	P/G	HG	HA	AG	AA	9192	9293
306	O Leary	LEE	29	1.2	0.5	8	0	0	5	6	14	12	12	10	1.5	0	0	0	0	-10	-7
330	Fairclough	LEE	3	2.5	1.8	40	4	0	16	39	37	45	32	32	1.13	1	0	3	0	43	-4
331	Bowman	LEE	59	1.4	0.7	0	0	0	0	0	0	0	0	0	-	0	0	0	0	0	-1
380	Wetherall	LEE	3	2.5	1.8	31	1	2	15	23	44	45	28	27	1.45	1	2	0	0	-	19
344	C Hill	LEI	-	1.4	0.6	35	1	-	-	-	-	-	-	-	-	-	-	-	-	-	-
347	J Willis	LEI	-	1.3	0.6	12	1	-	-	-	-	-	-	-	-	-	-	-	-	-	-
348	B Carey	LEI	-	1.4	0.6	27	-	-	-	-	-	-	-	-	-	-	-	-	-	-	-
358	N Mohan	LEI	-	1.4	0.6	-	-	-	-	-	-	-	-	-	-	-	-	-	-	-	-
332	Nicol	LIV	26	1.7	0.9	29	1	3	6	37	-4	13	-5	3	0.45	0	1	1	2	28	15
333	M Wright	LIV	37	1.7	0.8	30	1	1	7	40	-7	9	-7	0	0.3	1	1	0	0	19	-5
369	Ruddock	LIV	11	1.9	1.2	39	3	5	9	46	9	30	-1	11	0.77	1	5	2	0	5	1
376	Piechnik	LIV	62	1.2	0.5	1	0	0	0	3	-3	-2	0	0	-2	0	0	0	0	-	-11
335	**Curle**	M C	24	1.7	0.8	28	1	0	8	32	3	15	4	7	0.54	0	0	1	0	32	-6
336	D Brightwell	M C	22	1.5	0.6	20	1	0	7	20	11	17	10	14	0.85	1	0	0	0	-7	-9
337	Vonk	M C	26	1.7	0.8	32	1	1	9	42	-1	13	8	14	0.41	0	1	1	0	10	5
383	Kernaghan	M C	46	1.5	0.7	24	0	0	6	31	-7	5	-1	5	0.21	0	0	0	0	0	-3

CODE	NAME	CLUB	RANK	TEL £	SOL £	PLD	G	A	CS	GA	A	B	94A	94B	P/G	HG	HA	AG	AA	9192	9293
338	Bruce	M U	2	2.6	1.9	41	3	2	15	38	35	46	15	21	1.12	1	2	2	0	57	58
339	Pallister	M U	5	2.6	1.9	41	1	0	17	37	34	41	15	18	1	1	0	0	0	33	48
368	May	M U	7	2.6	1.9	40	1	0	15	36	27	37	-3	0	0.93	0	1	0	0	0	45
329	Nielson	NEW	45	1.3	0.6	10	0	0	3	10	2	6	2	6	0.6	0	0	0	0	0	0
341	S Howey	NEW	52	1.7	0.8	13	0	0	2	15	-7	2	-6	0	0.15	0	0	0	0	-	0
354	Peacock	NEW	13	2	1.2	39	3	2	13	50	15	28	19	23	0.72	1	1	2	1	16	-10
343	Butterworth	NOR	39	1.4	0.6	23	0	1	6	29	-3	8	-5	1	0.35	0	1	0	0	-6	-31
345	J Polston	NOR	34	1.4	0.6	23	0	1	6	27	-1	10	-4	2	0.43	0	0	0	1	-15	-8
349	Newman	NOR	-	1.4	0.6	32	2	0	0	0	-	-	-	-	-	-	-	-	-	27	10
364	Newsome	NOR	16	1.6	1.6	27	1	1	10	26	19	26	12	16	0.96	1	1	0	0	16	-20
384	Prior	NOR	52	1.4	0.6	10	0	0	3	14	-2	2	-5	-1	0.2	0	0	0	0	0	0
334	C Tiler	NOT	-	1.4	0.6	-	-	-	-	-	-	-	-	-	-	-	-	-	-	-9	-24
350	C Cooper	NOT	-	1.5	0.8	-	-	-	-	-	-	-	-	-	-	-	-	-	-	-	-
356	S Chettle	NOT	-	1.4	0.6	-	-	-	-	-	-	-	-	-	-	-	-	-	-	-18	-29
352	Maddix	QPR	59	1.2	0.5	0	0	0	0	0	0	0	0	0	-	0	0	0	0	-17	-6
353	A McDonald	QPR	39	1.6	0.6	12	1	2	3	17	2	8	0	0	0.67	0	2	1	0	26	-21

CODE	NAME	CLUB	RANK	TEL £	SOL £	PLD	G	A	CS	GA	A	B	94A	94B	P/G	HG	HA	AG	AA	9192	9293
375	Yates	QPR	56	1.6	0.6	25	0	0	6	36	-12	1	-13	-1	0.04	0	0	0	0	-	-
386	Ready	QPR	56	1.5	0.6	15	1	1	3	25	-8	1	-9	-1	0.07	0	1	1	0	0	0
321	A Pearce	S W	11	1.8	1.1	29	3	4	8	32	17	30	13	21	1.03	2	1	1	3	13	6
360	D Walker	S W	29	1.7	1	42	0	1	10	52	-10	12	-3	8	0.29	0	1	0	0	-	0
317	Monkou	SOT	52	1.5	0.6	34	4	0	6	56	-20	2	-5	5	0.06	3	0	1	0	-26	-9
361	S Wood	SOT	33	1.4	0.5	27	0	0	6	28	-4	11	1	9	0.41	0	0	0	0	0	-3
362	Moore	SOT	65	1.3	0.5	14	0	0	0	24	-24	-10	-8	-3	-0.71	0	0	0	0	19	-7
363	R Hall	SOT	62	1.3	0.6	3	0	0	0	5	-5	-2	0	0	-0.67	0	0	0	0	-15	9
342	Kevin Scott	TOT	43	1.3	0.6	29	1	0	7	39	-8	7	-15	-5	0.24	1	0	0	0	-	0
346	C Calderwood	TOT	51	1.2	0.5	26	0	0	4	31	-15	3	-10	-4	0.12	0	0	0	0	-	0
366	Cundy	TOT	59	1.2	0.5	0	0	0	0	0	0	0	0	0	-	0	0	0	0	-13	-14
367	Mabbutt	TOT	43	1.5	0.6	28	0	2	6	37	-9	7	-4	3	0.25	0	2	0	0	-18	-4
374	Nethercott	TOT	-	1.4	0.5	-	-	-	-	-	-	-	-	-	-	-	-	-	-	-	-
313	A Martin	W H	49	1.5	0.6	7	2	0	1	11	-1	4	-5	-1	0.57	2	0	0	0	-	0
314	S Potts	W H	29	1.5	0.7	41	0	0	14	57	-1	12	-12	-2	0.29	0	0	0	0	-	0
370	Blackwell	WIM	56	1.3	0.6	16	0	0	3	21	-9	1	-2	4	0.06	0	0	0	0	0	-10

CODE	NAME	CLUB	RANK	TEL £	SOL £	PLD	G	A	CS	GA	A	B	94A	94B	P/G	HG	HA	AG	AA	9192	9293
371	Fitzgerald	WIM	34	1.6	0.8	28	0	0	9	36	0	10	-9	-1	0.36	0	0	0	0	7	-9
372	B McAllister	WIM	52	1.6	0.7	12	0	1	3	18	-4	2	-5	-1	0.17	0	0	0	1	0	15
373	Scales	WIM	19	1.7	0.9	37	0	2	11	42	6	21	-4	7	0.57	0	2	0	0	3	10

midfielders

CODE	NAME	CLUB	RANK	TEL £	SOL £	PLD	G	A	CS	GA	A	B	94A	94B	P/G	HG	HA	AG	AA	9192	9293
401	G Parker	A V	63	1.5	0.8	17	2	3	-	-	12	12	3	3	0.71	0	1	2	2	8	29
402	K Richardson	A V	23	1.6	0.9	40	5	6	-	-	27	27	17	17	0.68	2	2	3	4	32	10
404	Yorke	A V	73	1.4	0.7	4	2	1	-	-	8	8	8	8	2	2	1	0	0	43	26
407	Beinlich	A V	89	1.2	0.5	5	1	1	-	-	5	5	5	5	1	0	0	1	1	0	0
408	Breitkreutz	A V	121	1.2	0.5	1	0	0	-	-	0	0	0	0	0	0	0	0	0	0	2
438	Townsend	A V	38	1.6	0.9	32	3	5	-	-	19	19	9	9	0.59	1	2	2	3	18	26
469	Houghton	A V	57	1.5	0.8	25	2	4	-	-	14	14	10	10	0.56	1	2	1	2	32	27
409	Merson	ARS	23	1.8	1.1	26	7	3	-	-	27	27	17	17	1.04	5	3	2	0	52	32
410	S Schwarz	ARS	-	1.6	0.9	-	-	-	-	-	-	-	-	-	-	-	-	-	-	-	-
412	Hillier	ARS	82	1.3	0.6	11	0	3	-	-	6	6	6	6	0.55	0	2	0	1	11	7
414	Davis	ARS	121	1.4	0.7	21	0	0	-	-	0	0	0	0	0	0	0	0	0	0	2
415	Carter	ARS	121	1.2	0.5	0	0	0	-	-	0	0	0	0	-	0	0	0	0	0	8

CODE	NAME	CLUB	RANK	TEL £	SOL £	PLD	G	A	CS	GA	A	B	94A	94B	P/G	HG	HA	AG	AA	9192	9293
416	Parlour	ARS	57	1.5	0.8	24	2	4	-	-	14	14	14	14	0.58	0	1	2	3	3	9
428	Morrow	ARS	102	1.2	0.5	7	0	2	-	-	4	4	0	0	0.57	0	2	0	0	-	2
429	McGoldrick	ARS	82	1.4	0.7	23	0	3	-	-	6	6	4	4	0.26	0	2	0	1	15	40
568	Jensen	ARS	112	1.4	0.7	27	0	1	-	-	2	2	0	0	0.07	0	0	0	1	0	0
582	Flatts	ARS	121	1.3	0.6	2	0	0	-	-	0	0	0	0	0	0	0	0	0	-	0
591	Selley	ARS	102	1.3	0.6	16	0	2	-	-	4	4	4	4	0.25	0	1	0	1	0	0
417	Wilcox	BLA	14	1.9	1.2	31	6	8	-	-	34	34	23	23	1.1	3	3	3	5	0	32
422	Sherwood	BLA	43	1.6	0.9	37	2	6	-	-	18	18	14	14	0.49	2	3	0	3	0	21
424	Atkins	BLA	89	1.3	0.6	8	1	1	-	-	5	5	2	2	0.63	1	0	0	1	0	17
426	Warhurst	BLA	-	1.7	1	9	0	1	-	-	-	-	-	-	-	-	-	-	-	16	22
462	Batty	BLA	82	1.6	0.9	34	0	3	-	-	6	6	4	4	0.18	0	1	0	2	18	9
500	Ripley	BLA	16	1.7	1	40	4	10	-	-	32	32	18	18	0.8	1	4	3	6	0	37
565	Makel	BLA	121	1.2	0.5	0	0	0	-	-	0	0	0	0	-	0	0	0	0	0	0
522	Wilkins	C P	26	1.6	0.9	39	1	11	-	-	25	25	12	12	0.64	1	5	0	6	15	14
526	G Southgate	C P	-	1.7	1	46	9	-	-	-	-	-	-	-	-	-	-	-	-	9	17
528	J Salako	C P	-	1.7	1	34	8	-	-	-	-	-	-	-	-	-	-	-	-	10	12

CODE	NAME	CLUB	RANK	TEL £	SOL £	PLD	G	A	CS	GA	A	B	94A	94B	P/G	HG	HA	AG	AA	9192	9293
530	D Matthew	C P	-	1.4	0.7	11	1	-	-	-	-	-	-	-	-	-	-	-	-	0	0
531	S Rodger	C P	-	1.5	0.8	37	3	-	-	-	-	-	-	-	-	-	-	-	-	2	16
533	S Osborn	C P	-	1.3	0.6	5	-	-	-	-	-	-	-	-	-	-	-	-	-	3	8
534	D Pitcher	C P	-	1.3	0.6	-	-	-	-	-	-	-	-	-	-	-	-	-	-	15	0
538	R Newman	C P	-	1.3	0.6	-	-	-	-	-	-	-	-	-	-	-	-	-	-	-	-
579	G Ndah	C P	-	1.3	0.6	-	-	-	-	-	-	-	-	-	-	-	-	-	-	-	-
588	B Bowry	C P	-	1.4	0.7	17	0	-	-	-	-	-	-	-	-	-	-	-	-	-	-
431	Hopkin	CHE	102	1.2	0.5	10	0	2	-	-	4	4	4	4	0.4	0	2	0	0	-	-
432	Dow	CHE	121	1.2	0.5	13	0	0	-	-	0	0	0	0	0	0	0	0	0	0	0
433	Burley	CHE	48	1.6	0.9	20	3	4	-	-	17	17	17	17	0.85	2	1	1	3	0	0
435	Newton	CHE	73	1.2	0.5	33	0	4	-	-	8	8	6	6	0.24	0	1	0	3	0	10
439	Wise	CHE	11	1.9	1.2	35	4	12	-	-	36	36	25	25	1.03	1	9	3	3	48	21
495	G Peacock	CHE	6	2.2	1.5	37	8	8	-	-	40	40	18	18	1.08	6	8	2	0	-	0
574	Spackman	CHE	121	1.2	0.5	6	0	0	-	-	0	0	0	0	0	0	0	0	0	-	0
440	J Darby	COV	55	1.4	0.7	23	5	0	-	-	15	15	9	9	0.65	2	0	3	0	0	0
441	Sheridan	COV	121	1.2	0.5	1	0	0	-	-	0	0	0	0	0	0	0	0	0	-	-

CODE	NAME	CLUB	RANK	TEL £	SOL £	PLD	G	A	CS	GA	A	B	94A	94B	P/G	HG	HA	AG	AA	9192	9293
443	S Robson	COV	121	1.2	0.5	1	0	0	-	-	0	0	0	0	0	0	0	0	0	13	4
444	J Williams	COV	48	1.6	0.9	28	3	4	-	-	17	17	3	3	0.61	0	0	1	0	0	39
445	Flynn	COV	38	1.5	0.8	34	3	5	-	-	19	19	15	15	0.56	2	5	1	0	3	0
446	Boland	COV	112	1.2	0.5	19	0	1	-	-	2	2	2	2	0.11	0	1	0	0	0	0
573	L Hurst	COV	121	1.2	0.5	0	0	0	-	-	0	0	0	0	-	0	0	0	0	-	16
597	Rennie	COV	70	1.2	0.5	35	1	3	-	-	9	9	9	9	0.26	1	2	0	1	-	2
598	Jenkinson	COV	112	1.2	0.5	10	0	1	-	-	2	2	2	2	0.2	0	0	0	1	-	0
413	Limpar	EVE	57	1.7	1	18	0	7	-	-	14	14	12	12	0.78	0	2	0	5	38	10
437	Stuart	EVE	48	1.6	0.9	26	3	4	-	-	17	17	17	17	0.65	3	2	0	2	8	41
447	Ebbrell	EVE	43	1.5	0.8	39	4	3	-	-	18	18	10	10	0.46	3	3	1	0	5	7
448	Mark Ward	EVE	64	1.4	0.7	26	1	4	-	-	11	11	4	4	0.42	1	2	0	2	13	11
450	Warzycha	EVE	121	1.2	0.5	3	0	0	-	-	0	0	0	0	0	0	0	0	0	17	13
452	Unsworth	EVE	121	1.2	0.5	7	0	0	-	-	0	0	0	0	0	0	0	0	0	0	0
544	Horne	EVE	77	1.2	0.5	28	1	2	-	-	7	7	7	7	0.25	1	1	0	1	5	5
581	Kenny	EVE	121	1.2	0.5	0	0	0	-	-	0	0	0	0	-	0	0	0	0	-	7
584	Preki	EVE	77	1.3	0.6	10	1	2	-	-	7	7	5	5	0.7	1	1	0	1	-	11

CODE	NAME	CLUB	RANK	TEL £	SOL £	PLD	G	A	CS	GA	A	B	94A	94B	P/G	HG	HA	AG	AA	9192	9293
430	Slater	IPS	77	1.4	0.7	28	1	2	-	-	7	7	5	5	0.25	1	0	0	2	0	0
453	Gregory	IPS	121	1.2	0.5	0	0	0	-	-	0	0	0	0	-	0	0	0	0	0	3
455	Milton	IPS	60	1.3	0.6	12	1	5	-	-	13	13	0	0	1.08	1	3	0	2	0	6
458	G Johnson	IPS	77	1.2	0.5	16	1	2	-	-	7	7	7	7	0.44	0	1	1	1	0	20
459	S Palmer	IPS	89	1.2	0.5	31	1	1	-	-	5	5	0	0	0.16	0	1	1	0	0	2
461	P Mason	IPS	64	1.3	0.6	19	3	1	-	-	11	11	3	3	0.58	0	1	3	0	-	0
549	Sedgley	IPS	38	1.4	0.7	42	5	2	-	-	19	19	11	11	0.45	3	0	2	2	-13	-8
567	G Williams	IPS	121	1.2	0.5	34	0	0	-	-	0	0	0	0	0	0	0	0	0	0	6
585	L Durrant	IPS	102	1.2	0.5	2	0	2	-	-	4	4	4	4	2	0	2	0	0	-	-
<u>463</u>	<u>Strachan</u>	LEE	34	1.6	0.9	32	3	6	-	-	21	21	4	4	0.66	2	5	1	1	38	28
464	Speed	LEE	5	2.4	1.7	35	10	7	-	-	44	44	19	19	1.26	5	3	5	4	37	27
<u>465</u>	**<u>G McAllister</u>**	LEE	6	2.2	1.5	42	8	8	-	-	40	40	13	13	0.95	7	5	1	3	25	29
466	Hodge	LEE	110	1.2	0.5	7	1	0	-	-	3	3	3	3	0.43	1	0	0	0	23	8
477	David White	LEE	28	1.9	1.2	28	6	3	-	-	24	24	21	21	0.86	3	3	3	0	64	62
536	C Palmer	LEE	34	1.5	0.8	37	5	3	-	-	21	21	12	12	0.57	2	2	3	1	23	7
558	M Blake	LEI	-	1.4	0.7	11	1	-	-	-	-	-	-	-	-	-	-	-	-	-	-

CODE	NAME	CLUB	RANK	TEL £	SOL £	PLD	G	A	CS	GA	A	B	94A	94B	P/G	HG	HA	AG	AA	9192	9293
560	S Agnew	LEI	-	1.5	0.8	40	3	-	-	-	-	-	-	-	-	-	-	-	-	-	-
562	**S Thompson**	LEI	-	1.7	1	34	8	-	-	-	-	-	-	-	-	-	-	-	-	-	-
564	J Joachim	LEI	-	2	1.3	31	12	-	-	-	-	-	-	-	-	-	-	-	-	-	-
569	L Philpott	LEI	-	1.3	0.6	12	-	-	-	-	-	-	-	-	-	-	-	-	-	-	-
572	D Oldfield	LEI	-	1.7	1	30	7	-	-	-	-	-	-	-	-	-	-	-	-	-	-
580	C Gibson	LEI	-	1.3	0.6	13	-	-	-	-	-	-	-	-	-	-	-	-	-	-	-
589	I Ormondroyd	LEI	-	1.6	0.9	36	6	-	-	-	-	-	-	-	-	-	-	-	-	-	-
451	Harkness	LIV	121	1.2	0.5	10	0	0	-	-	0	0	0	0	0	0	0	0	0	0	0
460	Matteo	LIV	89	1.3	0.6	10	1	1	-	-	5	5	0	0	0.5	1	1	0	0	0	0
467	Redknapp	LIV	43	1.6	0.9	29	4	3	-	-	18	18	10	10	0.62	1	3	3	0	2	16
468	McManaman	LIV	25	1.7	1	29	2	10	-	-	26	26	8	8	0.9	0	6	2	4	29	26
470	Molby	LIV	82	1.4	0.7	11	2	0	-	-	6	6	0	0	0.55	2	0	0	0	13	15
471	R Whelan	LIV	89	1.4	0.7	23	1	1	-	-	5	5	0	0	0.22	0	0	1	1	0	7
472	Walters	LIV	121	1.4	0.7	7	0	0	-	-	0	0	0	0	0	0	0	0	0	15	45
473	J Barnes	LIV	60	1.6	0.9	24	3	2	-	-	13	13	7	7	0.54	2	1	1	1	11	29
474	M Thomas	LIV	121	1.4	0.7	1	0	0	-	-	0	0	0	0	0	0	0	0	0	18	7

CODE	NAME	CLUB	RANK	TEL £	SOL £	PLD	G	A	CS	GA	A	B	94A	94B	P/G	HG	HA	AG	AA	9192	9293
478	Clough	LIV	-	1.7	1	26	7	3	-	-	-	-	-	-	-	-	-	-	-	23	34
553	P Stewart	LIV	102	1.5	0.8	7	0	2	-	-	4	4	0	0	0.57	0	2	0	0	33	11
578	Hutchison	LIV	102	1.4	0.7	7	0	2	-	-	4	4	2	2	0.57	0	2	0	0	-	24
411	Rocastle	M C	48	1.6	0.9	27	3	4	-	-	17	17	10	10	0.63	2	2	1	2	15	5
449	Beagrie	M C	20	1.7	1	38	5	7	-	-	29	29	18	18	0.76	2	5	3	2	21	9
476	Ingebrigtsen	M C	112	1.2	0.5	2	0	1	-	-	2	2	2	2	1	0	0	0	1	0	0
481	McMahon	M C	82	1.3	0.6	35	0	3	-	-	6	6	2	2	0.17	0	2	0	1	17	3
482	Simpson	M C	121	1.2	0.5	12	0	0	-	-	0	0	0	0	0	0	0	0	0	5	12
483	Groenendijk	M C	112	1.2	0.5	9	0	1	-	-	2	2	0	0	0.22	0	1	0	0	0	0
487	N Summerbee	M C	34	1.6	0.9	35	3	6	-	-	21	21	16	16	0.6	2	4	1	2	-	-
570	Lomas	M C	112	1.3	0.6	17	0	1	-	-	2	2	0	0	0.12	0	0	0	1	0	0
571	P Lake	M C	121	1.2	0.5	0	0	0	-	-	0	0	0	0	-	0	0	0	0	-	0
575	Flitcroft	M C	48	1.5	0.8	20	3	4	-	-	17	17	3	3	0.85	3	2	0	2	0	17
583	Karl	M C	89	1.4	0.7	4	1	1	-	-	5	5	5	5	1.25	0	1	1	0	-	-
485	R Giggs	M U	2	2.7	2	33	13	8	-	-	55	55	31	31	1.67	5	4	8	4	36	37
486	Kanchelskis	M U	16	2	1.3	28	6	7	-	-	32	32	22	22	1.14	3	5	3	2	27	13

CODE	NAME	CLUB	RANK	TEL £	SOL £	PLD	G	A	CS	GA	A	B	94A	94B	P/G	HG	HA	AG	AA	9192	9293
488	McClair	M U	70	1.6	0.9	13	1	3	-	-	9	9	4	4	0.69	1	1	0	2	64	37
491	Ince	M U	4	2.4	1.7	39	8	12	-	-	48	48	24	24	1.23	5	6	3	6	16	22
493	L Sharpe	M U	8	2	1.3	26	9	5	-	-	37	37	8	8	1.42	2	4	7	1	5	27
509	R Keane	M U	18	1.7	1	34	5	8	-	-	31	31	13	13	0.91	3	4	2	4	40	30
494	S Sellars	NEW	11	1.8	1.1	29	4	12	-	-	36	36	21	21	1.24	3	8	1	4	-	0
496	R Lee	NEW	7	2	1.3	41	7	9	-	-	39	39	21	21	0.95	4	5	3	4	-	0
497	L Clark	NEW	43	1.6	0.9	29	2	6	-	-	18	18	7	7	0.62	0	4	2	2	0	0
498	P Bracewell	NEW	89	1.4	0.7	32	1	1	-	-	5	5	3	3	0.16	1	1	0	0	-	0
501	S Watson	NEW	73	1.4	0.7	29	2	1	-	-	8	8	6	6	0.28	2	1	0	0	-	0
503	Fox	NEW	2	2.5	1.8	39	9	14	-	-	55	55	25	25	1.41	4	3	5	11	17	32
505	Holland	NEW	102	1.3	0.6	2	0	2	-	-	4	4	4	4	2	0	2	0	0	0	0
512	Papavasiliou	NEW	121	1.2	0.5	4	0	0	-	-	0	0	0	0	0	0	0	0	0	0	0
480	Megson	NOR	102	1.2	0.5	21	0	2	-	-	4	4	4	4	0.19	0	1	0	1	0	7
504	Crook	NOR	37	1.6	0.9	38	0	10	-	-	20	20	10	10	0.53	0	4	0	6	3	19
506	Goss	NOR	28	1.6	0.9	34	6	3	-	-	24	24	13	13	0.71	2	3	4	0	7	11
507	Ullathorne	NOR	82	1.2	0.5	11	2	0	-	-	6	6	6	6	0.55	1	0	1	0	11	0

CODE	NAME	CLUB	RANK	TEL £	SOL £	PLD	G	A	CS	GA	A	B	94A	94B	P/G	HG	HA	AG	AA	9192	9293
511	Sutch	NOR	121	1.2	0.5	1	0	0	-	-	0	0	0	0	0	0	0	0	0	0	12
513	Eadie	NOR	82	1.5	0.8	8	2	0	-	-	6	6	3	3	0.75	0	0	2	0	0	0
516	N Adams	NOR	73	1.4	0.7	19	0	4	-	-	8	8	8	8	0.42	0	3	0	1	20	35
596	Milligan	NOR	112	1.2	0.5	38	0	1	-	-	2	2	2	2	0.05	0	0	0	1	8	11
479	L Bohinen	NOT	-	1.5	0.8	-	-	-	-	-	-	-	-	-	-	-	-	-	-	-	-
499	B Roy	NOT	-	2.3	1.6	-	-	-	-	-	-	-	-	-	-	-	-	-	-	-	-
502	G Crosby	NOT	-	1.5	0.8	-	-	-	-	-	-	-	-	-	-	-	-	-	-	33	3
510	N Webb	NOT	-	1.5	0.8	-	-	-	-	-	-	-	-	-	-	-	-	-	-	4	23
515	S Stone	NOT	-	1.4	0.7	-	-	-	-	-	-	-	-	-	-	-	-	-	-	0	3
517	D Phillips	NOT	-	1.5	0.8	-	-	-	-	-	-	-	-	-	-	-	-	-	-	47	17
518	S Gemmill	NOT	-	1.5	0.8	-	-	-	-	-	-	-	-	-	-	-	-	-	-	28	13
519	I Woan	NOT	-	1.7	1	-	-	-	-	-	-	-	-	-	-	-	-	-	-	19	27
520	K Black	NOT	-	1.7	1	-	-	-	-	-	-	-	-	-	-	-	-	-	-	16	19
521	Barker	QPR	38	1.5	0.8	36	5	2	-	-	19	19	8	8	0.53	2	2	3	0	19	9
524	Impey	QPR	55	1.4	0.7	31	3	3	-	-	15	15	6	6	0.48	1	2	2	1	10	14
525	Holloway	QPR	68	1.3	0.6	21	0	5	-	-	10	10	6	6	0.48	0	4	0	1	4	10

CODE	NAME	CLUB	RANK	TEL £	SOL £	PLD	G	A	CS	GA	A	B	94A	94B	P/G	HG	HA	AG	AA	9192	9293
527	T Sinclair	QPR	33	1.6	0.9	28	4	5	-	-	22	22	12	12	0.79	2	0	2	5	-	-
532	Meaker	QPR	89	1.3	0.6	10	1	1	-	-	5	5	5	5	0.5	0	1	1	0	9	2
523	Sinton	S W	31	1.8	1.1	25	3	7	-	-	23	23	4	4	0.92	1	4	2	3	25	43
535	I Taylor	S W	-	1.5	0.8	-	-	-	-	-	-	-	-	-	-	-	-	-	-	-	-
537	**J Sheridan**	S W	38	1.6	0.9	19	3	5	-	-	19	19	14	14	1	3	3	0	2	24	17
540	Hyde	S W	64	1.3	0.6	30	1	4	-	-	11	11	4	4	0.37	0	3	1	1	0	7
541	Bart-Williams	S W	11	1.7	1	31	8	6	-	-	36	36	25	25	1.16	5	2	3	4	6	24
556	Ryan Jones	S W	22	1.5	0.8	23	6	5	-	-	28	28	10	10	1.22	3	2	3	3	0	0
566	Waddle	S W	31	1.8	1.1	19	3	7	-	-	23	23	0	0	1.21	3	6	0	1	0	23
542	**Le Tissier**	SOT	1	3.1	2.4	38	25	10	-	-	95	95	64	64	2.5	13	7	12	3	30	67
546	Maddison	SOT	20	1.5	0.8	41	7	4	-	-	29	29	13	13	0.71	5	2	2	2	0	20
547	Hurlock	SOT	121	1.2	0.5	2	0	0	-	-	0	0	0	0	0	0	0	0	0	2	0
548	Magilton	SOT	112	1.5	0.8	14	0	1	-	-	2	2	2	2	0.14	0	1	0	0	0	0
552	P Allen	SOT	70	1.2	0.5	29	1	3	-	-	9	9	5	5	0.31	1	2	0	1	17	13
593	Widdrington	SOT	89	1.2	0.5	11	1	1	-	-	5	5	3	3	0.45	1	0	0	1	-	0
456	Dozzell	TOT	8	1.6	0.9	29	9	5	-	-	37	37	13	13	1.28	3	2	6	3	0	37

CODE	NAME	CLUB	RANK	TEL £	SOL £	PLD	G	A	CS	GA	A	B	94A	94B	P/G	HG	HA	AG	AA	9192	9293
514	M Hazard	TOT	68	1.4	0.7	20	2	2	-	-	10	10	7	7	0.5	1	1	1	1	0	0
550	Howells	TOT	89	1.3	0.6	15	1	1	-	-	5	5	3	3	0.33	0	1	1	0	9	5
551	Samways	TOT	60	1.5	0.8	39	3	2	-	-	13	13	6	6	0.33	2	1	1	1	17	10
554	A Gray	TOT	110	1.2	0.5	1	1	0	-	-	3	3	3	3	3	0	0	1	0	21	5
555	Anderton	TOT	14	1.8	1.1	35	6	8	-	-	34	34	14	14	0.97	3	4	3	4	0	42
576	Turner	TOT	121	1.2	0.5	0	0	0	-	-	0	0	0	0	-	0	0	0	0	-	6
577	Caskey	TOT	43	1.6	0.9	18	4	3	-	-	18	18	7	7	1	3	2	1	1	0	0
418	D Williamson	W H	-	1.5	0.8	-	-	-	-	-	-	-	-	-	-	-	-	-	-	-	-
419	Martin Allen	W H	26	1.6	0.9	20	7	2	-	-	25	25	25	25	1.25	4	1	3	1	-	0
420	M Rush	W H	-	1.5	0.8	-	-	-	-	-	-	-	-	-	-	-	-	-	-	-	-
421	I Bishop	W H	64	1.6	0.9	36	1	4	-	-	11	11	9	9	0.31	0	3	1	1	-	0
423	P Butler	W H	89	1.2	0.5	26	1	1	-	-	5	5	0	0	0.19	1	1	0	0	-	0
425	D Gordon	W H	89	1.3	0.6	8	1	1	-	-	5	5	0	0	0.63	0	0	1	1	-	0
427	M Holmes	W H	18	1.6	0.9	33	3	11	-	-	31	31	22	22	0.94	2	7	1	4	-	0
436	J Moncur	W H	28	1.6	0.9	41	4	6	-	-	24	24	18	18	0.59	0	2	4	4	-	0
442	J Beauchamp	W H	-	1.6	0.9	-	-	-	-	-	-	-	-	-	-	-	-	-	-	-	-

CODE	NAME	CLUB	RANK	TEL £	SOL £	PLD	G	A	CS	GA	A	B	94A	94B	P/G	HG	HA	AG	AA	9192	9293
475	Marsh	W H	53	1.5	0.8	34	2	5	-	-	16	16	9	9	0.47	0	3	2	2	0	9
434	**V Jones**	WIM	53	1.5	0.8	33	2	5	-	-	16	16	8	8	0.48	0	3	2	2	19	18
557	McGee	WIM	121	1.2	0.5	0	0	0	-	-	0	0	0	0	-	0	0	0	0	6	0
559	Earle	WIM	8	2	1.3	42	9	5	-	-	37	37	30	30	0.88	5	5	4	0	54	41
561	Dobbs	WIM	121	1.2	0.5	3	0	0	-	-	0	0	0	0	0	0	0	0	0	-	9
563	Ardley	WIM	89	1.4	0.7	14	1	1	-	-	5	5	5	5	0.36	1	0	0	1	0	26
586	M Gayle	WIM	112	1.2	0.5	9	0	1	-	-	2	2	2	2	0.22	0	1	0	0	-	-
587	Fear	WIM	77	1.5	0.8	23	1	4	-	-	7	7	-3	-3	0.3	0	0	0	0	0	0

strikers

CODE	NAME	CLUB	RANK	TEL £	SOL £	PLD	G	A	CS	GA	A	B	94A	94B	P/G	HG	HA	AG	AA	9192	9293
601	Whittingham	A V	57	1.8	1.1	14	3	0	-	-	9	9	0	0	0.64	1	0	2	0	0	0
602	Atkinson	A V	25	2	1.3	29	8	7	-	-	38	38	8	8	1.31	6	4	2	3	15	41
606	Fenton	A V	63	1.6	0.9	8	1	0	-	-	3	3	3	3	0.38	0	0	1	0	-	-
632	**Saunders**	A V	28	2	1.3	37	10	2	-	-	34	34	20	20	0.92	5	1	5	1	34	52
603	**I Wright**	ARS	6	3.1	2.4	39	23	5	-	-	79	79	45	45	2.03	10	2	13	3	111	53
604	A Smith	ARS	46	1.6	0.9	21	3	4	-	-	17	17	9	9	0.81	2	2	1	2	50	15
605	K Campbell	ARS	15	1.8	1.1	29	14	5	-	-	52	52	29	29	1.79	5	3	9	2	55	26

CODE	NAME	CLUB	RANK	TEL £	SOL £	PLD	G	A	CS	GA	A	B	94A	94B	P/G	HG	HA	AG	AA	9192	9293
609	Newell	BLA	25	2.2	1.5	27	6	10	-	-	38	38	11	11	1.41	0	7	6	3	0	55
619	Gallacher	BLA	30	1.8	1.1	28	7	5	-	-	31	31	16	16	1.11	2	4	5	1	30	45
647	**Sutton**	BLA	2	3.3	2.6	41	25	15	-	-	105	105	62	62	2.56	13	6	12	9	4	30
670	**A Shearer**	BLA	3	3.6	2.9	35	31	5	-	-	103	103	53	53	2.94	19	1	12	4	49	56
664	B Launders	C P	-	1.4	0.7	-	-	-	-	-	-	-	-	-	-	-	-	-	-	-	-
689	C Armstrong	C P	-	2.3	1.6	43	23	-	-	-	-	-	-	-	-	-	-	-	-	0	51
690	P Williams	C P	-	1.6	0.9	21	7	-	-	-	-	-	-	-	-	-	-	-	-	38	9
693	B Dyer	C P	-	1.6	0.9	-	-	-	-	-	-	-	-	-	-	-	-	-	-	-	-
694	A Preece	C P	-	1.9	1.2	-	-	-	-	-	-	-	-	-	-	-	-	-	-	-	-
617	**M Stein**	CHE	19	2.4	1.7	18	13	3	-	-	45	45	45	45	2.5	8	1	5	2	0	0
643	Fleck	CHE	60	1.5	0.8	7	1	1	-	-	5	5	5	5	0.71	0	1	1	0	45	20
685	J Spencer	CHE	43	1.7	1	13	5	2	-	-	19	19	19	19	1.46	3	2	2	0	0	33
704	Shipperley	CHE	52	1.5	0.8	19	4	0	-	-	12	12	6	6	0.63	2	0	2	0	0	5
607	Wegerle	COV	32	1.6	0.9	22	6	5	-	-	28	28	8	8	1.27	3	0	3	5	0	14
681	**Ndlovu**	COV	17	2.1	1.4	42	11	9	-	-	51	51	14	14	1.21	8	4	2	0	5	29
692	M Quinn	COV	35	1.8	1.1	30	8	1	-	-	26	26	8	8	0.87	5	1	3	0	-	59

CODE	NAME	CLUB	RANK	TEL £	SOL £	PLD	G	A	CS	GA	A	B	94A	94B	P/G	HG	HA	AG	AA	9192	9293
621	Angell	EVE	63	1.4	0.7	13	1	0	-	-	3	3	3	3	0.23	1	0	0	0	0	0
622	**Cottee**	EVE	12	2	1.3	38	16	5	-	-	58	58	30	30	1.53	10	3	6	2	28	42
624	S Barlow	EVE	55	1.5	0.8	7	3	1	-	-	11	11	3	3	1.57	0	0	3	1	0	23
686	Rideout	EVE	42	1.5	0.8	21	6	1	-	-	20	20	6	6	0.95	4	1	2	0	0	9
626	Kiwomya	IPS	37	1.6	0.9	34	5	4	-	-	23	23	8	8	0.68	2	2	3	2	0	40
627	**Marshall**	IPS	25	1.8	1.1	28	10	4	-	-	38	38	18	18	1.36	8	4	2	0	0	-26
696	Guentchev	IPS	58	1.5	0.8	10	2	1	-	-	8	8	8	8	0.8	2	1	0	0	-	10
630	Rod Wallace	LEE	9	2.3	1.6	34	17	7	-	-	65	65	31	31	1.91	9	3	8	4	43	25
631	N Whelan	LEE	62	1.4	0.7	5	0	2	-	-	4	4	2	2	0.8	0	1	0	1	0	0
663	Deane	LEE	13	2.3	1.6	41	11	12	-	-	57	57	25	25	1.39	4	6	7	6	51	71
699	Strandli	LEE	67	1.3	0.6	1	0	1	-	-	2	2	0	0	2	0	1	0	0	0	8
703	Forrester	LEE	68	1.3	0.6	2	0	0	-	-	0	0	0	0	0	0	0	0	0	0	8
655	P Gee	LEI	-	1.4	0.7	9	3	-	-	-	-	-	-	-	-	-	-	-	-	-	-
674	S Walsh	LEI	-	1.6	0.9	10	5	-	-	-	-	-	-	-	-	-	-	-	-	-	-
678	I Roberts	LEI	-	1.6	0.9	26	13	-	-	-	-	-	-	-	-	-	-	-	-	-	-
697	D Speedie	LEI	-	1.6	0.9	41	13	-	-	-	-	-	-	-	-	-	-	-	-	-	-

CODE	NAME	CLUB	RANK	TEL £	SOL £	PLD	G	A	CS	GA	A	B	94A	94B	P/G	HG	HA	AG	AA	9192	9293
620	Fowler	LIV	21	2.4	1.7	26	12	3	-	-	42	42	14	14	1.62	6	2	6	1	0	0
633	Rush	LIV	14	2.2	1.5	41	14	6	-	-	54	54	37	37	1.32	9	1	5	5	15	48
629	Rosler	M C	46	1.9	1.2	12	5	1	-	-	17	17	17	17	1.42	3	0	2	1	-	-
635	N Quinn	M C	37	1.9	1.2	14	5	4	-	-	23	23	0	0	1.64	3	2	2	2	58	50
636	Sheron	M C	35	1.7	1	29	6	4	-	-	26	26	0	0	0.9	4	3	2	1	33	41
637	Mike	M C	63	1.3	0.6	2	1	0	-	-	3	3	0	0	1.5	0	0	1	0	0	0
640	P Walsh	M C	48	1.9	1.2	11	4	1	-	-	14	14	14	14	1.27	3	0	1	1	-	-
698	Griffiths	M C	45	1.6	0.9	12	4	3	-	-	18	18	8	8	1.5	2	1	2	2	-	-
628	**Cantona**	M U	5	3.1	2.4	34	18	13	-	-	80	80	33	33	2.35	10	8	8	5	13	77
638	M Hughes	M U	15	2.1	1.4	36	12	8	-	-	52	52	24	24	1.44	7	2	5	6	44	53
683	Dublin	M U	63	1.4	0.7	2	1	0	-	-	3	3	3	3	1.5	1	0	0	0	0	3
623	**Beardsley**	NEW	4	2.9	2.2	35	21	11	-	-	85	85	45	45	2.43	12	9	9	2	69	52
641	A Cole	NEW	1	3.6	2.9	40	34	15	-	-	132	132	67	67	3.3	22	6	12	9	-	0
642	Malcolm Allen	NEW	40	1.5	0.8	8	5	3	-	-	21	21	0	0	2.63	3	3	2	0	-	-
646	Mathie	NEW	55	1.5	0.8	4	3	1	-	-	11	11	6	6	2.75	2	0	1	1	0	0
687	Robins	NOR	47	1.8	1.1	11	1	6	-	-	15	15	9	9	1.36	1	3	0	3	0	59

CODE	NAME	CLUB	RANK	TEL £	SOL £	PLD	G	A	CS	GA	A	B	94A	94B	P/G	HG	HA	AG	AA	9192	9293
701	Ekoku	NOR	23	1.7	1	21	12	2	-	-	40	40	22	22	1.9	5	1	7	1	-	9
652	S Collymore	NOT	-	2.5	1.8	-	-	-	-	-	-	-	-	-	-	-	-	-	-	-	-
653	J Lee	NOT	-	1.5	0.8	-	-	-	-	-	-	-	-	-	-	-	-	-	-	-	-
654	R Rosario	NOT	-	1.7	1	-	-	-	-	-	-	-	-	-	-	-	-	-	-	31	22
656	L Glover	NOT	-	1.5	0.8	-	-	-	-	-	-	-	-	-	-	-	-	-	-	4	2
657	G Bull	NOT	-	1.4	0.7	-	-	-	-	-	-	-	-	-	-	-	-	-	-	-	-
658	Ferdinand	QPR	8	2.5	1.8	35	17	9	-	-	69	69	27	27	1.97	10	5	7	4	32	72
659	B Allen	QPR	37	1.7	1	14	7	1	-	-	23	23	0	0	1.64	2	1	5	0	6	38
660	Penrice	QPR	28	1.7	1	23	8	5	-	-	34	34	21	21	1.48	6	2	2	3	22	18
700	Devon White	QPR	34	1.5	0.8	14	7	3	-	-	27	27	21	21	1.93	4	1	3	2	-	0
611	Bright	S W	7	2.4	1.7	36	19	10	-	-	77	77	46	46	2.14	13	7	6	3	69	46
665	Hirst	S W	60	1.8	1.1	6	1	1	-	-	5	5	2	2	0.83	1	0	0	1	72	43
668	Jemson	S W	43	1.5	0.8	10	5	2	-	-	19	19	0	0	1.9	2	1	3	1	27	6
705	G Watson	S W	23	1.8	1.1	17	12	2	-	-	40	40	34	34	2.35	8	2	4	0	0	0
651	C Maskell	SOT	48	1.4	0.7	15	4	1	-	-	14	14	11	11	0.93	1	1	3	0	-	0
669	Dowie	SOT	30	1.6	0.9	39	5	8	-	-	31	31	17	17	0.79	3	5	2	3	33	47

CODE	NAME	CLUB	RANK	TEL £	SOL £	PLD	G	A	CS	GA	A	B	94A	94B	P/G	HG	HA	AG	AA	9192	9293
691	Banger	SOT	68	1.3	0.6	5	0	0	-	-	0	0	0	0	0	0	0	0	0	-	21
634	Rosenthal	TOT	52	1.6	0.9	12	2	3	-	-	12	12	12	12	1	2	1	0	2	9	24
649	**Sheringham**	TOT	18	2.7	2	19	13	4	-	-	47	47	16	16	2.47	6	4	7	0	57	90
667	Barmby	TOT	40	1.7	1	27	5	3	-	-	21	21	13	13	0.78	4	2	1	1	-	26
675	Beadle	TOT	68	1.3	0.6	0	0	0	-	-	0	0	0	0	-	0	0	0	0	0	0
612	S Jones	W H	58	1.4	0.7	4	2	1	-	-	8	8	8	8	2	1	1	1	0	-	0
613	**T Morley**	W H	19	1.8	1.1	40	13	3	-	-	45	45	26	26	1.13	6	2	7	1	-	0
616	Boere	W H	68	1.4	0.7	0	0	0	-	-	0	0	0	0	-	0	0	0	0	0	0
639	L Chapman	W H	32	1.6	0.9	27	8	2	-	-	28	28	11	11	1.04	3	0	5	2	60	53
676	**Fashanu**	WIM	22	2	1.3	35	11	4	-	-	41	41	22	22	1.17	7	2	4	2	57	28
677	A Clarke	WIM	52	1.5	0.8	12	2	3	-	-	12	12	9	9	1	1	1	1	2	11	17
679	Miller	WIM	68	1.3	0.6	0	0	0	-	-	0	0	0	0	-	0	0	0	0	17	7
680	Newhouse	WIM	68	1.3	0.6	0	0	0	-	-	0	0	0	0	-	0	0	0	0	0	3
682	**Holdsworth**	WIM	10	2.6	1.9	43	17	6	-	-	63	63	37	37	1.47	12	3	5	3	-	63
688	G Blissett	WIM	50	1.5	0.8	6	3	2	-	-	13	13	5	5	2.17	2	2	1	0	0	0

RANK	NAME	CLUB	CODE	TEL £	SOL £	PLD	G	A	CS	GA	A	B	94A	94B	P/G	HG	HA	AG	AA	9192	9293
goalkeepers																					
1	Seaman	ARS	102	2.7	2	39	0	4	20	24	64	63	29	30	1.62	0	3	0	1	-4	28
2	Schmeichel	M U	116	2.5	1.8	39	0	1	15	38	24	33	9	13	0.85	0	0	0	1	38	43
3	Ogrizovic	COV	107	1.8	1.1	33	0	1	11	32	14	25	10	17	0.76	0	1	0	0	18	-5
4	Beeney	LEE	115	2	1.3	22	0	1	9	20	18	22	4	5	1	0	0	0	1	-	0
5	Flowers	BLA	127	2.5	1.8	41	0	0	13	45	7	22	21	23	0.54	0	0	0	0	1	-17
6	P Srnicek	NEW	120	1.8	1.1	20	0	0	8	16	16	20	16	17	1	0	0	0	0	-	0
7	Lukic	LEE	111	2	1.3	20	0	0	9	19	17	19	22	21	0.95	0	0	0	0	43	-8
8	Bosnich	A V	139	2	1.3	28	0	0	9	28	8	18	9	14	0.64	0	0	0	0	0	21
9	Forrest	IPS	110	1.6	0.8	29	0	0	10	32	8	17	-1	4	0.59	0	0	0	0	0	-6
10	Kharin	CHE	137	1.6	0.7	40	0	1	11	48	-2	16	-1	8	0.4	0	1	0	0	-	-9
10	Coton	M C	114	1.6	0.7	31	0	1	10	37	5	16	11	12	0.52	0	0	0	1	17	0
10	Hooper	NEW	112	1.8	1.1	19	0	1	7	19	11	16	-5	-1	0.84	0	0	0	1	7	-3
10	Pressman	S W	136	1.6	0.8	28	0	1	8	30	4	16	-3	8	0.57	0	1	0	0	-	-
11	L Miklosko	W H	133	1.5	0.7	42	0	1	14	58	0	14	-13	-2	0.33	0	0	0	1	-	0
12	Segers	WIM	130	1.7	1	41	0	0	11	51	-7	12	-9	4	0.29	0	0	0	0	8	3

RANK	NAME	CLUB	CODE	TEL £	SOL £	PLD	G	A	CS	GA	A	B	94A	94B	P/G	HG	HA	AG	AA	9192	9293
13	Mimms	BLA	103	1.2	0.5	13	0	0	5	13	7	10	0	0	0.77	0	0	0	0	0	30
14	Gunn	NOR	119	1.5	0.6	41	0	3	10	58	-12	9	-17	-3	0.22	0	2	0	1	-6	-21
15	Steyskal	QPR	123	1.5	0.7	26	0	0	8	34	-2	8	-4	1	0.31	0	0	0	0	15	-7
16	G Walsh	M U	142	1.2	0.5	2	0	0	2		8	6	8	6	3	0	0	0	0	-	-
17	Thorstvedt	TOT	129	1.5	0.6	31	0	0	6	38	-14	5	-6	0	0.16	0	0	0	0	-25	-5
18	Dibble	M C	141	1.2	0.5	8	0	0	2	9	-1	3	-1	3	0.38	0	0	0	0	-	-
19	D James	LIV	131	1.7	0.8	13	0	0	2	15	-7	2	-7	2	0.15	0	0	0	0	0	2
20	Spink	A V	101	1.5	0.7	14	0	0	4	21	-5	1	-11	-7	0.07	0	0	0	0	11	2
20	Southall	EVE	109	1.6	0.7	42	0	0	11	63	-19	1	-21	-8	0.02	0	0	0	0	1	-1
20	Andrews	SOT	117	1.2	0.5	3	0	0	1	4	0	1	0	0	0.33	0	0	0	0	0	0
23	Gould	COV	140	1.2	0.5	9	0	0	2	13	-5	0	-1	0	0	0	0	0	0	0	-5
24	Hitchcock	CHE	105	1.3	0.5	2	0	0	0	5	-5	-3	0	0	-1.5	0	0	0	0	-9	5
24	Baker	IPS	135	1.6	0.5	15	0	0	4	26	-10	-3	-13	-7	-0.2	0	0	0	0	-	-11
24	C Woods	S W	126	1.6	0.8	10	0	0	2	17	-9	-3	0	0	-0.3	0	0	0	0	11	-12
27	Beasant	SOT	106	1.4	0.6	25	0	0	4	38	-22	-5	-17	-4	-0.2	0	0	0	0	-16	1
28	I Walker	TOT	128	1.4	0.6	11	0	0	2	21	-13	-6	-17	-8	-0.55	0	0	0	0	-10	-21

RANK	NAME	CLUB	CODE	TEL £	SOL £	PLD	G	A	CS	GA	A	B	94A	94B	P/G	HG	HA	AG	AA	9192	9293
29	Roberts	QPR	134	1.5	0.5	16	0	0	2	30	-22	-10	-9	-2	-0.63	0	0	0	0	-	-18
-	N Martyn	C P	124	1.5	0.7	46	0	-	-	-	-	-	-	-	-	-	-	-	-	2	-17
-	K Poole	LEI	104	1.4	0.6	16	-	-	-	-	-	-	-	-	-	-	-	-	-	-	-
-	G Ward	LEI	125	1.4	0.6	37	-	-	-	-	-	-	-	-	-	-	-	-	-	-	-
-	M Stensgard	LIV	118	1.7	0.8	-	-	-	-	-	-	-	-	-	-	-	-	-	-	-	-
-	M Crossley	NOT	122	1.4	0.6	-	-	-	-	-	-	-	-	-	-	-	-	-	-	-12	-25

full backs

RANK	NAME	CLUB	CODE	TEL £	SOL £	PLD	G	A	CS	GA	A	B	94A	94B	P/G	HG	HA	AG	AA	9192	9293
1	Le Saux	BLA	212	2.7	2	41	2	8	17	34	56	63	34	36	1.54	1	5	1	3	17	6
2	Irwin	M U	236	2.7	2	42	2	6	17	38	48	56	24	27	1.33	0	1	2	5	54	67
3	Berg	BLA	281	2.7	2	38	1	3	18	30	51	53	31	32	1.39	0	1	1	2	0	7
4	Winterburn	ARS	205	2.7	2	34	0	2	18	23	53	51	19	20	1.5	0	1	0	1	10	20
5	G Kelly	LEE	226	2.5	1.8	39	0	5	17	34	44	49	30	30	1.26	0	3	0	2	0	0
6	L Dixon	ARS	204	2.7	2	32	0	2	16	22	46	46	28	29	1.44	0	1	0	1	9	26
7	Dorigo	LEE	227	2.2	1.5	37	0	3	14	35	27	36	16	19	0.97	0	1	0	2	56	-1
8	P Parker	M U	237	2.5	1.8	39	0	0	15	35	25	34	14	17	0.87	0	0	0	0	28	28
9	S Morgan	COV	221	1.6	0.9	36	2	1	12	36	20	32	13	20	0.89	1	0	1	1	-	-

RANK	NAME	CLUB	CODE	TEL £	SOL £	PLD	G	A	CS	GA	A	B	94A	94B	P/G	HG	HA	AG	AA	9192	9293
10	**N Thompson**	IPS	224	1.8	0.9	32	0	5	12	37	21	29	7	10	0.91	0	4	0	1	0	31
10	J Beresford	NEW	239	2	1.3	34	0	3	11	33	17	29	10	17	0.85	0	2	0	1	-	0
10	Breacker	W H	208	1.7	1	40	3	5	13	56	15	29	-3	8	0.73	2	3	1	2	-	0
13	Barton	WIM	274	1.8	1.1	36	2	4	11	44	14	28	-2	10	0.78	2	2	0	2	18	8
14	Bowen	NOR	242	1.6	0.8	41	5	5	10	60	5	26	-13	2	0.63	3	1	2	4	-10	-12
15	Burrows	W H	231	1.7	0.8	27	1	1	11	30	19	24	1	5	0.89	1	0	0	1	45	5
16	S Clarke	CHE	214	1.5	0.7	39	0	2	11	45	3	20	-2	7	0.51	0	2	0	0	-10	-12
17	Rob Jones	LIV	230	1.8	1	37	0	7	8	48	-2	19	-8	5	0.51	0	3	0	4	12	9
17	Atherton	S W	261	1.6	0.7	40	0	1	11	45	1	19	29	29	0.48	0	1	0	1	22	-14
19	B Venison	NEW	238	2	1.3	36	0	0	11	40	4	18	-4	3	0.5	0	0	0	0	-	0
19	Elkins	WIM	271	1.6	0.9	18	1	6	4	23	8	18	8	18	1	1	3	0	3	-3	14
21	**J Dicks**	LIV	211	1.8	1	31	3	2	7	41	0	17	2	14	0.55	1	1	2	1	-	0
22	E Barrett	A V	202	1.8	0.8	39	0	0	12	47	1	16	-3	6	0.41	0	0	0	0	-13	25
22	**Staunton**	A V	203	2	1.1	24	2	2	6	30	4	16	-13	-3	0.67	2	0	0	2	23	46
24	F Sinclair	CHE	213	1.5	0.6	35	0	3	9	44	-2	15	4	11	0.43	0	1	0	2	-4	-2
24	Bardsley	QPR	252	1.6	0.8	32	0	6	8	45	-1	15	-8	2	0.47	0	5	0	1	14	6

RANK	NAME	CLUB	CODE	TEL £	SOL £	PLD	G	A	CS	GA	A	B	94A	94B	P/G	HG	HA	AG	AA	9192	9293
25	Borrows	COV	216	1.6	0.8	29	0	1	8	33	1	14	3	13	0.48	0	1	0	0	4	-3
26	T Phelan	M C	272	1.6	0.7	30	1	0	7	37	-6	10	3	9	0.33	1	0	0	0	22	4
27	Hinchcliffe	EVE	223	1.5	0.6	25	0	3	6	34	-4	9	0	5	0.36	0	2	0	1	30	9
27	**C Wilson**	QPR	251	1.6	0.7	42	3	1	10	64	-13	9	-10	2	0.21	3	0	0	1	10	-4
27	Joseph	WIM	273	1.6	0.8	13	0	0	5	14	6	9	1	1	0.69	0	0	0	0	4	9
30	Bjornbye	LIV	232	1.4	0.7	7	0	2	1	5	3	8	3	4	1.14	0	1	0	1	0	10
30	A Hill	M C	234	1.5	0.7	14	0	0	4	14	2	8	6	9	0.57	0	0	0	0	31	3
32	M Jackson	EVE	220	1.5	0.6	37	0	2	10	54	-10	7	-13	-2	0.19	0	2	0	0	10	18
32	R Elliot	NEW	247	1.7	0.9	12	0	1	3	13	1	7	-3	1	0.58	0	0	0	1	0	0
32	Kenna	SOT	262	1.6	0.8	40	2	6	6	63	-21	7	-4	7	0.18	2	1	0	5	10	-6
32	Austin	TOT	266	1.5	0.6	20	0	2	5	27	-3	7	-7	0	0.35	0	0	0	2	0	-11
32	Kimble	WIM	278	1.3	0.5	14	0	2	4	19	1	7	0	0	0.5	0	1	0	1	0	0
37	A Wright	BLA	209	2	1.2	8	0	1	2	8	2	6	-3	0	0.75	0	1	0	0	0	24
37	K Brown	W H	210	1.2	0.5	6	0	0	3	6	6	6	7	6	1	0	0	0	0	-	0
37	Rowland	W H	233	1.2	0.5	13	0	2	4	19	1	6	-8	-2	0.46	0	0	0	2	0	0
40	Holmes	EVE	284	1.5	0.6	15	0	1	5	22	0	5	-5	-3	0.33	0	0	0	1	-	0

RANK	NAME	CLUB	CODE	TEL £	SOL £	PLD	G	A	CS	GA	A	B	94A	94B	P/G	HG	HA	AG	AA	9192	9293
41	Culverhouse	NOR	243	1.4	0.6	42	1	0	10	61	-18	4	-21	-6	0.1	1	0	0	0	-15	-16
41	Kerslake	TOT	283	1.3	0.6	16	0	4	2	24	-8	4	-6	1	0.25	0	2	0	2	-	2
43	B Small	A V	277	1.3	0.6	9	0	0	2	10	-2	3	2	2	0.33	0	0	0	0	-	-12
44	Edgehill	M C	240	1.5	0.7	17	0	2	3	25	-9	2	0	7	0.12	0	2	0	0	0	0
45	Dodd	SOT	263	1.3	0.6	5	0	0	1	6	-2	1	0	1	0.2	0	0	0	0	-2	-7
46	Ray Wallace	LEE	229	1.2	0.5	0	0	0	0	0	0	0	0	0	-	0	0	0	0	0	-6
46	S Campbell	TOT	255	1.4	0.6	25	0	3	2	35	-21	0	-18	-9	0	0	1	0	2	0	0
48	Kubicki	A V	201	1.2	0.5	1	0	0	0	2	-2	-1	0	0	-1	0	0	0	0	6	0
48	S Charlton	SOT	260	1.4	0.6	30	1	1	5	46	-21	-1	-14	-4	-0.03	0	0	1	1	-	-
48	Edinburgh	TOT	270	1.5	0.6	23	0	1	3	32	-18	-1	-13	-3	-0.04	0	0	0	1	-9	-3
51	I Snodin	EVE	219	1.5	0.6	28	0	0	6	42	-18	-2	-25	-11	-0.07	0	0	0	0	0	-6
51	Brevett	QPR	253	1.2	0.5	4	0	0	0	6	-6	-2	-3	0	-0.5	0	0	0	0	0	-4
51	Coleman	S W	275	1.6	0.7	7	1	1	0	14	-9	-2	-9	-3	-0.29	0	1	1	0	0	0
54	Yallop	IPS	225	1.2	0.5	3	0	0	0	6	-6	-3	-3	-2	-1	0	0	0	0	0	3
55	G Hall	CHE	215	1.5	0.6	4	0	0	0	8	-8	-4	-3	-2	-1	0	0	0	0	-4	-4
56	Woodthorpe	NOR	241	1.4	0.6	19	0	1	3	33	-19	-6	-14	-4	-0.32	0	0	0	1	-9	6

RANK	NAME	CLUB	CODE	TEL £	SOL £	PLD	G	A	CS	GA	A	B	94A	94B	P/G	HG	HA	AG	AA	9192	9293
57	King	S W	259	1.6	0.7	8	0	0	1	17	-13	-7	-9	-6	-0.88	0	0	0	0	16	5
57	Benali	SOT	265	1.4	0.6	35	0	1	5	54	-32	-7	-13	-2	-0.2	0	1	0	0	14	4
-	J Humphrey	C P	254	1.5	0.6	32	1	-	-	-	-	-	-	-	-	-	-	-	-	-5	-5
-	**D Gordon**	C P	256	1.6	0.8	39	5	-	-	-	-	-	-	-	-	-	-	-	-	-	-
-	R Shaw	C P	258	1.5	0.6	30	2	-	-	-	-	-	-	-	-	-	-	-	-	-9	-10
-	Barnard	CHE	217	1.5	0.6	9	1	2	0	0	-	-	-	-	-	-	-	-	-	-	5
-	S Minto	CHE	218	1.6	0.7	-	-	-	-	-	-	-	-	-	-	-	-	-	-	-	-
-	Stockwell*	IPS	222	1.5	0.7	42	1	2	0	0	-	-	-	-	-	0	1	1	1	0	20
-	K Sharp*	LEE	228	1.5	0.6	7	0	0	0	0	-	-	-	-	-	0	0	0	0	0	0
-	Worthington*	LEE	264	1.9	1	30	1	5	0	0	-	-	-	-	-	1	4	0	1	25	13
-	G Coatsworth	LEI	244	1.3	0.6	17	2	-	-	-	-	-	-	-	-	-	-	-	-	-	-
-	M Whitlow	LEI	245	1.4	0.6	34	3	-	-	-	-	-	-	-	-	-	-	-	-	-	-
-	S Grayson	LEI	246	1.4	0.6	46	1	-	-	-	-	-	-	-	-	-	-	-	-	-	-
-	G Mills	LEI	267	1.3	0.6	22	-	-	-	-	-	-	-	-	-	-	-	-	-	-	-
-	I Brightwell*	M C	268	1.5	0.7	6	0	2	0	0	-	-	-	-	-	0	1	0	1	14	11
-	Haaland	NOT	235	1.4	0.6	-	-	-	-	-	-	-	-	-	-	-	-	-	-	-	-

RANK	NAME	CLUB	CODE	TEL £	SOL £	PLD	G	A	CS	GA	A	B	94A	94B	P/G	HG	HA	AG	AA	9192	9293
-	D Lyttle	NOT	248	1.4	0.6	-	-	-	-	-	-	-	-	-	-	-	-	-	-	-	-
-	**S Pearce**	NOT	249	1.8	1	-	-	-	-	-	-	-	-	-	-	-	-	-	-	18	3
-	B Laws	NOT	250	1.4	0.6	-	-	-	-	-	-	-	-	-	-	-	-	-	-	-7	-31

centre backs

RANK	NAME	CLUB	CODE	TEL £	SOL £	PLD	G	A	CS	GA	A	B	94A	94B	P/G	HG	HA	AG	AA	9192	9293
1	T Adams	ARS	307	2.7	2	35	0	2	20	21	63	58	29	29	1.66	0	1	0	1	5	28
2	Bruce	M U	338	2.6	1.9	41	3	2	15	38	35	46	15	21	1.12	1	2	2	0	57	58
3	Fairclough	LEE	330	2.5	1.8	40	4	0	16	39	37	45	32	32	1.13	1	0	3	0	43	-4
3	Wetherall	LEE	380	2.5	1.8	31	1	2	15	23	44	45	28	27	1.45	1	2	0	0	-	19
5	Pallister	M U	339	2.6	1.9	41	1	0	17	37	34	41	15	18	1	1	0	0	0	33	48
6	Babb	COV	320	1.8	1.1	40	3	2	13	39	26	40	2	14	1	1	1	2	1	-	0
7	A Linighan	ARS	308	2.3	1.5	20	0	2	12	11	41	37	3	4	1.85	0	0	0	2	-8	25
7	May	M U	368	2.6	1.9	40	1	0	15	36	27	37	-3	0	0.93	0	1	0	0	0	45
9	Bould	ARS	305	2.7	2	23	1	2	10	17	30	33	18	21	1.43	1	2	0	0	1	16
9	Keown	ARS	322	2.3	1.6	23	0	2	10	14	30	33	6	8	1.43	0	1	0	1	11	7
11	Ruddock	LIV	369	1.9	1.2	39	3	5	9	46	9	30	-1	11	0.77	1	5	2	0	5	1
11	A Pearce	S W	321	1.8	1.1	29	3	4	8	32	17	30	13	21	1.03	2	1	1	3	13	6

RANK	NAME	CLUB	CODE	TEL £	SOL £	PLD	G	A	CS	GA	A	B	94A	94B	P/G	HG	HA	AG	AA	9192	9293
13	C Hendry	BLA	310	2.6	1.9	23	0	0	10	15	25	28	16	18	1.22	0	0	0	0	0	42
13	**Wark**	IPS	325	1.6	0.8	38	3	1	13	47	16	28	-5	4	0.74	1	1	2	0	0	10
13	Peacock	NEW	354	2	1.2	39	3	2	13	50	15	28	19	23	0.72	1	1	2	1	16	-10
16	Newsome	NOR	364	1.6	1.6	27	1	1	10	26	19	26	12	16	0.96	1	1	0	0	16	-20
17	Teale	A V	303	1.8	1	36	1	0	12	40	11	23	1	7	0.64	0	0	1	0	12	24
17	D Linighan	IPS	328	1.6	0.7	38	3	0	13	50	11	23	-4	6	0.61	3	0	0	0	0	-2
19	Scales	WIM	373	1.7	0.9	37	0	2	11	42	6	21	-4	7	0.57	0	2	0	0	3	10
20	Kjeldberg	CHE	379	1.6	0.7	27	1	1	9	31	10	19	11	14	0.7	1	1	0	0	-	-
21	Marker	BLA	378	2.2	1.3	18	0	0	7	14	14	18	10	9	1	0	0	0	0	-	-7
22	P McGrath	A V	302	1.8	0.8	30	1	1	8	34	3	17	-4	3	0.57	0	1	1	0	13	39
22	D Brightwell	M C	336	1.5	0.6	20	1	0	7	20	11	17	10	14	0.85	1	0	0	0	-7	-9
24	**Curle**	M C	335	1.7	0.8	28	1	0	8	32	3	15	4	7	0.54	0	0	1	0	32	-6
25	P Whelan	IPS	326	1.5	0.6	28	0	0	10	34	6	14	-14	-5	0.5	0	0	0	0	0	-11
26	K Moran	BLA	311	2.4	1.7	19	1	0	5	19	4	13	1	6	0.68	1	0	0	0	0	43
26	Nicol	LIV	332	1.7	0.9	29	1	3	6	37	-4	13	-5	3	0.45	0	1	1	2	28	15
26	Vonk	M C	337	1.7	0.8	32	1	1	9	42	-1	13	8	14	0.41	0	1	1	0	10	5

RANK	NAME	CLUB	CODE	TEL £	SOL £	PLD	G	A	CS	GA	A	B	94A	94B	P/G	HG	HA	AG	AA	9192	9293
29	Youds	IPS	327	1.2	0.5	20	1	0	6	23	4	12	-9	-1	0.6	1	0	0	0	0	-12
29	O Leary	LEE	306	1.2	0.5	8	0	0	5	6	14	12	12	10	1.5	0	0	0	0	-10	-7
29	D Walker	S W	360	1.7	1	42	0	1	10	52	-10	12	-3	8	0.29	0	1	0	0	-	0
29	S Potts	W H	314	1.5	0.7	41	0	0	14	57	-1	12	-12	-2	0.29	0	0	0	0	-	0
33	S Wood	SOT	361	1.4	0.5	27	0	0	6	28	-4	11	1	9	0.41	0	0	0	0	0	-3
34	E Johnsen	CHE	316	1.5	0.6	27	1	0	8	36	-1	10	8	13	0.37	1	0	0	0	0	-11
34	J Polston	NOR	345	1.4	0.6	23	0	1	6	27	-1	10	-4	2	0.43	0	0	0	1	-15	-8
34	Fitzgerald	WIM	371	1.6	0.8	28	0	0	9	36	0	10	-9	-1	0.36	0	0	0	0	7	-9
37	G Hoddle	CHE	351	1.4	0.6	16	1	2	3	20	-1	9	1	3	0.56	1	1	0	1	-	0
37	M Wright	LIV	333	1.7	0.8	30	1	1	7	40	-7	9	-7	0	0.3	1	1	0	0	19	-5
39	Ablett	EVE	323	1.5	0.6	32	1	2	8	47	-8	8	-14	-5	0.25	1	1	0	1	11	-15
39	D Watson	EVE	324	1.5	0.6	26	1	0	7	35	-4	8	-8	-1	0.31	0	0	1	0	27	4
39	Butterworth	NOR	343	1.4	0.6	23	0	1	6	29	-3	8	-5	1	0.35	0	1	0	0	-6	-31
39	A McDonald	QPR	353	1.6	0.6	12	1	2	3	17	2	8	0	0	0.67	0	2	1	0	26	-21
43	Kevin Scott	TOT	342	1.3	0.6	29	1	0	7	39	-8	7	-15	-5	0.24	1	0	0	0	-	0
43	Mabbutt	TOT	367	1.5	0.6	28	0	2	6	37	-9	7	-4	3	0.25	0	2	0	0	-18	-4

RANK	NAME	CLUB	CODE	TEL £	SOL £	PLD	G	A	CS	GA	A	B	94A	94B	P/G	HG	HA	AG	AA	9192	9293
45	Nielson	NEW	329	1.3	0.6	10	0	0	3	10	2	6	2	6	0.6	0	0	0	0	0	0
46	Ehiogu	A V	301	1.7	0.7	14	0	0	5	19	1	5	-2	2	0.36	0	0	0	0	0	-2
46	D Lee	CHE	377	1.4	0.6	4	1	0	1	4	3	5	-1	0	1.25	1	0	0	0	-	6
46	Kernaghan	M C	383	1.5	0.7	24	0	0	6	31	-7	5	-1	5	0.21	0	0	0	0	0	-3
49	Donaghy	CHE	340	1.4	0.6	24	1	0	4	31	-12	4	-7	-2	0.17	1	0	0	0	19	4
49	A Martin	W H	313	1.5	0.6	7	2	0	1	11	-1	4	-5	-1	0.57	2	0	0	0	-	0
51	C Calderwood	TOT	346	1.2	0.5	26	0	0	4	31	-15	3	-10	-4	0.12	0	0	0	0	-	0
52	S Howey	NEW	341	1.7	0.8	13	0	0	2	15	-7	2	-6	0	0.15	0	0	0	0	-	0
52	Prior	NOR	384	1.4	0.6	10	0	0	3	14	-2	2	-5	-1	0.2	0	0	0	0	0	0
52	Monkou	SOT	317	1.5	0.6	34	4	0	6	56	-20	2	-5	5	0.06	3	0	1	0	-26	-9
52	B McAllister	WIM	372	1.6	0.7	12	0	1	3	18	-4	2	-5	-1	0.17	0	0	0	1	0	15
56	Yates	QPR	375	1.6	0.6	25	0	0	6	36	-12	1	-13	-1	0.04	0	0	0	0	-	-
56	Ready	QPR	386	1.5	0.6	15	1	1	3	25	-8	1	-9	-1	0.07	0	1	1	0	0	0
56	Blackwell	WIM	370	1.3	0.6	16	0	0	3	21	-9	1	-2	4	0.06	0	0	0	0	0	-10
59	Bowman	LEE	331	1.4	0.7	0	0	0	0	0	0	0	0	0	-	0	0	0	0	0	-1
59	Maddix	QPR	352	1.2	0.5	0	0	0	0	0	0	0	0	0	-	0	0	0	0	-17	-6

RANK	NAME	CLUB	CODE	TEL £	SOL £	PLD	G	A	CS	GA	A	B	94A	94B	P/G	HG	HA	AG	AA	9192	9293
59	Cundy	TOT	366	1.2	0.5	0	0	0	0	0	0	0	0	0	-	0	0	0	0	-13	-14
62	Piechnik	LIV	376	1.2	0.5	1	0	0	0	3	-3	-2	0	0	-2	0	0	0	0	-	-11
62	R Hall	SOT	363	1.3	0.6	3	0	0	0	5	-5	-2	0	0	-0.67	0	0	0	0	-15	9
64	Busst	COV	381	1.4	0.5	3	0	0	0	6	-6	-3	-4	-3	-1	0	0	0	0	0	1
65	Moore	SOT	362	1.3	0.5	14	0	0	0	24	-24	-10	-8	-3	-0.71	0	0	0	0	19	-7
-	E Young	C P	355	1.7	0.8	46	5	-	-	-	-	-	-	-	-	-	-	-	-	6	16
-	A Thorn	C P	357	1.5	0.6	10	-	-	-	-	-	-	-	-	-	-	-	-	-	-8	-6
-	C Coleman	C P	359	1.6	0.8	46	3	-	-	-	-	-	-	-	-	-	-	-	-	23	18
-	D Patterson	C P	365	1.5	0.6	-	-	-	-	-	-	-	-	-	-	-	-	-	-	-	-
-	E Smith	C P	382	1.5	0.6	-	-	-	-	-	-	-	-	-	-	-	-	-	-	-	-
-	C Hill	LEI	344	1.4	0.6	35	1	-	-	-	-	-	-	-	-	-	-	-	-	-	-
-	J Willis	LEI	347	1.3	0.6	12	1	-	-	-	-	-	-	-	-	-	-	-	-	-	-
-	B Carey	LEI	348	1.4	0.6	27	-	-	-	-	-	-	-	-	-	-	-	-	-	-	-
-	N Mohan	LEI	358	1.4	0.6	-	-	-	-	-	-	-	-	-	-	-	-	-	-	-	-
-	Newman	NOR	349	1.4	0.6	32	2	0	0	0	-	-	-	-	-	-	-	-	-	27	10
-	C Tiler	NOT	334	1.4	0.6	-	-	-	-	-	-	-	-	-	-	-	-	-	-	-9	-24

RANK	NAME	CLUB	CODE	TEL £	SOL £	PLD	G	A	CS	GA	A	B	94A	94B	P/G	HG	HA	AG	AA	9192	9293
-	C Cooper	NOT	350	1.5	0.8	-	-	-	-	-	-	-	-	-	-	-	-	-	-	-	-
-	S Chettle	NOT	356	1.4	0.6	-	-	-	-	-	-	-	-	-	-	-	-	-	-	-18	-29
-	Nethercott	TOT	374	1.4	0.5	-	-	-	-	-	-	-	-	-	-	-	-	-	-	-	-

midfielders

RANK	NAME	CLUB	CODE	TEL £	SOL £	PLD	G	A	CS	GA	A	B	94A	94B	P/G	HG	HA	AG	AA	9192	9293
1	**Le Tissier**	SOT	542	3.1	2.4	38	25	10	-	-	95	95	64	64	2.5	13	7	12	3	30	67
2	R Giggs	M U	485	2.7	2	33	13	8	-	-	55	55	31	31	1.67	5	4	8	4	36	37
2	Fox	NEW	503	2.5	1.8	39	9	14	-	-	55	55	25	25	1.41	4	3	5	11	17	32
4	Ince	M U	491	2.4	1.7	39	8	12	-	-	48	48	24	24	1.23	5	6	3	6	16	22
5	Speed	LEE	464	2.4	1.7	35	10	7	-	-	44	44	19	19	1.26	5	3	5	4	37	27
6	G Peacock	CHE	495	2.2	1.5	37	8	8	-	-	40	40	18	18	1.08	6	8	2	0	-	0
6	**G McAllister**	LEE	465	2.2	1.5	42	8	8	-	-	40	40	13	13	0.95	7	5	1	3	25	29
7	R Lee	NEW	496	2	1.3	41	7	9	-	-	39	39	21	21	0.95	4	5	3	4	-	0
8	L Sharpe	M U	493	2	1.3	26	9	5	-	-	37	37	8	8	1.42	2	4	7	1	5	27
8	Dozzell	TOT	456	1.6	0.9	29	9	5	-	-	37	37	13	13	1.28	3	2	6	3	0	37
8	Earle	WIM	559	2	1.3	42	9	5	-	-	37	37	30	30	0.88	5	5	4	0	54	41
11	Wise	CHE	439	1.9	1.2	35	4	12	-	-	36	36	25	25	1.03	1	9	3	3	48	21

RANK	NAME	CLUB	CODE	TEL £	SOL £	PLD	G	A	CS	GA	A	B	94A	94B	P/G	HG	HA	AG	AA	9192	9293
11	S Sellars	NEW	494	1.8	1.1	29	4	12	-	-	36	36	21	21	1.24	3	8	1	4	-	0
11	Bart-Williams	S W	541	1.7	1	31	8	6	-	-	36	36	25	25	1.16	5	2	3	4	6	24
14	Wilcox	BLA	417	1.9	1.2	31	6	8	-	-	34	34	23	23	1.1	3	3	3	5	0	32
14	Anderton	TOT	555	1.8	1.1	35	6	8	-	-	34	34	14	14	0.97	3	4	3	4	0	42
16	Ripley	BLA	500	1.7	1	40	4	10	-	-	32	32	18	18	0.8	1	4	3	6	0	37
16	Kanchelskis	M U	486	2	1.3	28	6	7	-	-	32	32	22	22	1.14	3	5	3	2	27	13
18	R Keane	M U	509	1.7	1	34	5	8	-	-	31	31	13	13	0.91	3	4	2	4	40	30
18	M Holmes	W H	427	1.6	0.9	33	3	11	-	-	31	31	22	22	0.94	2	7	1	4	-	0
20	Beagrie	M C	449	1.7	1	38	5	7	-	-	29	29	18	18	0.76	2	5	3	2	21	9
20	Maddison	SOT	546	1.5	0.8	41	7	4	-	-	29	29	13	13	0.71	5	2	2	2	0	20
22	Ryan Jones	S W	556	1.5	0.8	23	6	5	-	-	28	28	10	10	1.22	3	2	3	3	0	0
23	K Richardson	A V	402	1.6	0.9	40	5	6	-	-	27	27	17	17	0.68	2	2	3	4	32	10
23	Merson	ARS	409	1.8	1.1	26	7	3	-	-	27	27	17	17	1.04	5	3	2	0	52	32
25	McManaman	LIV	468	1.7	1	29	2	10	-	-	26	26	8	8	0.9	0	6	2	4	29	26
26	Wilkins	C P	522	1.6	0.9	39	1	11	-	-	25	25	12	12	0.64	1	5	0	6	15	14
26	Martin Allen	W H	419	1.6	0.9	20	7	2	-	-	25	25	25	25	1.25	4	1	3	1	-	0

RANK	NAME	CLUB	CODE	TEL £	SOL £	PLD	G	A	CS	GA	A	B	94A	94B	P/G	HG	HA	AG	AA	9192	9293
28	David White	LEE	477	1.9	1.2	28	6	3	-	-	24	24	21	21	0.86	3	3	3	0	64	62
28	Goss	NOR	506	1.6	0.9	34	6	3	-	-	24	24	13	13	0.71	2	3	4	0	7	11
28	J Moncur	W H	436	1.6	0.9	41	4	6	-	-	24	24	18	18	0.59	0	2	4	4	-	0
31	Sinton	S W	523	1.8	1.1	25	3	7	-	-	23	23	4	4	0.92	1	4	2	3	25	43
31	Waddle	S W	566	1.8	1.1	19	3	7	-	-	23	23	0	0	1.21	3	6	0	1	0	23
33	T Sinclair	QPR	527	1.6	0.9	28	4	5	-	-	22	22	12	12	0.79	2	0	2	5	-	-
34	Strachan	LEE	463	1.6	0.9	32	3	6	-	-	21	21	4	4	0.66	2	5	1	1	38	28
34	C Palmer	LEE	536	1.5	0.8	37	5	3	-	-	21	21	12	12	0.57	2	2	3	1	23	7
34	N Summerbee	M C	487	1.6	0.9	35	3	6	-	-	21	21	16	16	0.6	2	4	1	2	-	-
37	Crook	NOR	504	1.6	0.9	38	0	10	-	-	20	20	10	10	0.53	0	4	0	6	3	19
38	Townsend	A V	438	1.6	0.9	32	3	5	-	-	19	19	9	9	0.59	1	2	2	3	18	26
38	Flynn	COV	445	1.5	0.8	34	3	5	-	-	19	19	15	15	0.56	2	5	1	0	3	0
38	Sedgley	IPS	549	1.4	0.7	42	5	2	-	-	19	19	11	11	0.45	3	0	2	2	-13	-8
38	Barker	QPR	521	1.5	0.8	36	5	2	-	-	19	19	8	8	0.53	2	2	3	0	19	9
38	**J Sheridan**	S W	537	1.6	0.9	19	3	5	-	-	19	19	14	14	1	3	3	0	2	24	17
43	Sherwood	BLA	422	1.6	0.9	37	2	6	-	-	18	18	14	14	0.49	2	3	0	3	0	21

RANK	NAME	CLUB	CODE	TEL £	SOL £	PLD	G	A	CS	GA	A	B	94A	94B	P/G	HG	HA	AG	AA	9192	9293
43	Ebbrell	EVE	447	1.5	0.8	39	4	3	-	-	18	18	10	10	0.46	3	3	1	0	5	7
43	Redknapp	LIV	467	1.6	0.9	29	4	3	-	-	18	18	10	10	0.62	1	3	3	0	2	16
43	L Clark	NEW	497	1.6	0.9	29	2	6	-	-	18	18	7	7	0.62	0	4	2	2	0	0
43	Caskey	TOT	577	1.6	0.9	18	4	3	-	-	18	18	7	7	1	3	2	1	1	0	0
48	Burley	CHE	433	1.6	0.9	20	3	4	-	-	17	17	17	17	0.85	2	1	1	3	0	0
48	J Williams	COV	444	1.6	0.9	28	3	4	-	-	17	17	3	3	0.61	0	0	1	0	0	39
48	Stuart	EVE	437	1.6	0.9	26	3	4	-	-	17	17	17	17	0.65	3	2	0	2	8	41
48	Rocastle	M C	411	1.6	0.9	27	3	4	-	-	17	17	10	10	0.63	2	2	1	2	15	5
48	Flitcroft	M C	575	1.5	0.8	20	3	4	-	-	17	17	3	3	0.85	3	2	0	2	0	17
53	Marsh	W H	475	1.5	0.8	34	2	5	-	-	16	16	9	9	0.47	0	3	2	2	0	9
53	**V Jones**	WIM	434	1.5	0.8	33	2	5	-	-	16	16	8	8	0.48	0	3	2	2	19	18
55	J Darby	COV	440	1.4	0.7	23	5	0	-	-	15	15	9	9	0.65	2	0	3	0	0	0
55	Impey	QPR	524	1.4	0.7	31	3	3	-	-	15	15	6	6	0.48	1	2	2	1	10	14
57	Houghton	A V	469	1.5	0.8	25	2	4	-	-	14	14	10	10	0.56	1	2	1	2	32	27
57	Parlour	ARS	416	1.5	0.8	24	2	4	-	-	14	14	14	14	0.58	0	1	2	3	3	9
57	Limpar	EVE	413	1.7	1	18	0	7	-	-	14	14	12	12	0.78	0	2	0	5	38	10

RANK	NAME	CLUB	CODE	TEL £	SOL £	PLD	G	A	CS	GA	A	B	94A	94B	P/G	HG	HA	AG	AA	9192	9293
60	Milton	IPS	455	1.3	0.6	12	1	5	-	-	13	13	0	0	1.08	1	3	0	2	0	6
60	J Barnes	LIV	473	1.6	0.9	24	3	2	-	-	13	13	7	7	0.54	2	1	1	1	11	29
60	Samways	TOT	551	1.5	0.8	39	3	2	-	-	13	13	6	6	0.33	2	1	1	1	17	10
63	G Parker	A V	401	1.5	0.8	17	2	3	-	-	12	12	3	3	0.71	0	1	2	2	8	29
64	Mark Ward	EVE	448	1.4	0.7	26	1	4	-	-	11	11	4	4	0.42	1	2	0	2	13	11
64	P Mason	IPS	461	1.3	0.6	19	3	1	-	-	11	11	3	3	0.58	0	1	3	0	-	0
64	Hyde	S W	540	1.3	0.6	30	1	4	-	-	11	11	4	4	0.37	0	3	1	1	0	7
64	I Bishop	W H	421	1.6	0.9	36	1	4	-	-	11	11	9	9	0.31	0	3	1	1	-	0
68	Holloway	QPR	525	1.3	0.6	21	0	5	-	-	10	10	6	6	0.48	0	4	0	1	4	10
68	M Hazard	TOT	514	1.4	0.7	20	2	2	-	-	10	10	7	7	0.5	1	1	1	1	0	0
70	Rennie	COV	597	1.2	0.5	35	1	3	-	-	9	9	9	9	0.26	1	2	0	1	-	2
70	McClair	M U	488	1.6	0.9	13	1	3	-	-	9	9	4	4	0.69	1	1	0	2	64	37
70	P Allen	SOT	552	1.2	0.5	29	1	3	-	-	9	9	5	5	0.31	1	2	0	1	17	13
73	Yorke	A V	404	1.4	0.7	4	2	1	-	-	8	8	8	8	2	2	1	0	0	43	26
73	Newton	CHE	435	1.2	0.5	33	0	4	-	-	8	8	6	6	0.24	0	1	0	3	0	10
73	S Watson	NEW	501	1.4	0.7	29	2	1	-	-	8	8	6	6	0.28	2	1	0	0	-	0

RANK	NAME	CLUB	CODE	TEL £	SOL £	PLD	G	A	CS	GA	A	B	94A	94B	P/G	HG	HA	AG	AA	9192	9293
73	N Adams	NOR	516	1.4	0.7	19	0	4	-	-	8	8	8	8	0.42	0	3	0	1	20	35
77	Horne	EVE	544	1.2	0.5	28	1	2	-	-	7	7	7	7	0.25	1	1	0	1	5	5
77	Preki	EVE	584	1.3	0.6	10	1	2	-	-	7	7	5	5	0.7	1	1	0	1	-	11
77	Slater	IPS	430	1.4	0.7	28	1	2	-	-	7	7	5	5	0.25	1	0	0	2	0	0
77	G Johnson	IPS	458	1.2	0.5	16	1	2	-	-	7	7	7	7	0.44	0	1	1	1	0	20
77	Fear	WIM	587	1.5	0.8	23	1	4	-	-	7	7	-3	-3	0.3	0	0	0	0	0	0
82	Hillier	ARS	412	1.3	0.6	11	0	3	-	-	6	6	6	6	0.55	0	2	0	1	11	7
82	McGoldrick	ARS	429	1.4	0.7	23	0	3	-	-	6	6	4	4	0.26	0	2	0	1	15	40
82	Batty	BLA	462	1.6	0.9	34	0	3	-	-	6	6	4	4	0.18	0	1	0	2	18	9
82	Molby	LIV	470	1.4	0.7	11	2	0	-	-	6	6	0	0	0.55	2	0	0	0	13	15
82	McMahon	M C	481	1.3	0.6	35	0	3	-	-	6	6	2	2	0.17	0	2	0	1	17	3
82	Ullathorne	NOR	507	1.2	0.5	11	2	0	-	-	6	6	6	6	0.55	1	0	1	0	11	0
82	Eadie	NOR	513	1.5	0.8	8	2	0	-	-	6	6	3	3	0.75	0	0	2	0	0	0
89	Beinlich	A V	407	1.2	0.5	5	1	1	-	-	5	5	5	5	1	0	0	1	1	0	0
89	Atkins	BLA	424	1.3	0.6	8	1	1	-	-	5	5	2	2	0.63	1	0	0	1	0	17
89	S Palmer	IPS	459	1.2	0.5	31	1	1	-	-	5	5	0	0	0.16	0	1	1	0	0	2

RANK	NAME	CLUB	CODE	TEL £	SOL £	PLD	G	A	CS	GA	A	B	94A	94B	P/G	HG	HA	AG	AA	9192	9293
89	Matteo	LIV	460	1.3	0.6	10	1	1	-	-	5	5	0	0	0.5	1	1	0	0	0	0
89	R Whelan	LIV	471	1.4	0.7	23	1	1	-	-	5	5	0	0	0.22	0	0	1	1	0	7
89	Karl	M C	583	1.4	0.7	4	1	1	-	-	5	5	5	5	1.25	0	1	1	0	-	-
89	P Bracewell	NEW	498	1.4	0.7	32	1	1	-	-	5	5	3	3	0.16	1	1	0	0	-	0
89	Meaker	QPR	532	1.3	0.6	10	1	1	-	-	5	5	5	5	0.5	0	1	1	0	9	2
89	Widdrington	SOT	593	1.2	0.5	11	1	1	-	-	5	5	3	3	0.45	1	0	0	1	-	0
89	Howells	TOT	550	1.3	0.6	15	1	1	-	-	5	5	3	3	0.33	0	1	1	0	9	5
89	P Butler	W H	423	1.2	0.5	26	1	1	-	-	5	5	0	0	0.19	1	1	0	0	-	0
89	D Gordon	W H	425	1.3	0.6	8	1	1	-	-	5	5	0	0	0.63	0	0	1	1	-	0
89	Ardley	WIM	563	1.4	0.7	14	1	1	-	-	5	5	5	5	0.36	1	0	0	1	0	26
102	Morrow	ARS	428	1.2	0.5	7	0	2	-	-	4	4	0	0	0.57	0	2	0	0	-	2
102	Selley	ARS	591	1.3	0.6	16	0	2	-	-	4	4	4	4	0.25	0	1	0	1	0	0
102	Hopkin	CHE	431	1.2	0.5	10	0	2	-	-	4	4	4	4	0.4	0	2	0	0	-	-
102	L Durrant	IPS	585	1.2	0.5	2	0	2	-	-	4	4	4	4	2	0	2	0	0	-	-
102	P Stewart	LIV	553	1.5	0.8	7	0	2	-	-	4	4	0	0	0.57	0	2	0	0	33	11
102	Hutchison	LIV	578	1.4	0.7	7	0	2	-	-	4	4	2	2	0.57	0	2	0	0	-	24

RANK	NAME	CLUB	CODE	TEL £	SOL £	PLD	G	A	CS	GA	A	B	94A	94B	P/G	HG	HA	AG	AA	9192	9293
102	Holland	NEW	505	1.3	0.6	2	0	2	-	-	4	4	4	4	2	0	2	0	0	0	0
102	Megson	NOR	480	1.2	0.5	21	0	2	-	-	4	4	4	4	0.19	0	1	0	1	0	7
110	Hodge	LEE	466	1.2	0.5	7	1	0	-	-	3	3	3	3	0.43	1	0	0	0	23	8
110	A Gray	TOT	554	1.2	0.5	1	1	0	-	-	3	3	3	3	3	0	0	1	0	21	5
112	Jensen	ARS	568	1.4	0.7	27	0	1	-	-	2	2	0	0	0.07	0	0	0	1	0	0
112	Boland	COV	446	1.2	0.5	19	0	1	-	-	2	2	2	2	0.11	0	1	0	0	0	0
112	Jenkinson	COV	598	1.2	0.5	10	0	1	-	-	2	2	2	2	0.2	0	0	0	1	-	0
112	Ingebrigtsen	M C	476	1.2	0.5	2	0	1	-	-	2	2	2	2	1	0	0	0	1	0	0
112	Groenendijk	M C	483	1.2	0.5	9	0	1	-	-	2	2	0	0	0.22	0	1	0	0	0	0
112	Lomas	M C	570	1.3	0.6	17	0	1	-	-	2	2	0	0	0.12	0	0	0	1	0	0
112	Milligan	NOR	596	1.2	0.5	38	0	1	-	-	2	2	2	2	0.05	0	0	0	1	8	11
112	Magilton	SOT	548	1.5	0.8	14	0	1	-	-	2	2	2	2	0.14	0	1	0	0	0	0
112	McGayle	WIM	586	1.2	0.5	9	0	1	-	-	2	2	2	2	0.22	0	1	0	0	-	-
121	Breitkreutz	A V	408	1.2	0.5	1	0	0	-	-	0	0	0	0	0	0	0	0	0	0	2
121	Davis	ARS	414	1.4	0.7	21	0	0	-	-	0	0	0	0	0	0	0	0	0	0	2
121	Carter	ARS	415	1.2	0.5	0	0	0	-	-	0	0	0	0	-	0	0	0	0	0	8

RANK	NAME	CLUB	CODE	TEL £	SOL £	PLD	G	A	CS	GA	A	B	94A	94B	P/G	HG	HA	AG	AA	9192	9293
121	Flatts	ARS	582	1.3	0.6	2	0	0	-	-	0	0	0	0	0	0	0	0	0	-	0
121	Makel	BLA	565	1.2	0.5	0	0	0	-	-	0	0	0	0	-	0	0	0	0	0	0
121	Dow	CHE	432	1.2	0.5	13	0	0	-	-	0	0	0	0	0	0	0	0	0	0	0
121	Spackman	CHE	574	1.2	0.5	6	0	0	-	-	0	0	0	0	0	0	0	0	0	-	0
121	Sheridan	COV	441	1.2	0.5	1	0	0	-	-	0	0	0	0	0	0	0	0	0	-	-
121	S Robson	COV	443	1.2	0.5	1	0	0	-	-	0	0	0	0	0	0	0	0	0	13	4
121	L Hurst	COV	573	1.2	0.5	0	0	0	-	-	0	0	0	0	-	0	0	0	0	-	16
121	Warzycha	EVE	450	1.2	0.5	3	0	0	-	-	0	0	0	0	0	0	0	0	0	17	13
121	Unsworth	EVE	452	1.2	0.5	7	0	0	-	-	0	0	0	0	0	0	0	0	0	0	0
121	Kenny	EVE	581	1.2	0.5	0	0	0	-	-	0	0	0	0	-	0	0	0	0	-	7
121	Gregory	IPS	453	1.2	0.5	0	0	0	-	-	0	0	0	0	-	0	0	0	0	0	3
121	G Williams	IPS	567	1.2	0.5	34	0	0	-	-	0	0	0	0	0	0	0	0	0	0	6
121	Harkness	LIV	451	1.2	0.5	10	0	0	-	-	0	0	0	0	0	0	0	0	0	0	0
121	Walters	LIV	472	1.4	0.7	7	0	0	-	-	0	0	0	0	0	0	0	0	0	15	45
121	M Thomas	LIV	474	1.4	0.7	1	0	0	-	-	0	0	0	0	0	0	0	0	0	18	7
121	Simpson	M C	482	1.2	0.5	12	0	0	-	-	0	0	0	0	0	0	0	0	0	5	12

RANK	NAME	CLUB	CODE	TEL £	SOL £	PLD	G	A	CS	GA	A	B	94A	94B	P/G	HG	HA	AG	AA	9192	9293
121	P Lake	M C	571	1.2	0.5	0	0	0	-	-	0	0	0	0	-	0	0	0	0	-	0
121	Papavasiliou	NEW	512	1.2	0.5	4	0	0	-	-	0	0	0	0	0	0	0	0	0	0	0
121	Sutch	NOR	511	1.2	0.5	1	0	0	-	-	0	0	0	0	0	0	0	0	0	0	12
121	Hurlock	SOT	547	1.2	0.5	2	0	0	-	-	0	0	0	0	0	0	0	0	0	2	0
121	Turner	TOT	576	1.2	0.5	0	0	0	-	-	0	0	0	0	-	0	0	0	0	-	6
121	McGee	WIM	557	1.2	0.5	0	0	0	-	-	0	0	0	0	-	0	0	0	0	6	0
121	Dobbs	WIM	561	1.2	0.5	3	0	0	-	-	0	0	0	0	0	0	0	0	0	-	9
-	S Schwarz	ARS	410	1.6	0.9	-	-	-	-	-	-	-	-	-	-	-	-	-	-	-	-
-	Warhurst	BLA	426	1.7	1	9	0	1	-	-	-	-	-	-	-	-	-	-	-	16	22
-	G Southgate	C P	526	1.7	1	46	9	-	-	-	-	-	-	-	-	-	-	-	-	9	17
-	J Salako	C P	528	1.7	1	34	8	-	-	-	-	-	-	-	-	-	-	-	-	10	12
-	D Matthew	C P	530	1.4	0.7	11	1	-	-	-	-	-	-	-	-	-	-	-	-	0	0
-	S Rodger	C P	531	1.5	0.8	37	3	-	-	-	-	-	-	-	-	-	-	-	-	2	16
-	S Osborn	C P	533	1.3	0.6	5	-	-	-	-	-	-	-	-	-	-	-	-	-	3	8
-	D Pitcher	C P	534	1.3	0.6	-	-	-	-	-	-	-	-	-	-	-	-	-	-	15	0
-	R Newman	C P	538	1.3	0.6	-	-	-	-	-	-	-	-	-	-	-	-	-	-	-	-

RANK	NAME	CLUB	CODE	TEL £	SOL £	PLD	G	A	CS	GA	A	B	94A	94B	P/G	HG	HA	AG	AA	9192	9293
-	G Ndah	C P	579	1.3	0.6	-	-	-	-	-	-	-	-	-	-	-	-	-	-	-	-
-	B Bowry	C P	588	1.4	0.7	17	0	-	-	-	-	-	-	-	-	-	-	-	-	-	-
-	M Blake	LEI	558	1.4	0.7	11	1	-	-	-	-	-	-	-	-	-	-	-	-	-	-
-	S Agnew	LEI	560	1.5	0.8	40	3	-	-	-	-	-	-	-	-	-	-	-	-	-	-
-	**S Thompson**	LEI	562	1.7	1	34	8	-	-	-	-	-	-	-	-	-	-	-	-	-	-
-	J Joachim	LEI	564	2	1.3	31	12	-	-	-	-	-	-	-	-	-	-	-	-	-	-
-	L Philpott	LEI	569	1.3	0.6	12	-	-	-	-	-	-	-	-	-	-	-	-	-	-	-
-	D Oldfield	LEI	572	1.7	1	30	7	-	-	-	-	-	-	-	-	-	-	-	-	-	-
-	C Gibson	LEI	580	1.3	0.6	13	-	-	-	-	-	-	-	-	-	-	-	-	-	-	-
-	I Ormondroyd	LEI	589	1.6	0.9	36	6	-	-	-	-	-	-	-	-	-	-	-	-	-	-
-	Clough	LIV	478	1.7	1	26	7	3	-	-	-	-	-	-	-	-	-	-	-	23	34
-	L Bohinen	NOT	479	1.5	0.8	-	-	-	-	-	-	-	-	-	-	-	-	-	-	-	-
-	B Roy	NOT	499	2.3	1.6	-	-	-	-	-	-	-	-	-	-	-	-	-	-	-	-
-	G Crosby	NOT	502	1.5	0.8	-	-	-	-	-	-	-	-	-	-	-	-	-	-	33	3
-	N Webb	NOT	510	1.5	0.8	-	-	-	-	-	-	-	-	-	-	-	-	-	-	4	23
-	S Stone	NOT	515	1.4	0.7	-	-	-	-	-	-	-	-	-	-	-	-	-	-	0	3

RANK	NAME	CLUB	CODE	TEL £	SOL £	PLD	G	A	CS	GA	A	B	94A	94B	P/G	HG	HA	AG	AA	9192	9293
-	D Phillips	NOT	517	1.5	0.8	-	-	-	-	-	-	-	-	-	-	-	-	-	-	47	17
-	S Gemmill	NOT	518	1.5	0.8	-	-	-	-	-	-	-	-	-	-	-	-	-	-	28	13
-	I Woan	NOT	519	1.7	1	-	-	-	-	-	-	-	-	-	-	-	-	-	-	19	27
-	K Black	NOT	520	1.7	1	-	-	-	-	-	-	-	-	-	-	-	-	-	-	16	19
-	I Taylor	S W	535	1.5	0.8	-	-	-	-	-	-	-	-	-	-	-	-	-	-	-	-
-	D Williamson	W H	418	1.5	0.8	-	-	-	-	-	-	-	-	-	-	-	-	-	-	-	-
-	M Rush	W H	420	1.5	0.8	-	-	-	-	-	-	-	-	-	-	-	-	-	-	-	-
-	J Beauchamp	W H	442	1.6	0.9	-	-	-	-	-	-	-	-	-	-	-	-	-	-	-	-

strikers

RANK	NAME	CLUB	CODE	TEL £	SOL £	PLD	G	A	CS	GA	A	B	94A	94B	P/G	HG	HA	AG	AA	9192	9293
1	A Cole	NEW	641	3.6	2.9	40	34	15	-	-	132	132	67	67	3.3	22	6	12	9	-	0
2	**Sutton**	BLA	647	3.3	2.6	41	25	15	-	-	105	105	62	62	2.56	13	6	12	9	4	30
3	**A Shearer**	BLA	670	3.6	2.9	35	31	5	-	-	103	103	53	53	2.94	19	1	12	4	49	56
4	**Beardsley**	NEW	623	2.9	2.2	35	21	11	-	-	85	85	45	45	2.43	12	9	9	2	69	52
5	**Cantona**	M U	628	3.1	2.4	34	18	13	-	-	80	80	33	33	2.35	10	8	8	5	13	77
6	**I Wright**	ARS	603	3.1	2.4	39	23	5	-	-	79	79	45	45	2.03	10	2	13	3	111	53
7	Bright	S W	611	2.4	1.7	36	19	10	-	-	77	77	46	46	2.14	13	7	6	3	69	46

RANK	NAME	CLUB	CODE	TEL £	SOL £	PLD	G	A	CS	GA	A	B	94A	94B	P/G	HG	HA	AG	AA	9192	9293
8	Ferdinand	QPR	658	2.5	1.8	35	17	9	-	-	69	69	27	27	1.97	10	5	7	4	32	72
9	Rod Wallace	LEE	630	2.3	1.6	34	17	7	-	-	65	65	31	31	1.91	9	3	8	4	43	25
10	**Holdsworth**	WIM	682	2.6	1.9	43	17	6	-	-	63	63	37	37	1.47	12	3	5	3	-	63
12	**Cottee**	EVE	622	2	1.3	38	16	5	-	-	58	58	30	30	1.53	10	3	6	2	28	42
13	Deane	LEE	663	2.3	1.6	41	11	12	-	-	57	57	25	25	1.39	4	6	7	6	51	71
14	Rush	LIV	633	2.2	1.5	41	14	6	-	-	54	54	37	37	1.32	9	1	5	5	15	48
15	K Campbell	ARS	605	1.8	1.1	29	14	5	-	-	52	52	29	29	1.79	5	3	9	2	55	26
15	M Hughes	M U	638	2.1	1.4	36	12	8	-	-	52	52	24	24	1.44	7	2	5	6	44	53
17	**Ndlovu**	COV	681	2.1	1.4	42	11	9	-	-	51	51	14	14	1.21	8	4	2	0	5	29
18	**Sheringham**	TOT	649	2.7	2	19	13	4	-	-	47	47	16	16	2.47	6	4	7	0	57	90
19	**M Stein**	CHE	617	2.4	1.7	18	13	3	-	-	45	45	45	45	2.5	8	1	5	2	0	0
19	**T Morley**	W H	613	1.8	1.1	40	13	3	-	-	45	45	26	26	1.13	6	2	7	1	-	0
21	Fowler	LIV	620	2.4	1.7	26	12	3	-	-	42	42	14	14	1.62	6	2	6	1	0	0
22	**Fashanu**	WIM	676	2	1.3	35	11	4	-	-	41	41	22	22	1.17	7	2	4	2	57	28
23	Ekoku	NOR	701	1.7	1	21	12	2	-	-	40	40	22	22	1.9	5	1	7	1	-	9
23	G Watson	S W	705	1.8	1.1	17	12	2	-	-	40	40	34	34	2.35	8	2	4	0	0	0

RANK	NAME	CLUB	CODE	TEL £	SOL £	PLD	G	A	CS	GA	A	B	94A	94B	P/G	HG	HA	AG	AA	9192	9293
25	Atkinson	A V	602	2	1.3	29	8	7	-	-	38	38	8	8	1.31	6	4	2	3	15	41
25	Newell	BLA	609	2.2	1.5	27	6	10	-	-	38	38	11	11	1.41	0	7	6	3	0	55
25	**Marshall**	IPS	627	1.8	1.1	28	10	4	-	-	38	38	18	18	1.36	8	4	2	0	0	-26
28	**Saunders**	A V	632	2	1.3	37	10	2	-	-	34	34	20	20	0.92	5	1	5	1	34	52
28	Penrice	QPR	660	1.7	1	23	8	5	-	-	34	34	21	21	1.48	6	2	2	3	22	18
30	Gallacher	BLA	619	1.8	1.1	28	7	5	-	-	31	31	16	16	1.11	2	4	5	1	30	45
30	Dowie	SOT	669	1.6	0.9	39	5	8	-	-	31	31	17	17	0.79	3	5	2	3	33	47
32	Wegerle	COV	607	1.6	0.9	22	6	5	-	-	28	28	8	8	1.27	3	0	3	5	0	14
32	L Chapman	W H	639	1.6	0.9	27	8	2	-	-	28	28	11	11	1.04	3	0	5	2	60	53
34	Devon White	QPR	700	1.5	0.8	14	7	3	-	-	27	27	21	21	1.93	4	1	3	2	-	0
35	M Quinn	COV	692	1.8	1.1	30	8	1	-	-	26	26	8	8	0.87	5	1	3	0	-	59
35	Sheron	M C	636	1.7	1	29	6	4	-	-	26	26	0	0	0.9	4	3	2	1	33	41
37	Kiwomya	IPS	626	1.6	0.9	34	5	4	-	-	23	23	8	8	0.68	2	2	3	2	0	40
37	N Quinn	M C	635	1.9	1.2	14	5	4	-	-	23	23	0	0	1.64	3	2	2	2	58	50
37	B Allen	QPR	659	1.7	1	14	7	1	-	-	23	23	0	0	1.64	2	1	5	0	6	38
40	Malcolm Allen	NEW	642	1.5	0.8	8	5	3	-	-	21	21	0	0	2.63	3	3	2	0	-	-

RANK	NAME	CLUB	CODE	TEL £	SOL £	PLD	G	A	CS	GA	A	B	94A	94B	P/G	HG	HA	AG	AA	9192	9293
40	Barmby	TOT	667	1.7	1	27	5	3	-	-	21	21	13	13	0.78	4	2	1	1	-	26
42	Rideout	EVE	686	1.5	0.8	21	6	1	-	-	20	20	6	6	0.95	4	1	2	0	0	9
43	J Spencer	CHE	685	1.7	1	13	5	2	-	-	19	19	19	19	1.46	3	2	2	0	0	33
43	Jemson	S W	668	1.5	0.8	10	5	2	-	-	19	19	0	0	1.9	2	1	3	1	27	6
45	Griffiths	M C	698	1.6	0.9	12	4	3	-	-	18	18	8	8	1.5	2	1	2	2	-	-
46	A Smith	ARS	604	1.6	0.9	21	3	4	-	-	17	17	9	9	0.81	2	2	1	2	50	15
46	Rosler	M C	629	1.9	1.2	12	5	1	-	-	17	17	17	17	1.42	3	0	2	1	-	-
47	Robins	NOR	687	1.8	1.1	11	1	6	-	-	15	15	9	9	1.36	1	3	0	3	0	59
48	P Walsh	M C	640	1.9	1.2	11	4	1	-	-	14	14	14	14	1.27	3	0	1	1	-	-
48	C Maskell	SOT	651	1.4	0.7	15	4	1	-	-	14	14	11	11	0.93	1	1	3	0	-	0
50	G Blissett	WIM	688	1.5	0.8	6	3	2	-	-	13	13	5	5	2.17	2	2	1	0	0	0
52	Shipperley	CHE	704	1.5	0.8	19	4	0	-	-	12	12	6	6	0.63	2	0	2	0	0	5
52	Rosenthal	TOT	634	1.6	0.9	12	2	3	-	-	12	12	12	12	1	2	1	0	2	9	24
52	A Clarke	WIM	677	1.5	0.8	12	2	3	-	-	12	12	9	9	1	1	1	1	2	11	17
55	S Barlow	EVE	624	1.5	0.8	7	3	1	-	-	11	11	3	3	1.57	0	0	3	1	0	23
55	Mathie	NEW	646	1.5	0.8	4	3	1	-	-	11	11	6	6	2.75	2	0	1	1	0	0

RANK	NAME	CLUB	CODE	TEL £	SOL £	PLD	G	A	CS	GA	A	B	94A	94B	P/G	HG	HA	AG	AA	9192	9293
57	Whittingham	A V	601	1.8	1.1	14	3	0	-	-	9	9	0	0	0.64	1	0	2	0	0	0
58	Guentchev	IPS	696	1.5	0.8	10	2	1	-	-	8	8	8	8	0.8	2	1	0	0	-	10
58	S Jones	W H	612	1.4	0.7	4	2	1	-	-	8	8	8	8	2	1	1	1	0	-	0
60	Fleck	CHE	643	1.5	0.8	7	1	1	-	-	5	5	5	5	0.71	0	1	1	0	45	20
60	Hirst	S W	665	1.8	1.1	6	1	1	-	-	5	5	2	2	0.83	1	0	0	1	72	43
62	N Whelan	LEE	631	1.4	0.7	5	0	2	-	-	4	4	2	2	0.8	0	1	0	1	0	0
63	Fenton	A V	606	1.6	0.9	8	1	0	-	-	3	3	3	3	0.38	0	0	1	0	-	-
63	Angell	EVE	621	1.4	0.7	13	1	0	-	-	3	3	3	3	0.23	1	0	0	0	0	0
63	Mike	M C	637	1.3	0.6	2	1	0	-	-	3	3	0	0	1.5	0	0	1	0	0	0
63	Dublin	M U	683	1.4	0.7	2	1	0	-	-	3	3	3	3	1.5	1	0	0	0	0	3
67	Strandli	LEE	699	1.3	0.6	1	0	1	-	-	2	2	0	0	2	0	1	0	0	0	8
68	Forrester	LEE	703	1.3	0.6	2	0	0	-	-	0	0	0	0	0	0	0	0	0	0	8
68	Banger	SOT	691	1.3	0.6	5	0	0	-	-	0	0	0	0	0	0	0	0	0	-	21
68	Beadle	TOT	675	1.3	0.6	0	0	0	-	-	0	0	0	0	-	0	0	0	0	0	0
68	Boere	W H	616	1.4	0.7	0	0	0	-	-	0	0	0	0	-	0	0	0	0	0	0
68	Miller	WIM	679	1.3	0.6	0	0	0	-	-	0	0	0	0	-	0	0	0	0	17	7

RANK	NAME	CLUB	CODE	TEL £	SOL £	PLD	G	A	CS	GA	A	B	94A	94B	P/G	HG	HA	AG	AA	9192	9293
68	Newhouse	WIM	680	1.3	0.6	0	0	0	-	-	0	0	0	0	-	0	0	0	0	0	3
-	B Launders	C P	664	1.4	0.7	-	-	-	-	-	-	-	-	-	-	-	-	-	-	-	-
-	C Armstrong	C P	689	2.3	1.6	43	23	-	-	-	-	-	-	-	-	-	-	-	-	0	51
-	P Williams	C P	690	1.6	0.9	21	7	-	-	-	-	-	-	-	-	-	-	-	-	38	9
-	B Dyer	C P	693	1.6	0.9	-	-	-	-	-	-	-	-	-	-	-	-	-	-	-	-
-	A Preece	C P	694	1.9	1.2	-	-	-	-	-	-	-	-	-	-	-	-	-	-	-	-
-	P Gee	LEI	655	1.4	0.7	9	3	-	-	-	-	-	-	-	-	-	-	-	-	-	-
-	S Walsh	LEI	674	1.6	0.9	10	5	-	-	-	-	-	-	-	-	-	-	-	-	-	-
-	I Roberts	LEI	678	1.6	0.9	26	13	-	-	-	-	-	-	-	-	-	-	-	-	-	-
-	D Speedie	LEI	697	1.6	0.9	41	13	-	-	-	-	-	-	-	-	-	-	-	-	-	-
-	S Collymore	NOT	652	2.5	1.8	-	-	-	-	-	-	-	-	-	-	-	-	-	-	-	-
-	J Lee	NOT	653	1.5	0.8	-	-	-	-	-	-	-	-	-	-	-	-	-	-	-	-
-	R Rosario	NOT	654	1.7	1	-	-	-	-	-	-	-	-	-	-	-	-	-	-	31	22
-	L Glover	NOT	656	1.5	0.8	-	-	-	-	-	-	-	-	-	-	-	-	-	-	4	2
-	G Bull	NOT	657	1.4	0.7	-	-	-	-	-	-	-	-	-	-	-	-	-	-	-	-

F.A. CARLING PREMIERSHIP FINAL LEAGUE TABLE 1993/94

F.A. Carling Premiership

1993-94	PLD	W	D	L	F	A	W	D	L	F	A	Pts
Manchester United	42	14	6	1	39	13	13	5	3	41	25	92
Blackburn Rovers	42	14	5	2	31	11	11	4	6	32	25	84
Newcastle United	42	14	4	3	51	14	9	4	8	31	27	77
Arsenal	42	10	8	3	25	15	8	9	4	28	13	71
Leeds United	42	13	6	2	37	18	5	10	6	28	21	70
Wimbledon	42	12	5	4	35	21	6	6	9	21	32	65
Sheffield Wed	42	10	7	4	48	24	6	9	6	28	30	64
Liverpool	42	12	4	5	33	23	5	5	11	26	32	60
Queen's Park Rangers	42	8	7	6	32	29	8	5	8	30	32	60
Aston Villa	42	8	5	8	23	18	7	7	7	23	32	57
Coventry City	42	9	7	5	23	17	5	7	9	20	28	56
Norwich City	42	4	9	8	26	29	8	8	5	39	32	53
West Ham United	42	6	7	8	26	31	7	6	8	21	27	52
Chelsea	42	11	5	5	31	20	2	7	12	18	33	51
Tottenham Hotspur	42	4	8	9	29	33	7	4	10	25	26	45
Manchester City	42	6	10	5	24	22	3	8	10	14	27	45
Everton	42	8	4	9	26	30	4	4	13	16	33	44
Southampton	42	9	2	10	30	31	3	5	13	19	35	43
Ipswich Town	42	5	8	8	21	32	4	8	9	14	26	43
Sheffield United	42	6	10	5	24	23	2	8	11	18	37	42
Oldham Athletic	42	5	8	8	24	33	4	5	12	18	35	40
Swindon Town	42	4	7	10	25	45	1	8	12	22	55	30

Goals 1993-94

	Home	Away	Total
Newcastle United	51	31	82
Manchester United	39	41	80
Sheffield Wed	48	28	76
Leeds United	37	28	65
Norwich City	26	39	65
Blackburn Rovers	31	32	63
Queen's Park Rangers	32	30	62
Liverpool	33	26	59
Wimbledon	35	21	56
Tottenham Hotspur	29	25	54
Arsenal	25	28	53
Chelsea	31	18	49
Southampton	30	19	49
West Ham United	26	21	47
Swindon Town	25	22	47
Aston Villa	23	23	46
Coventry City	23	20	43
Everton	26	16	42
Sheffield United	24	18	42
Oldham Athletic	24	18	42
Manchester City	24	14	38
Ipswich Town	21	14	35

Goals Conceded 1993-94

	Home	Away	Total
Arsenal	15	13	28
Blackburn Rovers	11	25	36
Manchester United	13	25	38
Leeds United	18	21	39
Newcastle United	14	27	41
Coventry City	17	28	45
Manchester City	22	27	49
Aston Villa	18	32	50
Wimbledon	21	32	53
Chelsea	20	33	53
Sheffield Wed	24	30	54
Liverpool	23	32	55
West Ham United	31	27	58
Ipswich Town	32	26	58
Tottenham Hotspur	33	26	59
Sheffield United	23	37	60
Queen's Park Rangers	29	32	61
Norwich City	29	32	61
Everton	30	33	63
Southampton	31	35	66
Oldham Athletic	33	35	68
Swindon Town	45	55	**100**

Clean Sheets 1993-94

	Home	Away	Total
Arsenal	11	10	21
Blackburn Rovers	13	5	18
Leeds United	11	7	18
Manchester United	11	6	17
Newcastle United	11	4	15
West Ham United	7	7	14
Ipswich Town	6	8	14
Aston Villa	9	4	13
Coventry City	6	7	13
Wimbledon	7	5	12
Manchester City	6	6	12
Sheffield United	6	6	12
Chelsea	9	2	11
Everton	5	6	11
Sheffield Wed	7	3	10
Queen's Park Rangers	5	5	10
Norwich City	5	5	10
Liverpool	6	3	9
Tottenham Hotspur	3	4	7
Southampton	3	3	6
Oldham Athletic	3	3	6
Swindon Town	2	2	4

F.A. CARLING PREMIERSHIP – DEFENCE POINTS

		CS	GA	A	B
1	Arsenal	21	28	56	56
2	Blackburn Rovers	18	36	36	42
3	Leeds United	18	39	33	39
4	Manchester United	17	38	30	38
5	Newcastle United	15	41	19	31
6	Coventry City	13	45	7	23
7	Aston Villa	13	50	2	18
8	Manchester City	12	49	-1	17
9	Wimbledon	12	53	-5	13
10	West Ham United	14	58	-2	12
11	Ipswich Town	14	58	-2	12
12	Chelsea	11	53	-9	11
13	Sheffield Wed	10	54	-14	8
14	Sheffield United	12	60	-12	6
15	Liverpool	9	55	-19	5
16	Queen's Park Rangers	10	61	-21	1
17	Norwich City	10	61	-21	1
18	Everton	11	63	-19	1
19	Tottenham Hotspur	7	59	-31	-3
20	Southampton	6	66	-42	-12
21	Oldham Athletic	6	68	-44	-14
22	Swindon Town	4	100	-84	-50

f.a. carling premiership

fixtures 1994–95

saturday, august 20th 1994

Arsenal	v	Manchester City
Chelsea	v	Norwich City
Coventry City	v	Wimbledon
Crystal Palace	v	Liverpool
Everton	v	Aston Villa
Ipswich Town	v	Nottingham Forest
Manchester United	v	Queens Park Rangers
Sheffield Wednesday	v	Tottenham Hotspur
Southampton	v	Blackburn Rovers
West Ham United	v	Leeds United

sunday, august 21st 1994

Leicester City	v	Newcastle United (4:00)

monday, august 22nd 1994

Nottingham Forest	v	Manchester United (8:00)

tuesday, august 23rd 1994

Blackburn Rovers	v	Leicester City (7:45)
Leeds United	v	Arsenal (7:45)
Wimbledon	v	Ipswich Town (7:45)

wednesday, august 24th 1994

Aston Villa	v	Southampton (7:45)
Manchester City	v	West Ham United (7:45)
Newcastle United	v	Coventry City (7:45)
Norwich City	v	Crystal Palace (7:45)
Queens Park Rangers	v	Sheffield Wednesday (7:45)
Tottenham Hotspur	v	Everton (7:45)

saturday, august 27th 1994

Aston Villa	v	Crystal Palace
Blackburn Rovers	v	Coventry City
Leeds United	v	Chelsea
Manchester City	v	Everton
Newcastle United	v	Southampton
Norwich City	v	West Ham United
Nottingham Forest	v	Leicester City
Queens Park Rangers	v	Ipswich Town
Tottenham Hotspur	v	Manchester United
Wimbledon	v	Sheffield Wednesday

sunday, august 28th 1994

Liverpool	v	Arsenal (4:00)

monday, august 29th 1994

Coventry City	v	Aston Villa (8:00)

tuesday, august 30th 1994

Crystal Palace	v	Leeds United (7:45)
Everton	v	Nottingham Forest
Ipswich Town	v	Tottenham Hotspur (7:45)

wednesday, august 31st 1994

Arsenal	v	Blackburn Rovers (7:45)
Chelsea	v	Manchester City (7:45)
Leicester City	v	Queens Park Rangers (7:45)
Manchester United	v	Wimbledon (8:00)
Sheffield Wednesday	v	Norwich City (7:45)
Southampton	v	Liverpool
West Ham United	v	Newcastle United (7:45)

saturday, september 10th 1994

Aston Villa	v	Ipswich Town
Blackburn Rovers	v	Everton
Liverpool	v	West Ham United
Manchester City	v	Crystal Palace
Newcastle United	v	Chelsea
Norwich City	v	Arsenal
Nottingham Forest	v	Sheffield Wednesday
Queens Park Rangers	v	Coventry City
Wimbledon	v	Leicester City

sunday, september 11th 1994

Leeds United	v	Manchester United (4:00)

monday, september 12th 1994

Tottenham Hotspur	v	Southampton (8:00)

saturday, september 17th 1994

Coventry City	v	Leeds United
Crystal Palace	v	Wimbledon
Everton	v	Queens Park Rangers
Leicester City	v	Tottenham Hotspur
Manchester United	v	Liverpool
Sheffield Wednesday	v	Manchester City
Southampton	v	Nottingham Forest
West Ham United	v	Aston Villa

sunday, september 18th 1994

Arsenal	v	Newcastle United
Chelsea	v	Blackburn Rovers (4:00)

monday, september 19th 1994

Ipswich Town	v	Norwich City (8:00)

saturday, september 24th 1994

Blackburn Rovers	v	Aston Villa
Coventry City	v	Southampton
Crystal Palace	v	Chelsea
Everton	v	Leicester City
Ipswich Town	v	Manchester United
Manchester City	v	Norwich City
Newcastle United	v	Liverpool
Queens Park Rangers	v	Wimbledon
Tottenham Hotspur	v	Nottingham Forest

sunday, september 25th 1994

West Ham United	v	Arsenal (4:00)

monday, september 26th 1994

Sheffield Wednesday	v	Leeds United (8:00)

saturday, october 1st 1994

Arsenal	v	Crystal Palace
Aston Villa	v	Newcastle United
Leeds United	v	Manchester City
Liverpool	v	Sheffield Wednesday
Manchester United	v	Everton
Norwich City	v	Blackburn Rovers
Southampton	v	Ipswich Town
Wimbledon	v	Tottenham Hotspur

sunday, october 2nd 1994

Chelsea	v	West Ham United
Nottingham Forest	v	Queens Park Rangers (4:00)

monday, october 3rd 1994

Leicester City	v	Coventry City (8:00)

saturday, october 8th 1994

Chelsea	v	Leicester City
Coventry City	v	Ipswich Town
Liverpool	v	Aston Villa
Manchester City	v	Nottingham Forest
Norwich City	v	Leeds United
Sheffield Wednesday	v	Manchester United
Southampton	v	Everton
Tottenham Hotspur	v	Queens Park Rangers
Wimbledon	v	Arsenal

sunday, october 9th 1994

Newcastle United	v	Blackburn Rovers (4:00)

monday, october 10th 1994

West Ham United	v	Crystal Palace (8:00)

saturday, october 15th 1994

Arsenal	v	Chelsea
Aston Villa	v	Norwich City
Blackburn Rovers	v	Liverpool
Crystal Palace	v	Newcastle United
Everton	v	Coventry City
Leeds United	v	Tottenham Hotspur

Leicester City	v	Southampton
Manchester United	v	West Ham United
Queens Park Rangers	v	Manchester City

sunday, october 16th 1994

Ipswich Town	v	Sheffield Wednesday (4:00)

monday, october 17th 1994

Nottingham Forest	v	Wimbledon (8:00)

saturday, october 22nd 1994

Arsenal	v	Coventry City
Aston Villa	v	Nottingham Forest
Chelsea	v	Ipswich Town
Crystal Palace	v	Everton
Leeds United	v	Leicester City
Liverpool	v	Wimbledon
Manchester City	v	Tottenham Hotspur
Newcastle United	v	Sheffield Wednesday
Norwich City	v	Queens Park Rangers
West Ham United	v	Southampton

sunday, october 23rd 1994

Blackburn Rovers	v	Manchester United (4:00)

saturday, october 29th 1994

Coventry City	v	Manchester City
Everton	v	Arsenal
Ipswich Town	v	Liverpool
Leicester City	v	Crystal Palace
Manchester United	v	Newcastle United
Nottingham Forest	v	Blackburn Rovers
Queens Park Rangers	v	Aston Villa
Sheffield Wednesday	v	Chelsea
Southampton	v	Leeds United
Tottenham Hotspur	v	West Ham United

sunday, october 30th 1994

Wimbledon	v	Norwich City (4:00)

monday, october 31st 1994

Queens Park Rangers	v	Liverpool (8:00)

tuesday, november 1st 1994

Everton	v	West Ham United
Ipswich Town	v	Leeds United (7:45)

wednesday, november 2nd 1994

Coventry City	v	Crystal Palace (7:45)
Nottingham Forest	v	Newcastle United
Sheffield Wednesday	v	Blackburn Rovers (7:45)
Southampton	v	Norwich City
Wimbledon	v	Aston Villa (7:45)

saturday, november 5th 1994

Blackburn Rovers	v	Tottenham Hotspur
Chelsea	v	Coventry City
Crystal Palace	v	Ipswich Town
Leeds United	v	Wimbledon
Liverpool	v	Nottingham Forest
Manchester City	v	Southampton
Newcastle United	v	Queens Park Rangers
Norwich City	v	Everton
West Ham United	v	Leicester City

sunday, november 6th 1994

Arsenal	v	Sheffield Wednesday
Aston Villa	v	Manchester United (4:00)

wednesday, november 9th 1994

Liverpool	v	Chelsea (7:45)

thursday, november 10th 1994

Manchester United	v	Manchester City (8:00)

saturday, november 19th 1994

Coventry City	v	Norwich City
Ipswich Town	v	Blackburn Rovers
Manchester United	v	Crystal Palace
Nottingham Forest	v	Chelsea
Queens Park Rangers	v	Leeds United

Sheffield Wednesday	v	West Ham United
Southampton	v	Arsenal
Tottenham Hotspur	v	Aston Villa
Wimbledon	v	Newcastle United

sunday, november 20th 1994

Leicester City	v	Manchester City (4:00)

monday, november 21st 1994

Everton	v	Liverpool (8:00)

wednesday, november 23rd 1994

Leicester City	v	Arsenal (7:45)
Tottenham Hotspur	v	Chelsea (7:45)

saturday, november 26th 1994

Arsenal	v	Manchester United
Aston Villa	v	Sheffield Wednesday
Blackburn Rovers	v	Queens Park Rangers
Chelsea	v	Everton
Crystal Palace	v	Southampton
Leeds United	v	Nottingham Forest
Liverpool	v	Tottenham Hotspur
Manchester City	v	Wimbledon
Newcastle United	v	Ipswich Town
Norwich City	v	Leicester City
West Ham United	v	Coventry City

saturday, december 3rd 1994

Coventry City	v	Liverpool
Ipswich Town	v	Manchester City
Leicester City	v	Aston Villa
Manchester United	v	Norwich City
Nottingham Forest	v	Arsenal
Queens Park Rangers	v	West Ham United
Sheffield Wednesday	v	Crystal Palace
Southampton	v	Chelsea
Tottenham Hotspur	v	Newcastle United
Wimbledon	v	Blackburn Rovers

monday, december 5th 1994

Everton	v	Leeds United (8:00)

saturday, december 10th 1994

Aston Villa	v	Everton
Blackburn Rovers	v	Southampton
Leeds United	v	West Ham United
Liverpool	v	Crystal Palace
Manchester City	v	Arsenal
Newcastle United	v	Leicester City
Norwich City	v	Chelsea
Nottingham Forest	v	Ipswich Town
Queens Park Rangers	v	Manchester United
Wimbledon	v	Coventry City

monday, december 12th 1994

Tottenham Hotspur	v	Sheffield Wednesday (8:00)

friday, december 16th 1994

Ipswich Town	v	Wimbledon (7:45)

saturday, december 17th 1994

Arsenal	v	Leeds United
Chelsea	v	Liverpool
Coventry City	v	Newcastle United
Crystal Palace	v	Norwich city
Everton	v	Tottenham Hotspur
Leicester City	v	Blackburn Rovers
Manchester United	v	Nottingham Forest
Sheffield Wednesday	v	Queens Park Rangers
Southampton	v	Aston Villa
West Ham United	v	Manchester City

wednesday, december 21st 1994

Newcastle United	v	Everton (7:45)

monday, december 26th 1994

Arsenal	v	Aston Villa (12:00)
Chelsea	v	Manchester United (12:00)

Coventry City	v	Nottingham Forest
Crystal Palace	v	Queens Park Rangers (12:00)
Everton	v	Sheffield Wednesday
Leeds United	v	Newcastle United
Leicester City	v	Liverpool (11:30)
Manchester City	v	Blackburn Rovers
Norwich City	v	Tottenham Hotspur
Southampton	v	Wimbledon (12:00)
West Ham United	v	Ipswich Town (12:00)

tuesday, december 27th 1994

Nottingham Forest	v	Norwich City
Tottenham Hotspur	v	Crystal Palace

wednesday, december 28th 1994

Aston Villa	v	Chelsea (7:45)
Blackburn Rovers	v	Leeds United (7:45)
Ipswich Town	v	Arsenal (7:45)
Liverpool	v	Manchester City (7:45)
Manchester United	v	Leicester City (8:00)
Queens Park Rangers	v	Southampton (7:45)
Sheffield Wednesday	v	Coventry City (7:45)
Wimbledon	v	West Ham United (7:45)

saturday, december 31st 1994

Arsenal	v	Queens Park Rangers
Chelsea	v	Wimbledon
Coventry City	v	Tottenham Hotspur
Crystal Palace	v	Blackburn Rovers
Everton	v	Ipswich Town
Leeds United	v	Liverpool
Leicester City	v	Sheffield Wednesday
Manchester City	v	Aston Villa
Norwich City	v	Newcastle United
Southampton	v	Manchester United
West Ham United	v	Nottingham Forest

monday, january 2nd 1995

Aston Villa	v	Leeds United
Blackburn Rovers	v	West Ham United
Ipswich Town	v	Leicester City

Liverpool	v	Norwich city
Newcastle United	v	Manchester City
Nottingham Forest	v	Crystal Palace
Sheffield Wednesday	v	Southampton
Tottenham Hotspur	v	Arsenal
Wimbledon	v	Everton

tuesday, january 3rd 1995

Manchester United	v	Coventry City (8:00)
Queens Park Rangers	v	Chelsea (7:45)

saturday, january 14th 1995

Arsenal	v	Everton
Aston Villa	v	Queens Park Rangers
Blackburn Rovers	v	Nottingham Forest
Chelsea	v	Sheffield Wednesday
Crystal Palace	v	Leicester City
Leeds United	v	Southampton
Liverpool	v	Ipswich Town
Manchester City	v	Coventry City
Newcastle United	v	Manchester United
Norwich City	v	Wimbledon
West Ham United	v	Tottenham Hotspur

saturday, january 21st 1995

Coventry City	v	Arsenal
Everton	v	Crystal Palace
Ipswich Town	v	Chelsea
Leicester City	v	Leeds United
Manchester United	v	Blackburn Rovers
Nottingham Forest	v	Aston Villa
Queens Park Rangers	v	Norwich City
Sheffield Wednesday	v	Newcastle United
Southampton	v	West Ham United
Tottenham Hotspur	v	Manchester City
Wimbledon	v	Liverpool

tuesday, january 24th 1995

Arsenal	v	Southampton (7:45)
Blackburn Rovers	v	Ipswich Town (7:45)
Crystal Palace	v	Manchester United (7:45)
Leeds United	v	Queens Park Rangers (7:45)

Liverpool	v	Everton (7:45)

wednesday, january 25th 1995

Aston Villa	v	Tottenham Hotspur (7:45)
Chelsea	v	Nottingham Forest (7:45)
Manchester City	v	Leicester City (7:45)
Newcastle United	v	Wimbledon (7:45)
Norwich City	v	Coventry City (7:45)
West Ham United	v	Sheffield Wednesday (7:45)

saturday, february 4th 1995

Coventry City	v	Chelsea
Everton	v	Norwich City
Ipswich Town	v	Crystal Palace
Leicester City	v	West Ham United
Manchester United	v	Aston Villa
Nottingham Forest	v	Liverpool
Queens Park Rangers	v	Newcastle United
Sheffield Wednesday	v	Arsenal
Southampton	v	Manchester City
Tottenham Hotspur	v	Blackburn Rovers
Wimbledon	v	Leeds United

saturday, february 11th 1995

Arsenal	v	Leicester City
Aston Villa	v	Wimbledon
Blackburn Rovers	v	Sheffield Wednesday
Chelsea	v	Tottenham Hotspur
Crystal Palace	v	Coventry City
Leeds United	v	Ipswich town
Liverpool	v	Queens Park Rangers
Manchester City	v	Manchester United
Newcastle United	v	Nottingham Forest
Norwich City	v	Southampton
West Ham United	v	Everton

saturday, february 18th 1995

Coventry City	v	West Ham United
Everton	v	Chelsea
Ipswich Town	v	Newcastle United
Leicester City	v	Norwich City
Manchester United	v	Arsenal

Nottingham Forest	v	Leeds United
Queens Park Rangers	v	Blackburn Rovers
Sheffield Wednesday	v	Aston Villa
Southampton	v	Crystal Palace
Tottenham Hotspur	v	Liverpool
Wimbledon	v	Manchester City

tuesday, february 21st 1995

Arsenal	v	Nottingham Forest (7:45)
Blackburn Rovers	v	Wimbledon (7:45)
Crystal Palace	v	Sheffield Wednesday (7:45)
Leeds United	v	Everton (7:45)

wednesday, february 22nd 1995

Aston Villa	v	Leicester City (7:45)
Chelsea	v	Southampton (7:45)
Liverpool	v	Coventry City (7:45)
Manchester City	v	Ipswich Town (7:45)
Newcastle United	v	Tottenham Hotspur (7:45)
Norwich City	v	Manchester United (7:45)
West Ham United	v	Queens Park Rangers (7:45)

saturday, february 25th 1995

Blackburn Rovers	v	Norwich City
Coventry City	v	Leicester City
Crystal Palace	v	Arsenal
Everton	v	Manchester United
Ipswich Town	v	Southampton
Manchester City	v	Leeds United
Newcastle United	v	Aston Villa
Queens Park Rangers	v	Nottingham Forest
Sheffield Wednesday	v	Liverpool
Tottenham Hotspur	v	Wimbledon
West Ham United	v	Chelsea

saturday, march 4th 1995

Aston Villa	v	Blackburn Rovers
Chelsea	v	Crystal Palace
Leeds United	v	Sheffield Wednesday
Leicester City	v	Everton
Liverpool	v	Newcastle United
Manchester United	v	Ipswich Town

Norwich City	v	Manchester City
Nottingham Forest	v	Tottenham Hotspur
Southampton	v	Coventry City
Wimbledon	v	Queens Park Rangers

sunday, march 5th 1995

Arsenal	v	West Ham United

tuesday, march 7th 1995

Blackburn Rovers	v	Arsenal (7:45)
Leeds United	v	Crystal Palace (7:45)
Wimbledon	v	Manchester United (7:45)

wednesday, march 8th 1995

Aston Villa	v	Coventry City (7:45)
Liverpool	v	Southampton (7:45)
Manchester City	v	Chelsea (7:45)
Newcastle United	v	West Ham United (7:45)
Norwich City	v	Sheffield Wednesday (7:45)
Nottingham Forest	v	Everton
Queens Park Rangers	v	Leicester City (7:45)
Tottenham Hotspur	v	Ipswich Town (7:45)

saturday, march 11th 1995

Arsenal	v	Liverpool
Chelsea	v	Leeds United
Coventry City	v	Blackburn Rovers
Crystal Palace	v	Aston Villa
Everton	v	Manchester City
Ipswich Town	v	Queens Park Rangers
Leicester City	v	Nottingham Forest
Manchester United	v	Tottenham Hotspur
Sheffield Wednesday	v	Wimbledon
Southampton	v	Newcastle United
West Ham United	v	Norwich City.

saturday, march 18th 1995

Aston Villa	v	West Ham United
Blackburn Rovers	v	Chelsea
Leeds United	v	Coventry City
Liverpool	v	Manchester United
Manchester City	v	Sheffield Wednesday

Newcastle United	v	Arsenal
Norwich City	v	Ipswich Town
Nottingham Forest	v	Southampton
Queens Park Rangers	v	Everton
Tottenham Hotspur	v	Leicester City
Wimbledon	v	Crystal Palace

saturday, april 1st 1995

Arsenal	v	Norwich City
Chelsea	v	Newcastle United
Coventry City	v	Queens Park Rangers
Crystal Palace	v	Manchester City
Everton	v	Blackburn Rovers
Ipswich Town	v	Aston villa
Leicester City	v	Wimbledon
Manchester United	v	Leeds United
Sheffield Wednesday	v	Nottingham Forest
Southampton	v	Tottenham Hotspur
West Ham United	v	Liverpool

saturday, april 8th 1995

Aston Villa	v	Manchester City
Blackburn Rovers	v	Crystal Palace
Ipswich Town	v	Everton
Liverpool	v	Leeds United
Manchester United	v	Southampton
Newcastle United	v	Norwich City
Nottingham Forest	v	West Ham United
Queens Park Rangers	v	Arsenal
Sheffield Wednesday	v	Leicester City
Tottenham Hotspur	v	Coventry City
Wimbledon	v	Chelsea

saturday, april 15th 1995

Arsenal	v	Ipswich Town
Chelsea	v	Aston Villa
Coventry City	v	Sheffield Wednesday
Crystal Palace	v	Tottenham Hotspur
Everton	v	Newcastle United
Leeds United	v	Blackburn Rovers
Leicester City	v	Manchester United
Manchester City	v	Liverpool

Norwich City	v	Nottingham Forest
Southampton	v	Queens Park Rangers
West Ham United	v	Wimbledon

monday, april 17th 1995

Aston Villa	v	Arsenal
Blackburn Rovers	v	Manchester City
Ipswich Town	v	West Ham United
Liverpool	v	Leicester City
Manchester United	v	Chelsea
Newcastle United	v	Leeds United
Nottingham Forest	v	Coventry City
Queens Park Rangers	v	Crystal Palace
Sheffield Wednesday	v	Everton
Tottenham Hotspur	v	Norwich City
Wimbledon	v	Southampton

saturday, april 29th 1995

Arsenal	v	Tottenham Hotspur
Chelsea	v	Queens Park Rangers
Coventry City	v	Manchester United
Crystal Palace	v	Nottingham Forest
Everton	v	Wimbledon
Leeds United	v	Aston Villa
Leicester City	v	Ipswich Town
Manchester City	v	Newcastle United
Norwich City	v	Liverpool
Southampton	v	Sheffield Wednesday
West Ham United	v	Blackburn Rovers

saturday,J may 6th 1995

Arsenal	v	Wimbledon
Aston Villa	v	Liverpool
Blackburn Rovers	v	Newcastle United
Crystal Palace	v	West Ham United
Everton	v	Southampton
Ipswich Town	v	Coventry City
Leeds United	v	Norwich City
Leicester City	v	Chelsea
Manchester United	v	Sheffield Wednesday
Nottingham Forest	v	Manchester City
Queens Park Rangers	v	Tottenham Hotspur

saturday, may 13th 1995

Chelsea	v	Arsenal
Coventry City	v	Everton
Liverpool	v	Blackburn Rovers
Manchester City	v	Queens Park Rangers
Newcastle United	v	Crystal Palace
Norwich City	v	Aston Villa
Sheffield Wednesday	v	Ipswich Town
Southampton	v	Leicester City
Tottenham Hotspur	v	Leeds United
West Ham United	v	Manchester United
Wimbledon	v	Nottingham Forest

rearranged fixtures:

....

....

....

....

....

....

....

....

....

....

....

....

....

....

....

how to set up your own league

If you're a keen Fantasy Leaguer then you should really be thinking about setting up your own mini league. We have been running mini leagues for three seasons - this is the original and most exciting way to play Fantasy League. Kick things off with a dramatic Player Auction, where you get to decide who goes under the hammer and for how much. Will you be able to outbid everyone for Andy Cole? Everyone owns a squad of fifteen stars and each week of the season we send you your own Fantasy League report which shows your league table and a player-by-player breakdown of every manager's team. You'll be able to make as many changes as you like - do swap deals with other managers, buy a free agent or bring on a sub - it's up to you!

Here's how to set up your league with Fantasy League:

1 Fill in the order form. At this stage all we need from you is the number of people in your league.

2 As soon as we receive your order form, we will despatch your Auction Pack. This will include a guide to running your Auction, Managers Packs for each manager, Player Lists of over 450 Premier League players, full Fantasy League rules, etc.

3 Hold your Auction. The most important day of your Fantasy League season, and the most fun. Everything is explained in your Auction Pack. All you have to do is decide on a date and a venue.The Auction should last about two hours. Once its over, you send us back all your team sheets.

4 Once we receive your team sheets, you're up and running for the next weekend's Premier League games. From then on, we send you a First Class mailed report every week of the season to a designated address. You will receive weekly League Table & Team Breakdowns, free entry into National Manager of The Month and National Hall of Fame as well as regular newsletters.

Name ....

Address ....

....

....

.... PostCode ....

How many in your league? *(5 to 15)* ....

No. of teams @ £17.50 each ....
(includes 20 team changes for your league)

Total amount (chq/cc etc.) £ ....

payment details

I am paying: ☐ by cheque *(payable to* ***fantasy league****)*

☐ by credit card

Name on Card ....

Address ....

....

.... PostCode ....

Card Number

☐☐☐☐☐☐☐☐☐☐☐☐☐☐☐☐

Expiry Date

☐☐ ☐☐ ☐☐

return to:

fantasy league P.O. Box 1977, London N6 4NQ

sign up for the season!

CUT ALONG THIS LINE

win cup final tickets!

Get the answers to these three simple questions right and you will have a chance to win one of FIVE sets of pairs of free tickets to the 1995 FA Cup Final.

The questions refer to the three seasons 1991/92, 1992/93 and 1993/94. **We are after the best TOTAL performances across these three seasons.**

Not so simple. then – but have a go anyway.
Circle the letter against your choice and return the entry form toTransworld at the address below:

1. **Who has scored the most points?**
   - A Chris Sutton
   - B Ian Rush
   - C Ryan Giggs

2. **Who has kept the most clean sheets?**
   - A Flowers
   - B Lukic
   - C Schmeichel

3. **Who has provided the most assists?**
   - A Newell
   - B Cantona
   - C Le Tissier

The winner will be the first five correct entries drawn after the closing date.
No correspondence will be entered into – the referee's decision is final. Closing date for entries 28th February 1995.

Return this form to:

Publicity Department. Transworld Publishers Ltd,

61-63 Uxbridge Road, London W5 5SA.

Envelopes should be marked

FANTASY LEAGUE COMPETITION

notes

notes

notes

notes

notes